ŚAṂKARA ON DISCIPLESHIP

A ŚAṂKARA SOURCE-BOOK

VOLUME V

by

A.J. Alston

SHANTI SADAN

29 Chepstow Villas
LONDON

First published in 1989 by Shanti Sadan

British Library Cataloguing in Publication Data
Sankaracarya
Śaṃkara on Discipleship -(A Śaṃkara
Source Book; v.5)
1. Advaita Vedanta
I. Title
II. Alston, A.J. (Anthony John) 1919-
III. Series
181'.482

ISBN 0 85424 037 3

29 Chepstow Villas,
London W11 3DR

Printed and bound by Baker Brothers (Litho) Ltd, Pontefract, West Yorkshire.

P R E F A C E

This is the fifth volume of a six-volume series forming a Source-Book presenting the most important texts of the classical philosopher of Advaita Vedanta, Śaṃkara. As in previous volumes, a Conspectus of the Source-Book as a whole is appended at the back. Though each individual volume in the series covers a well-defined topic and can be read on its own, it was felt that the serious student would want to possess the whole series. For this reason the Bibliography at the back of the present volume includes only those works not already mentioned in the Bibliography to Volume I. The list of Abbreviations has been lengthened slightly to accommodate a few works that appear with some frequency in the present volume.

Some readers have told me that they have difficulty in finding their way about the work, so I thought I might say a word about the sign-posting. The heading of each page has a Roman numeral followed by an Arabic numeral on the left (e.g. XII.2). The Roman numeral shows the chapter, the Arabic numeral the section within the chapter. The scheme of chapters and sections within the volume can be seen from the Contents at the beginning, the wider context of the place of the chapter within the work as a whole can be seen from the Conspectus at the back. Each section is broken down into a series of Extracts, taken from different parts of Śaṃkara's works. Their beginning is indicated by an Arabic numeral at the left of the first paragraph. Their end is marked by a row of asterisks, and the last Note before the asterisks gives the source of the Extract in Śaṃkara's works.

Since there are a number of references to the Āpastamba Dharma Sūtras in the present volume, and references to this work can be confusing, it seems worth pointing out that, unless otherwise specified, the references are to Praśnas, Kaṇḍikās and Aphorisms, not to Paṭalas. Thus the recurring reference II.ii.2-3 indicates Praśna II, Kaṇḍikā ii, Aphorisms 2 and 3, page 183 in Chinnaswami's edition. On the other hand Śaṃkara's Vivaraṇa is spoken of as being on the Adhyātma Paṭala, which in fact consists of the 14 Aphorisms of the 22nd and 23rd Kaṇḍikās of the first Praśna.

Some of the material in the present volume is mainly of historical interest. But it also contains an abundance of fine passages, admirable, at least in the original, for their literary quality and for their noble sentiments. No one who had read this book could think that Śaṃkara or Advaita Vedanta dispensed with ethics.

My obligations as translator are as mentioned in previous volumes.

A. J. Alston
London, 1989

CONTENTS

TRANSLITERATED SANSKRIT WORDS

The following table gives the most elementary indications of the value of the vowels that are variable in English (but regular in Sanskrit) and of the unfamiliar symbols and groupings of letters found in transliterated Sanskrit words. It is *not* intended as an accurate guide to correct pronunciation, for which see M. Coulson, *Sanskrit*, Teach yourself Books, pp.4-21.

a = **u in but**
ā = **a in father**
ai = **ê in French crême**
au = **au in audit**
c = **ch in chant**
ch = **ch aspirated (said with extra breath)**
ḍ = **d in drake**
e = **ay in hay, (better. French é elongated)**
h = **immediately after a consonant aspirates it without altering the value. (bh,ph)**
ḥ = **strong h**
i = **i in hit**
ī = **ea in eat**

jñ = **ja or gya (as big yard)**
ṃ = **m before b, p, v and y and at the end of a word; elsewhere = n**
ṅ = **n in king**
ṇ = **n in tendril**
ñ = **n (except in jñ, q.v.)**
o = **o in note**
ṛ = **ri in rich**
s = **s in such (not as in "as")**
ś = **sh in shut**
ṣ = **sh in shut**
ṭ = **t in try**
u = **u in put**
u = **oo in boot**

CHAPTER XII

ADOPTING THE PATH

1. THE WHEEL OF TRANSMIGRATION

With the opening of the present chapter we pass over to the practical side of Śaṃkara's teaching, to which the theoretical part, in his eyes, only constituted a mere preparation. In the present chapter there will be Extracts exhibiting Śaṃkara's graphic descriptions of the plight of man bound on the wheel of transmigration, together with texts in which he expounds the results of living without obeying the Vedic injunctions to perform rituals without any meditation on their symbolic significance, or performing them with insufficient meditation to attain liberation by the indirect path.

The Extracts will be given in two groups without much preliminary explanation. Group A will deal with the fruits of self-interested action in general, group B with the results of ritualistic action in particular. The Extracts in this latter group are dominated by the Brahma Sūtra tradition, which in turn goes back to the Chāndogya Upanishad. In the earliest versions of this teaching, the vehicle of the soul was water. But long before Śaṃkara's day the Sāṃkhya philosophers (1) had evolved the more precise theory of a subtle body composed of all five subtle elements (tanmātra), the repository of the "traces" (saṃskāra) of "impregnations" (vāsanā) of the thoughts and deeds of the soul, clothed in which the soul passed from one physical body to another. (2) This idea is fused in the Brahma Sūtra tradition with the old Vedic teaching that the soul created a new "self" through ritualistic action for a new life after the death of the physical body: (3) the outcome is the teaching that the liquid libations poured into the sacrificial fire form a watery body in which the sacrificer experiences temporary felicity on the moon but returns to earth in rain when that body is exhausted. This is interwoven with the doctrine that the soul has a subtle body composed of *all* the elements in their subtle form which contains the saṃskāras and vāsanās which impel it towards further experiences in new physical bodies according to the merit or demerit of its past thoughts and deeds. Another old doctrine, the view that the vehicle of the soul is fire, surfaces towards the end of Group B (4) and has to be reconciled with the more developed doctrine of a subtle body composed of all five elements.

The Extracts in Group A, which include at least two magnificent purple passages in the loaded style of Sanskrit literary prose and bring the evils of identification with the body vividly before the mind of the reader, will perhaps be of more interest to the modern student than those of Group B, where Śaṃkara is found dealing with a part of the Upanishadic and Brahma Sūtra doctrine which was not of prime concern to him. It is of even less practical concern today, since the Vedic ritual is hardly performed in modern India. (5) Nevertheless, we get some interesting glimpses of the views current in Śaṃkara's day, which he seems to have shared at the level of practical experience, on such topics as the purpose of the performance of Vedic ritual and the fate of the soul that does not obtain release after death, which means the fate of practically every one, as even strivance for release is stated to be very rare. (6)

TEXTS ON THE WHEEL OF TRANSMIGRATION: GROUP A

1. What are the five factors of action? First, the vehicle (body). It is the seat for the manifestation of desire, aversion, pleasure, pain, knowledge and the like. (7) Second, the agent, the experiencer, which conforms to the states of its external adjuncts (body and mind). (8) Third, the organ, of diverse kinds, meaning faculties such as those of hearing whereby sound is heard, along with the faculties (of touch, taste, sight and smell) which perceive the other elements, together with the five faculties of action, as well as the lower (manas) and higher (buddhi) mental organs, making twelve organs in all. Fourthly, the different activities of the vital principle, such as breathing in and breathing out. And fifthly the divine power in the form of the support of Āditya (the sun-deity presiding over vision etc.) and other deities presiding over the preceding four factors.

Whatever act in conformity with or against the Vedic injunctions a man does through body, speech or mind, or whatever biological event like blinking and so on takes place in his body – even the latter being determined by the merit and demerit of former deeds and hence falling in some sense within the domain of action – whatever act, in short, occurs at all, is analysable into these five above-mentioned factors.

Perhaps you will ask how one can speak of actions performed by body, speech and mind if these other five factors are the sole causes of action. But there is no difficulty here. All action, whether in harmony with Vedic injunctions or against them, is chiefly action of either body, speech or mind. The biological functions, here including seeing and hearing and the other powers of perception, are mere subordinate features of the main action, which is either of the body or else of speech or else of the mind in every case. Hence these three classes of action, namely, action in harmony with the Vedic injunctions, actions prohibited by the Veda and involuntary biological events (9) are all included together when we speak of "action" being performed by the body and other factors. When the "fruits" of such action come to be experienced, they will be experienced in the realm of the body, speech or mind, according to whether the original act was of body, speech or mind. Hence, since the classification of acts into acts of body, speech or mind was a mere *internal* classification, there is no contradiction when it is said that *all* actions are analysable into the above-mentioned five factors of agent, vehicle, organ, Vital Energy and adjuvant divine power.

Hence if a person erroneously identifies his Self with these five factors, and thinks that he himself is the agent of some act which has really been performed by them, he is ignorant, for his intellect will not have been properly educated by the teachings of the Upanishads and Teacher. Even he who maintains that the Self is other than the body and the senses and the mind and is the bare agent using them as his instruments, he also lacks the true spiritual culture, and knows the true nature neither of the Self nor of action. Such a person has a miserable, perverted, stunted mentality, exactly calculated to bring on further births and deaths. Such a one, says the text, does not see, even though he sees. That is, he is like the one suffering from strabism and who sees not one but a whole collection of moons, or like the one who imagines that the moon is rushing through the sky when he sees it in the midst of swiftly moving clouds, or like one seated in a palanquin who thinks he is running because the bearers are running. (10)

* * * * *

2. What is the reason for the suspicion that the gods and other beings place obstacles in the way of attaining the benefits of knowledge of the Absolute? Well, the Veda shows that man contracts debts to the gods and other beings from the mere fact of being born, for this is what is implied in the passage "to the seers (ṛṣi) through celibacy, to the gods through sacrifice, to the ancestors through progeny." (11) The present Upanishad passage, too, speaks of man as "like an animal to the gods;" and the same is implied in the later passage, "Now this Self (the ignorant man) is an object of enjoyment to all beings." (12) Hence the suspicion is quite justifiable that the gods, acting in the manner of creditors wishing to preserve their means of livelihood, may cast obstacles in the way to prevent their dependents, men, from attaining immortality. Indeed, the gods protect their animals as if they were their own bodies, and a later text will show that the gods and other beings derive the greater part of their livelihood from the ritual performed by men, from which point of view one man is equal to many animals. The present text will say "Therefore they do not like it that human beings should know this" and the later text will say "Just as one wishes safety to one's body, so do all beings wish safety to him who knows it as such." (13) The mention of "dislike" and "safety" shows that the gods think that when a man comes to know the Absolute he ceases to be dependent on others and therefore ceases to belong to the world of any deity or to function as his beast of burden. Therefore it is very likely that the gods should cast obstacles in the way of him who wished to know the Absolute and prevent him acquiring that consummation. For they do not lack power.

To this the following objection might be advanced. It might be objected that if the gods could throw obstacles which could prevent the fruition of one kind of action they could also prevent the fruition of action in other spheres too, notably that of rituals. But this would undermine all belief in the means to prosperity and liberation from rebirth taught by the Veda. Moreover, the Lord Himself, being possessed of infathomable powers, would be better than any one else at casting obstacles. And the theory would affect all results attributable to time, ritual, spells, herbs and fulfilment of ascetic vows, which are accepted as having their peculiar power to attract or impel; and this, too, would undermine all faith in carrying out the behests of the Veda.

But all this we deny. For objects are invariably produced according to definite laws. And we also observe the variety present in the world. (14) Both these features would be impossible if anything were capable of behaving entirely spontaneously. We accept that action is a factor in the later emergence of pleasure and pain and other experiences, as this is agreed upon by the Vedas, by the derivative literature, by common worldly belief and by reason alike. And hence we deny that the gods or the Lord or a force like time work to upset the causality of action. For all action depends on the co-operation of different factors. Men's good and bad deeds cannot take place without the co-operation of the gods (as deities presiding over natural forces), time, the Lord and other factors. And even when they have taken place, actions cannot bring their appropriate fruits to the agent without the same factors being at work. For it is the very nature of action to require the presence of co-operating factors and instruments. Hence the gods and the Lord co-operate in favour of action and cannot be supposed to make obstacles to prevent its producing its appropriate results.

There is, moreover, an irreducible element in actions themselves which the co-operating factors must support. The relative predominance or subordination of the act itself and of factors such as the power of presiding deities and the nature of the material used varies in different cases and is hard to determine, and this is what drives people into confusion on the subject. Some say that the action alone and not its co-operating factors determines the nature of the future results. Others say that the future result is entirely the work of presiding deities. Others say it is produced by the force called time. Others lay the emphasis on the nature of the materials used or on other factors. Others, again, say that it is the resultant of all these forces working together. It is clear that the Veda and the derivative literature accept the predominance of the act itself in this regard, as we have such texts as, "He becomes holy through holy deeds and sinful through sinful deeds." (15) It is true that each of the co-operating factors is supreme as regards its own function while the others are only auxiliaries in that particular sphere, yet it is the act itself that invariably predominates in determining the future result, as its predominance in this regard is established by the Veda and by reason alike. (16)

* * * * *

3. The text now goes on to explain what it is that originates action. First of all it mentions knowledge (jñāna). By "knowledge" it means knowledge in the quite general sense of that by which every object without exception is known. Secondly it means "the known", an equally general sense to mean all that can be known. Thirdly it mentions "the knower". This latter is the experiencer, characterized by an external adjunct (body, senses and mind), and fictitiously imagined through nescience. (17) This triad is the originator of all action without exception. For it is only when knowledge, knower and known are present that there can arise that need for production or removal which brings all action into being.

The text then goes on to explain how action, initiated by the five factors beginning with the vehicle (the body), and analysed into three classes, namely actions of the body, speech and mind, may also be analysed into the three factors of instrument, object and agent. The "instrument" means the organ, whether external like the senses of perception or internal like the intellect. The "object" means that which is above all desired by the agent and towards which his action is directed. And the agent means him who sets the instruments of action in motion. This, as the text puts it, is the "threefold complex necessary for action." (18)

* * * * *

4. But when they (the Vaiśeṣikas) say that the soul performs action through its own memory, will and effort, which are the causes of the action, this is wrong. For these alleged memory, desire and effort that the soul is supposed to have are themselves but illusions resting on mere erroneous notions. They are invariably associated with impressions (saṃskāra) arising from illusory notions of the experience of the pleasant and the unpleasant results of actions.

In the present birth merit and demerit are amassed and their fruits experienced solely through attachment and aversion arising from false identification with the body-mind organism. And we are bound to infer that the same must have been the case in the previous birth too, and also in those before it, so that transmigration is a beginningless and endless process resting on nescience. And this shows that the total cessation of transmigratory experience can only occur through devotion to the path of knowledge, associated with the renunciation of all action. And because self-identification with the body is based on nescience, when nescience is brought to an end one is no longer embodied and transmigratory experience no longer continues. (19)

* * * * *

5. And so the whole world, which depends for whatever existence it has on this continued performance of meditation and ritual, which is of the nature of means and ends and of actions and their results, which goes out of existence and comes back into existence anew every instant, is impure, hollow, changeful like a running river, comparable to the series of flashes that *seems* to constitute a steady flame, insubstantial like the stalk of a plantain, comparable to foam, to the water of a mirage, to a dream and the like, being kept in being solely by the stream of the acts and impressions of acts (vāsanā) of its teeming living beings — this whole world, thus constituted, cannot be eradicated by those who identify themselves with it, and to them it seems eternal and solid. (20)

* * * * *

6. In the world one estimates the size of the (hidden) roots of a tree from the size of its visible yield (lit. its cotton). And in the same way, the sixth Vallī of the Upanishad is begun with a view to determine the true nature of the root, the Absolute, by a consideration of the nature of the visible tree, the world of transmigration.

Of the tree of this world of transmigration, embracing all from the realm of the Unmanifest Principle to the realm of the inanimate, the root is on high, that is, in the highest abode of Viṣṇu. It is called a tree because it can be cut down. (21) It is an unmitigated series of evils, such as birth, old age, death, grief and many another. Every instant it changes its constitution, for its nature is to vanish on sight, like the water of a mirage or a city seen in the clouds. It ends in non-existence, like a (felled) tree. It is hollow like the stalk of a plantain. It is the source of many hundreds of vain speculations to the heretical mind. Its nature does not yield itself to the investigator as a definite "this". Its root and origin is the supreme principle, the Absolute, to be known through the Upanishads. It springs from the unmanifest seed of ignorance, desire and action. It comes forth as the Golden Embryo (Hiraṇyagarbha) consisting in the twin powers of knowledge and action belonging to the Absolute in its "lower form". (22) Its trunk is composed of the subtle bodies of all living creatures. Its proud bearing arises from the constant sprinkling of the water-drops of desire for this thing and that thing. Its shoots and buds are the objects of the senses. Its leaves are the Veda, the derivative literature (smṛti), reason, learning and instruction. Its fair flowers are the many pious acts of sacrifice, charity and austerity. It offers innumerable fruits to support the life of its denizens, which taste variously of pleasure and pain. Its firm roots have waxed, gnarled and mighty, through being sprinkled with the water of desire for its fruits. It has nests for the sojourning of all its inhabitants from Brahmā onwards in the form of the various worlds called Satya, etc. It is clamorous with the manifold sounds of cries of joy and sorrow escaping the lips of living beings, of singing and instrumental music, of cries of "No, no! Let me go, let me go," either laughed out or groaned out in the course of sporting and wrestling. It stands to be cut down by the weapon of non-attachment arising from the vision of the Self laid down in the Upanishads. (23) It is an "Aśvattha" in the sense of a "wont-stand-tomorrow tree," (24) by nature eternally on the move, impelled by the winds of desire and action. It has low-hanging branches in the form of heaven, hell, animals and ghosts. It is eternal in the sense of being beginningless and therefore long-standing (but not in the sense of being indestructible).

The root of this tree of transmigratory experience is glorious, pure, all-luminous, of the very nature of the Self as Consciousness. And that is the Absolute (brahman) because it is the greatest (25) of all. (26)

* * * * *

7. But those who take part in the round of transmigration revolve round in the midst of ignorance, of thick darkness, swaddled in the bonds of a thousand longings for sons and cattle and worldly goods. Thinking themselves to be wise and to be great experts in the secular and sacred sciences, they pursue a crooked and devious course. Lacking true discrimination, they wander about afflicted by old age, death and disease, like a large crowd of blind people being led by others as blind along a rocky road leading to a great disaster.

On account of their blind infatuation, the next world never crosses the path of their thoughts, neither do they think of the means to attain it taught by the Veda, as those who are without spiritual discrimination never do. For they are heedless, their minds are given over to thinking only of what is needed in connection with sons and cattle and the like, they are dazzled by the glamour of wealth and covered in darkness. They habitually regard this physical world with its women, food, drink and other objects of enjoyment as all that is, and deny the existence of a world beyond. Such people are born again and again, and come again and again into my power, (27) into the power of death. That is, they remain involved in the unbroken chain of suffering constituted by birth, death and the other hardships of transmigratory existence. That is exactly the condition of the very great majority of the people. (28)

* * * * *

8. The section of the Veda dealing with rituals is instituted for the sake of the man who has the conviction that in some sense or other a permanent Self exists and will be joined with other bodies, and who wants to know how to obtain the desirable and avoid the undesirable in regard to life in those bodies. It gives him detailed information on the point. But this does nothing to remove ignorance of the Self in the form of supposing oneself to be an agent and enjoyer, which is the cause of the desire to pursue the pleasant and shun the unpleasant. It does not, that is, in any way convey the knowledge that one is quite other than the agent and enjoyer and is in fact the real Self, none other than the Absolute (brahmātma-svarūpa). And until this ignorance *is* removed, a person will remain afflicted with natural desire and aversion for the results of deeds, and, under their impulse, will tend to transgress even the injunctions and prohibitions of the Veda, and heap up by thought, word and deed a great deal of demerit which will cause him much trouble both at present and in future lives, all on account of the natural tendency towards evil. And on this path he can descend right down into the vegetable realms.

At some stage, however, the tendencies implanted by the holy teachings (29) will assert themselves. Then he will begin to accumulate a preponderance of merit through thought, word and deed, which is the means to welfare. Spiritual welfare is of two kinds — that derived from mere performance of good deeds, and that derived from performance of good deeds in association with meditation. (30) The first leads only to a sojourn in the realm of the ancestors (pitṛ), the second to the world of the gods (deva) and finally to the "World of Brahmā". (31) And there is the Vedic passage in the same sense, "He who sacrifices to the Self is better than he who sacrifices to the gods," (32) and there are such passages from the derivative literature as "Works prescribed in the Veda are of two kinds." (33) And when the deeds of merit and the deeds of demerit are evenly balanced there results birth as a man. Thus this process of transmigratory life rolls on, embracing all from the creator-god Brahmā to immobile objects, associated with such evils as the innate ignorance of the Self, impelled on by merit and demerit, based on name, form and action. And all this universe, which is now manifest as means and ends, was unmanifest before its production. This world of transmigratory experience, which consists essentially in the superimposition of action, its factors and results onto the Self through nescience, proceeds on in a cycle like seed and sprout. And this Upanishad was composed to bring to an end the metaphysical ignorance of anyone who had become disenchanted with the world of transmigratory experience and who had come to realize it was a beginningless, endless evil. It does this by communicating to him metaphysical knowledge of the Absolute, which is the opposite of metaphysical ignorance. (34)

* * * * *

9. The Lord describes transmigratory experience (saṃsāra) under the image of a tree in order to induce indifference towards it. For without indifference to worldly life no one is qualified for knowledge of the true nature of the Lord (Bhagavan).

The root of the tree of transmigratory life is said to be "above" in order to show that it lies in a principle beyond time which is the ground of empirical phenomena, itself eternal and inexhaustible.

(XII.1) ADOPTING THE PATH (TEXTS)

The Lord declares that this tree of transmigratory life has its root above, taking the root to be the Absolute as associated with the power of Māyā (māyā-śakti) in its unmanifest form. And there are precedents for this in the Upanishads, such as the text "With root above and branches below." (35)

In the Purāṇas, too, we find the following passage: (36) "Age-old is the tree of Brahmā. Its roots lie in the Unmanifest Principle and it can only grow thanks to the presence of this latter. Its trunk is mind, its hollows the senses, its branches the great elements and its leaves the sense-objects. Good and evil deeds are its fair flowers, pain and pleasure the fruits. It sustains all creatures, and is the pleasure-ground where Brahmā ever wanders at will. If one once cuts it down with the supreme sword of knowledge one attains to the joy of the Self from which there is no return."

It is this tree to which the present verse (Bhagavad Gītā XV.1) refers. It has its roots above. It represents transmigratory life, illusory in character. Its branches hang below. They are the "Great Principle" (mahat), the principle of (cosmic) Ego-Consciousness (ahaṃkāra), and the subtle elements (tanmātra) and the rest, and are spoken of figuratively as branches. It is known as an "Aśvattha" tree (aspen-leafed fig-tree) because it undergoes destruction every instant and hence "will not stand tomorrow." (37) It is called "imperishable" (akṣara) because it consists in the illusory cycle of transmigratory experiences which have been in progress from beginningless time. It is the well-known "tree of transmigratory life" based on a beginningless and endless series of bodies, and in this sense "imperishable" (i.e. though not beyond being cut down by the sword of spiritual knowledge).

Another mark of this "tree of transmigratory life" is that it has the Vedic hymns (chanda) for its leaves, the hymns of the Ṛg, Yajur and Sāma

Vedas. (38) The hymns are figuratively spoken of as leaves, and are called in Sanskrit "chandas" because they are the tree's "covering" (chādana). As the leaves serve to protect a tree, so do the Vedas serve to protect the "tree of transmigratory life" by proclaiming what leads to merit and what to demerit. He who understands the nature of the tree of transmigratory life together with its root understands the true meaning of the Veda. For when this is known not a jot remains to be known elsewhere. The text eulogizes knowledge of the tree together with its root, implying by the phrase "understands the true meaning of the Veda" that the person concerned is omniscient. (39)

Now the tree-metaphor is carried on further and the roles of some of the smaller parts of the "tree" explained. The "branches" of the tree stretch down from the realm of human beings and the like to the inanimate realms and upwards to the realm of Brahmā, the world-creator. (40) They represent the fruits of meditation and ritual as laid down in the Veda. They are nourished by the "constituents" (guṇa), that is, sattva, rajas and tamas, the very material from which they are formed (upādāna). The sense-objects consisting in sound, etc., are taken as the shoots, springing from the branches and other parts which represent the body and the other external physical circumstances arising from the fruits of previous deeds. The nature of the ultimate "root" or material cause (upādāna-kāraṇa) of the tree has already been declared. (41) Hence the text can now speak of secondary "roots", namely the tendencies (vāsanā) arising from attachments and aversions implanted by former experience. These tendencies, in their turn, promote further good and bad actions. They occupy a middle position, lower than that of the gods, (42) pervasive in their effects, intimately related with all activity, good and bad, in the sense that future action arises when they arise. These tendencies operate, as the text emphasizes, "in the world of man." For it is well known that deliberate action is peculiarly the province of man.

The next verse (i.e. Bhagavad Gītā XV.3) adds further details about the tree of transmigratory life already described. It is never perceived here on earth in the form just described. For its nature is to undergo destruction the instant it is perceived, like a dream or a mirage or a magic display (māyā) or a city in the clouds. It has no end, is never done with. (43) It has no beginning in the sense that no one has a clear conception "*this* was the point at which it began." Nor can any one perceive the whole of its duration between beginning and end.

First one must cut down this Aśvattha tree with its firmly entrenched roots, by the sword of non-attachment (asaṅga). Non-attachment means rising above the desire for sons and wealth and for a higher "world". One must destroy this tree of transmigratory life along with its roots (i.e. secondary roots) by the sword of non-attachment as strengthened by a resolute determination to attain to the supreme Self and as sharpened by repeated application to the grind-stone of spiritual discrimination and spiritual affirmation.

Then one must seek out the abode of Viṣṇu. (44) This "seeking out" is a matter of enquiry, the meaning being that the abode of Viṣṇu is (not something to be attained through movement of any kind but) something to be known. Those who "reach" this abode of Viṣṇu do not return to transmigratory life.

How does this abode have to be sought out? The text goes on to explain that it has to be sought out with the feeling "I will attain to the primeval spirit (puruṣa)," that is, by taking refuge in Him.

Who is that spirit? The text explains that it is that spirit from which arose this age-old illusory show (māyā) of transmigratory life, issuing forth like an illusion (māyā) conjured up by a strolling magician. (45)

* * * * *

10. The "Prājāpatyas" (mentioned in the text) are the offspring of Prajāpati (Brahmā) in a previous birth. Who are they? "The gods (deva) and demons (asura)," which means the faculities of Prajāpati (Brahmā) such as speech and the rest, (which here means our own faculties).

If they are faculties, why does the text speak of them as gods and demons? We reply that they are called gods in so far as they are brought into being by meditation and ritualistic merit stemming from the Veda. But in so far as they are generated by secular knowledge and activity arising from natural perception and inference applied to visible ends they are called demons (asura). The name "asura" arises either because they rejoice in their own life-breath (asu) or because they are the opposite of the gods (sura). (46) Because the "demons" are "generated by secular knowledge and activity applied to visible ends" they are more numerous than the "gods". The human faculties make more frequent efforts in the pursuit of knowledge and action on a natural secular basis than they do in the pursuit of knowledge and action following Vedic revelation. For in the former case the ends are visible. The gods are therefore spoken of as "fewer", because efforts inspired by Vedic revelation are less frequent, demanding, as they do, a total consecration of attention.

These "gods" and "demons", situated in the body of Prajāpati, become rivals in the pursuit of "these worlds", (states of consciousness) attained through knowledge and action, both sacred and secular. Their "rivalry" consists in their successively emerging dominant and then undergoing suppression. Sometimes the faculties are dominated by a mood dictated by knowledge and action following Vedic revelation. And when they are, then the "demoniac" mood of those faculties, dictated by secular knowledge and activity following from perception and inference and directed to visible ends, is suppressed. This represents a victory for the "gods" and a defeat for the "demons". Sometimes, on the contrary, the "god-like" mood is suppressed and the "demoniac" emerges dominant. This represents a victory for the "demons" and a defeat for the "gods".

When the "gods" secure victories of this kind, the soul progresses on by access of merit right up to the attainment of the state of Prajāpati. When the "demons" secure victories of this kind, the soul sinks through access of demerit right on down to the condition of a plant. When the two sides are equally balanced, human birth results. (47)

* * * * *

11. The unenlightened man is eligible for the ritual laid down in the Veda, which may be performed with or without accompanying symbolic meditations and which varies according to caste and stage of life. On this path (i.e. of ritual) he may rise higher and higher from the condition of man up to that of Hiraṇyagarbha. If, however, he ignores the injunctions and prohibitions of the Veda and acts merely according to his natural inclinations he will sink from the human level to that of vegetation. (48)

* * * * *

12. Since (the bodies of) all living beings are modifications of food, and since all alike are descended from Brahmā, why is man alone singled out in the present connection? On account of his pre-eminence. What is that pre-eminence? The fact that he has the capacity for ritualistic action and spiritual knowledge. For man alone has the requisite faculties for this, man alone desires the fruit of it, and in his case alone is there no circumstance to debar him from it. (49) For we have such other Vedic texts as, "The Self is supremely evident in man. He has a higher degree of intelligence than other beings. He speaks what he knows. He sees what he knows. He sees into the future. He knows what is and what is not his ultimate goal. He desires (50) to attain the immortal through the mortal instrument. In this sense he is (said to be) equipped with intelligence. All that other animals are really aware of is their hunger and thirst."(51)

TEXTS ON THE WHEEL OF TRANSMIGRATION: GROUP B

13. Next the Upanishad proceeds to answer the question, "How can that single couple consisting, on the one hand, of the realm of 'the moon', 'form' and 'food', and on the other of 'the formless', 'the Vital Energy', 'the sun' (52) produce (all these manifold) creatures?" This couple, it is replied, constitute time or the year, and that is Prajāpati. For the year is the sum of the days and nights and special occasions brought by the moon and the sun. And since the year is identical with the Cosmic Vital Energy and Food it is said to have the double nature (of these two).

How is this? The year, called Prajāpati, includes two passages. They are well known as the Southern and the Northern Passage, being the two periods of six months in which the sun moves southwards and northwards respectively in the sky. By doing so, it arranges for the worlds of those who only perform rituals and for those who perform rituals in conjunction with meditation on their symbolic significance respectively.

Now the text elaborates on this. Those Brahmins who follow action in the form of sacrificial ritual and good works ((iṣṭā-pūrte) alone, who resort only to action and not to the eternal principle beyond action, they gain access to the world of the moon. That is to say, they gain access to that part of Prajāpati which is constituted by food. For (a sojourn on) the moon is something produced by action. And when the fruits of their deeds are exhausted there on the moon, they return to this world. For we have the text, "They enter either this world or a lower one." (53)

Because this is so, these seers (ṛṣi) who have heaven in mind, who desire children and adopt the householder's life, attain the Southern Path, which is to attain to the moon, which is Prajāpati in the form of food. For this "Path of the Ancestors", which means "world-of-the-moon-reached-by-the-path-of-the-ancestors", is verily (in the realm of) food.(54)

* * * * *

14. The word "then" serves to introduce a different subject, the householders living in villages. By "villages" (55) is meant a characterization of householders in general, contrasting them with forest-dwellers, just in the same way as "living in the forests" is a general epithet for retired folk living in the forests and for wandering ascetics, both contrasted with householders. The text says, "These householders living in villages who occupy themselves with Vedic ritual like the Agnihotra and good works like the construction of wells and tanks and rest-houses and the like, and also charity, consisting in the distribution according to one's means of necessaries to worthy recipients in the precincts of one's household altar, and obedience to the Teacher and protection of one's dependents, daily repetition of one's

Veda and so forth". We have to fill in such details because the use of the word "iti" shows that only the general kind of things meant has been indicated.

These souls, being without spiritual insight, proceed at death to the deity who presides over smoke. He conducts them from smoke to the deity presiding over the night. From the night they are conducted to the deity presiding over the fortnight of the waning moon, and from there they proceed to the six months in which the trajectory of the sun moves towards the south — that is to say, to the group of six deities adopting those months. But these ritualists under discussion do not pass on to the year (as do those on the Path of Light after negotiating the deities presiding over the six months when the sun is moving towards the north)...

From the months they proceed to the world of the ancestors (pitṛ-loka) and from there to the ether and from the ether to the moon. What is it, then, that these ritualists finally attain? It is this moon we see in the sky, Soma, the King of the Brahmins. This moon is the food devoured by Indra and the other gods, (56) from whence it follows that they, too, who have followed the path beginning with smoke, are devoured by the gods. Does this mean that the performance of Vedic ritual and the rest is only for their discomfiture if they are eventually to become food devoured by the gods? Not so, for the expression "food for the gods" merely means "servants of the gods". It does not mean that they are literally gobbled up by the gods, but only that they become servants of the gods, as women and domestic animals serve us. The word "food" is widely used to mean servants, as when we say "Women are the food of kings" or "Cattle are the food of kings" or "Farmers are the food of kings."

Women, domestic animals, servants and the like, though "enjoyed" by others, are not themselves entirely bereft of pleasure. In the same way, the ritualists, though "enjoyed" by the gods, also sport with them happily. Further, they acquire a watery body in the lunar sphere that is capable of enjoying pleasures. It has already been explained (57) how the waters, called "Faith", when offered into the "sacrificial fire" of the shining world (dyu-loka), become "Soma the King". These waters, offspring of ritual acts, proceed to the shining world, accompanied by the other material elements (making up the subtle body), and, having become "moonlike" in quality, engender bodies for those who have carried out the Vedic and other (enjoined) activities mentioned above.

On the occasion of the last sacrifice (of one's present life), the offering of the body on the funeral pyre, when the body is being burnt by the flames, the "waters" (arising from the libations offered at the sacrifices he has performed)(58) unite with the smoke arising from the funeral pyre of the sacrificer and wrap themselves round him and proceed to the moon, where they form an external body for him, as if of clay trussed in by grasses. Through this body he proceeds to enjoy the fruits of his ritualistic and other (good) acts.

Such souls dwell on the sphere of the moon until the merit for their enjoyment there is exhausted, and they return to earth again by the path to be described. From the use (in the text) of the word "again" we deduce that they have been to the sphere of the moon and returned many times before. Hence, having stored up merit in this world by the performance of Vedic ritual and other meritorious practices, they go to the moon, and on the exhaustion of that merit they return, without being able to remain on the moon an instant longer than their merit warrants. For with the exhaustion of their merit their very wherewithal to stay on the moon is exhausted, like the exhaustion of oil in a lamp.

Here a question might be raised. Does descent take place on the exhaustion of *all* the merit through which one ascended to the moon, or is there a remnant left over? If you ask the questioner to state more clearly what is at issue, he will say that if *all* the merit and demerit of one in the sphere of the moon were exhausted while he was still there, that might result in (the absurd consequence) that he would be liberated. (59) We might reply that it might only mean that he stayed there on the sphere of the moon, without prejudice to the question of whether he was liberated or not. But the opponent would claim that it would still imply that the sacrificer could not return here on earth to enjoy experiences in another body, and that this would contradict the passages in the Smṛti about a "remnant". (60)

To all this our reply is that the sacrificer's life might well include many acts besides those of Vedic ritual, for example good works and charity as defined above, and that these would cause further embodiment and further experience in the world of men. As the merit and demerit from these acts could not be experienced in the sphere of the moon, they would remain unexhausted, and there would be no conflict with the teaching that all the merit that caused ascent to the sphere of the moon would be exhausted there by being experienced. Nor would there be any contradiction with the teaching in the Smṛti about a remnant, as the word "remnant" covers merit and demerit derived from any kind of actions whatever.

And this is enough to dispose of the questioner's objection that if all the merit derived from rituals, good works and charity, which caused ascent to the sphere of the moon, had to be consumed before descent from the moon, this would (absurdly) imply liberation. It must be remembered that it is likely that every living being will have acquired merit and demerit that will demand to be experienced in births of a totally different and mutually contradictory kind. Nor can all merit and demerit be eliminated by experience in a single birth. The Smṛti teaches that every such (extremely pernicious) act as murder of a Brahmin sets up many future births. Acts apart from rituals, good works and charity do produce a residue of merit and demerit resulting in rebirth, as is proved by the fact that those who attain to birth as plants or in other senseless conditions cannot (in that life) produce the merit that would raise them to anything higher. Without this residue, the foetus hanging upside down in the womb would never reach the world, as it is incapable of action producing merit or demerit. From all this it follows that all one's merit and demerit cannot be exhausted in a single birth.

Some hold (61) that acts cause a new birth by destroying the previous repository of all merit and demerit at death. This view is not willing to grant the possibility of the distinction implied in "one part of the merit and demerit remains in being without initiating a rebirth; another part initiates a new birth." It maintains that death brings out into the open all merit and demerit, just as a lamp illumines everything within its range.

We cannot admit this doctrine because we adhere to the principle that everything is (ultimately) the Self of everything else. If everything is the Self of everything else, nothing can totally be destroyed, because destruction is limited to a particular place, time and cause, and nothing can become totally manifest for the same reason. Consider the case, too, of souls bearing the marks of previously experienced births as man, peacock and monkey, and thus having many mutually incompatible latent tendencies (vāsanā). These latent tendencies would not all be destroyed if the merit and demerit appropriate to rebirth as a monkey actually caused rebirth as a monkey, and neither would the total merit and demerit which might cause other births. For if *all* latent tendencies arising from experience in previous bodies were destroyed, then, when a new birth as a monkey had been originated as a result of the merit and demerit acquired in a previous birth as a monkey, then the new-born monkey would never acquire the power of clinging to its mother's body in the fashion of a baby-monkey while the mother moved from branch to branch, as this act would never have been practised in the present birth. Nor can you say that such a soul must have been a monkey in its immediately previous birth. The Veda, too, says "His knowledge, secular and sacred, his ritualistic works and his acquired skills and aptitudes follow him." (62) Hence it follows that the doctrine that latent tendencies and all merit and demerit are destroyed at death is untenable, and the teaching of the existence of a "remnant" of merit and demerit is quite justified.Hence our view that all the merit from rituals, good works and charity which cause ascent to the sphere of the moon is exhausted through enjoyment in the sphere of the moon does not conflict with the continuation of transmigratory life afterwards, as the latter proceeds on the basis of a "remnant" of the *total* merit and demerit from all actions, which continues in being after the above-mentioned particular benefit is exhausted.

What is that journey by which they return? We answer, they return back as they came. But is it not a fact that the outward journey was to proceed from the six months of the Southern Passage of the sun to the world of the ancestors, from the world of the ancestors to the ether (ākāśa) and from the ether to the moon, whereas the return is different, since it is said one there proceeds from the ether to the wind? We reply that there is nothing wrong here, as the passage to the ether and the earth is the same in both cases. And the text "return as they came" is not meant to specify exactly how they return: it only means that as they went so they returned again, though possibly by a different route. "As they came" is just a very general indication.

The meaning is that they reach the material ether. The waters that engendered their special body in the sphere of the moon now dissolve, when the merit that originally caused them to ascend there has been exhausted through enjoyment. Melting like a pot of clarified butter in fire, the waters dissolve into the space between earth and heaven (antarikṣa) (63) in subtle form, like the ether. From having the nature of this space, the waters change and become wind. Resting in the wind, becoming wind, they hurtle about, hither and thither. And the one whose special merit has become exhausted becomes wind with them. Having become wind, he afterwards becomes smoke with them, and from being smoke he becomes cirrus cloud. From cirrus cloud, he becomes a rain-cloud and rains down on the high places of the earth. The text means that the one possessed now only of the remnant of his merit and demerit falls to the earth as rain. These souls are then reborn here as rice, herbs, trees, sesamum and beans. (64) The text breaks into the plural here to show that there are many souls of this kind whose merit in the sphere of the moon becomes exhausted, whereas the singular number was used before, because all were alike as long as they were in the rain-cloud and other earlier stages.

The "escape" of these souls is said to be "extremely difficult" because they fall in rain showers on many an awkward place like the side of a mountain, an inaccessible river, the sea, the jungle, desert-land and the like. Carried down from the sides of mountains by mountain streams, they reach first the rivers and then the sea and then are swallowed by monsters of the deep. And whatever monster swallows them up will in turn be swallowed by another, and then they will be dissolved back with him into the sea. Then they will be sucked up by the sea-water clouds and will again fall in rain-showers on desert-ground or on the sides of inaccessible mountains, and there they will stay until eventually drunk by, say, a snake or a deer inhabiting such wild places, and these will be eventually eaten by other animals. In this way they will revolve. Sometimes they will pass into inedible plants and just wither away. Even if they pass into edible vegetables, they will be fortunate to find their way to be eaten by a seed-bearing animal, as plants are many ....

To become rice or barley or other edible grain and to connect up with a seed-bearing animal is more difficult still. For instance, if they happen to be eaten by young children in whom the seed is still locked up, or by impotent old men, they will just be crushed in mid-passage. For food-eaters are legion, and not all of them bear seed. When at last, by accident, (65) they happen to be eaten by a seed-bearing being, they assume his form and their further action for merit or demerit becomes possible.

How? Whenever a person eats food that is impregnated with the soul of one who has performed sacrifices and descended from the sphere of the moon, and imparts the seed to a woman at the right time, then the soul (as the Upanishad puts it) "assumes something of that person's form." Endowed largely with the forms of the limbs of the procreator, the soul of the sacrificer enters the womb of the woman. For the seed is conditioned by the bodily form of the one who imparts it. For we have another Vedic text, "(The seed) is heat generated from all the limbs." (66) So the soul assumes the form of the procreator. Thus from a man is born a man, from a bull a creature of the bull-species and never of any other species ....

(XII.1) ADOPTING THE PATH (TEXTS)

As for those others, who do not perform sacrifices and hence do not ascend to the sphere of the moon, they also (sometimes) become rice and barley and other forms of food on account of their heinous sins. But their "escape" and return to the condition of man is not "difficult" like that of those who perform the sacrifices. This is because they have acquired their embodiment as rice or barley or the like directly through their own merit and demerit. But when the merit and demerit warranting this form of experience has become exhausted, and their plant-body of rice or the like has undergone destruction, then they transfer in conscious condition to new bodies (of a lowly insect kind) such as a leech. For there is that other Vedic passage, "He has particular cognition (at death), and he proceeds on under the light of this cognition." (67)

Although they go to their new body with their senses withdrawn, yet they have a certain dream-like consciousness through the latent impressions stirred by the merit and demerit that cause the transference to the new body, as this text shows. In a similar way, the passages to the path beginning with the flame and the path beginning with smoke are made with a certain dream-like consciousness aroused, because the cause of their passing is merit and demerit that has assumed an active form. But when the practitioners of Vedic ritual have once been transformed into (lit. taken birth as) rice and the like, they cannot still be conscious when they acquire contact with the seed-bearing man and the woman. For they cannot retain consciousness during the reaping and threshing and pounding of the grain (before it is eaten).

Now, you might think that, as there is not much difference in principle between descending from the sphere of the moon and entering another body, those who descended from the moon would be just as conscious when they entered another body as the leech in passing from leaf to leaf. And this, you might think, would involve the difficulty that those who performed Vedic ritual and good works would have to experience a terrible hell between the time of their leaving the sphere of the moon and their taking birth as a Brahmin. And the Veda would have ordained resort to ritual and good works for the harm of the sacrificer instead of for his good. And if the Vedic ritual wrought harm for the sacrificer, this would undermine the authority of the Veda.

But this view is unfounded. For it neglects the possibility that there is a difference between the ascent to the sphere of the moon and descent from it, just as there is a difference between climbing a tree and falling off it. When transition from one body to another (is like a leech stretching its body over to pass from one leaf to the next and so) is immediate and caused by merit and demerit that have assumed active form, the presence of consciousness is intelligible, as it will have been aroused by the merit and demerit in active form. One might compare this with the case of one climbing a tree to get at the fruit, and, accordingly, there may well be consciousness for those passing on the path of the flame, as well as for those ascending to the moon by the path beginning with smoke. But there are no reasons of this kind suggesting that those descending from the sphere of the moon feel any consciousness, any more than a person who falls from a tree does.

Consider also the case of those who have been struck by a mallet or the like and have had their senses, the source of their empirical consciousness, stunned and blocked, and who yet can travel from one place to another on their own momentum. (68) Similar is the case of those who are returning down from the moon to another body, after their watery bodies have been crushed and their senses withdrawn on the exhaustion of the merit which caused their heavenly enjoyments. They descend back down to earth in a state of suspended animation. The descent is chiefly caused by the water that had served as the seed of their body in the sphere of the moon, which still remains in attendance (in dissolved or "subtle" form), and they are eventually connected with plant-bodies, the selection of which is determined by their merit and demerit. But they have no particularized consciousness, as their senses are withdrawn. They remain in suspended animation during the operations of reaping, threshing, pounding, cooking, eating, transformation into liquid seed and imparting of seed, as the merit and demerit initiating the next life are not yet active. Because the water that formed the seed of the body in the sphere of the moon is still with them during all these operations, their case is different from that of those who transfer from one body to the next in the manner of a leech, so that there is no contradiction with the Veda when it says that the latter retain their consciousness. On the contrary, we have shown that as long as they are in mid-passage they are in suspended animation and have no particularized consciousness.

Nor is there any reason to infer that because Vedic sacrifices involve slaughter of animals they must produce demerit as well as merit. For such slaughter is actually enjoined by the Veda. We reject the notion that slaughter enjoined in the Veda causes demerit, on the authority of the Vedic text, "Doing harm to no living creature *except on sacred ground*." (69) But even if it did cause demerit, it is quite intelligible that the demerit should be wiped away by the sacred verses that accompany the ritual, just as poison and other harmful forces can be neutralized by charms.

Amongst those who perform sacrifices, only those whose conduct here in this world is of a high ethical standard are said to be "men of fair conduct." Only when cruelty, lies and deception are absent can we say that a man's ritualistic actions lead to merit. Such people swiftly attain a good birth, free from the demerit arising from cruelty, through the merit that remains over when their special merit which took them to the sphere of the moon has been exhausted. They are born as a priest (brāhmaṇa), warrior (kṣatriya) or husbandman (vaiśya) as their merit warrants.

As for those who perform rituals but are unethical in their way of life, their ritualistic action does not lead to merit. They swiftly attain a bad birth according to their aggregate of merit and demerit, a loathsome birth devoid of all connection with merit, as a dog or a hog or a low-born outcaste.

If those others, the twice-born ones, (70) do not deviate from the path of their own peculiar duty and continue with rituals, good works and charity as defined above, then they come and go by the path beginning with smoke in a continuing cycle, like a bucket mounted on a machine at a well. And if they should happen to gain success on the path of symbolic meditation on the ritual (71) they proceed by the path beginning with the flame (which leads to the world of Brahmā from which there is no return).

But if they devote themselves neither to meditations on the symbolism of the ritual nor to ritualistic practice in its plain form allied to good works and charity, then they do not go (at death) either by the path beginning with the flame or by the path beginning with smoke. They turn into insignificant insects like mosquitoes and flies, and return to earth as such many times. Having fallen from both paths, they are just repeatedly born and repeatedly die. The text says "Be born and die" to express their continuous round of births and deaths, the command being assumed to proceed from the Lord. In the case of these creatures, all time is passed in these momentary births and deaths. No time is passed either in ritualistic activity and amassing merit or in enjoyment of merit. This is the third (possible) state of those undergoing transmigration in the world, the state of insignificant insects, the other two having been just mentioned above. It is because those on the southern path (the path beginning with smoke) come back again to the world, while the third class do not even go on the southern path because they are not qualified either for meditation or rituals, that the world of Brahmā (final end of the "northern" path) never becomes filled up....

All this being so, the text invites us to reflect on the extremely troublesome nature of transmigratory life and to learn to hold it in horror. The insignificant insects spend their time undergoing momentary flashes of pain in birth and death, as if placed without hope of rescue in a bottomless and unnavigable ocean, and we should therefore hold this form of transmigratory life in utter abhorrence and cherish the will to avoid it at all costs. (72)

* * * * *

15, In the first Quarter (of the third Book of the Brahmā Sūtras) the author expounds some different itineraries traversed by the soul in the course of transmigration according to the doctrine of the Knowledge of the Five Fires (pañcāgni-vidyā), because the topic so expounded helps to generate indifference to worldly experience, as is shown by the phrase at the end of the Upanishadic exposition, "One should acquire disgust for it." (73)

(XII.1) ADOPTING THE PATH (TEXTS)

The individual soul, accompanied by the Vital Energy and the sense-organs and the mind retaining (the impressions of) his knowledge, secular and sacred, his ritualistic works and his acquired skills and aptitudes, (74) abandons one body and acquires another, as we learn from the passage dealing with transmigration (75) which begins "Then the organs come to it" and ends "It forms a new and better body." And it is also clear (from mere reason) that something of this nature must occur, as the experience of the fruit of one's meritorious and sinful deeds would not be possible otherwise.

We now take up the question of whether the soul is or is not specially enshrouded by the elements in subtle form to serve as the seed for its future body. One might initially suppose that it was not so enshrouded, as the text in question (76) mentions the presence of organs but not of the elements in subtle form. It says, "Taking the bright organs," thereby indicating that the soul's equipment consists of the organs alone, particularly as it goes on to speak of the organs of sight, etc. And the elements in subtle form are everywhere easily available. Wherever the new body has to be instituted they will be present, so that it would be useless to bring them specially. So we conclude that the soul proceeds on its travels not specially enshrouded in the elements in their subtle form.

Against this view the Teacher says: "The soul hastens forth to attain a new body enshrouded." It goes off, that is to say, specially enshrouded in the elements in their subtle form to serve as the seed of the future body. Why? "Because," he says, "of the question and its answer." The question referred to is: "Do you know how at the fifth oblation the water comes to have a human voice?" And the reply explains how the oblations of Faith, Soma, rain, food and human seed are offered in the five fires consisting respectively of the world of the gods, the rain-deity (parjanya), the earth, man and woman, and concludes with the statement "In the fifth oblation water comes to have a human voice." (77) Hence we conclude that the soul "hastens forth" enshrouded in water.

But is it not a fact that there is another Vedic text which says "Like a leech on a piece of grass"? (78) The soul, like a leech (stretching out from leaf to leaf) does not leave one body until it has already touched the next. (79) But there is no contradiction, because all this text means by its simile of the leech is that the soul, already enshrouded in the water-element, stretches itself out (like a leech) through its yearning towards the new body set up for it through the effects of its past actions.

This being the Vedic teaching on the way in which one passes to a new body, no attention should be paid to human conjectures on the subject which differ from it, as they stand in contradiction with the Veda. Such, amongst others, are the Sāṃkhya view that the organs (in their cosmic aspect as Cosmic Ego, etc.) and the soul are all-pervading,and that attainment of a new body means no more than that the organs begin to function there (where the new body is) under the causal influence of past action; or the Buddhist view that it is just the soul that begins to act again (under the influence of past action), while a new body and new senses spring up miraculously on the occasion of each new experience; or the view of the Vaiśeṣikas that it is only the mind that passes to the new abode for experience (not the body — because the soul, being all-pervading, is already present within the new body without requiring to move); or the view of the Jainas that it is the soul alone that moves from one body to another, like a parrot passing from tree to tree. (80)

* * * * *

16. With the word "But" the author of the Sūtras begins his refutation of the objection. (81) Water itself is compounded of three basic elements, (82) as the text on "making threefold" shows. Wherever, therefore, water is admitted as a component in any substance, fire and earth must necessarily be admitted to be present too.

Now, the human body, too, has a threefold composition. For fire, water and earth (lit. food) are found in its products, and it is likewise "threefold" in point of harbouring the three humours wind, bile and phlegm. It is quite impossible that the body should be composed of water alone to the exclusion of other elements. So the words of the dialogue "Water acquires a human voice" (84) are a figurative expression in which the word "water" is used to stand for the body in general, in which the water-element predominates. The phrase does not mean that the body consists of water alone. Liquids in the form of blood and various juices are seen to have a predominant place in all human bodies.

But is it not rather the earth (lit. food) element that seems to predominate in the body? Well, we are not concerned with what *seems*. Whatever be the case with appearances, the *fact* is that the water element predominates over the others. Water is even found to predominate in the seed form of the body, in the form of the semen (of the father) and blood (of the mother).

A further point to note here is that previous ritualistic merit is what brings into being a new body. But ritualistic action, as in the case of the Agnihotra offering and the like, is based on fluid substances like Soma, butter and milk. And the author of the Sūtras will point out later (85) how it is the water-substances supporting the merit that are referred to by the word "Faith" and which are "offered", together with the sacrificer's ritualistic merit, into the "fire" constituted by heaven (dyu-loka). This familiar conception is yet another reason for accepting the preponderance of water in the body. And because of this predominance it follows that there is justification for taking the word "water" to stand for *all* the seeds of the body, even though the latter consist of all (five of) the different subtle elements. (86)

* * * * *

17. Those who perform sacrifices such as the Agnihotra and Darśapūrṇamāsa, etc., are possessed of "water" in the form of the curds, milk and other liquid substances that they use for these rituals, since these substances consist chiefly of water. Offered in the Āhavanīya fire, (87) the subtle portions of those libations assume the form of the "hidden future efficacy of the sacrifices" (apūrva) and cling to the performers of the sacrifice. The bodies of the latter are eventually offered to the flames on the funeral pyre by the priests with the words "May he proceed to the realm of heaven! Svāhā!" Then this "water", which has now assumed the form of the "hidden future efficacy of the sacrifice," associated with the sacrificer's Faith (88) and ritualistic works, enshrouds the souls who have performed ritualistic sacrifices and takes them to yonder world, there to bestow on them the fruits of their ritualistic acts. This is the meaning of the text, "They offer Faith as a libation." (89)

And in a similar way, there are other passages such as the sequel to the six questions (asked of Yājñavalka by Janaka) about the Agnihotra beginning "These two oblations (of the morning and evening Agnihotra)when completed rise up" (90) which show how the two Agnihotra libations (offered daily at dawn and dusk) proceed to another world to set their fruits in motion. Hence the implication is that the individual souls hasten forth enshrouded in the "water" of their libations to experience the fruits of ritualistic acts. (91)

* * * * *

18. But here the object is to explain the development of merit from rituals and enjoin the Meditation on the Five Fires (92) beginning with the fire of heaven (dyu-loka) in order to enjoy the results of special merit. For this is the means to the attainment of the Northern Path. (93) So an eulogy of the fire of heaven and the rest is made.

Those Vital Airs that act as Hotṛ priests here in the body become Indra and the other gods when they develop into their form as deities. They serve as Hotṛ priests for the fire of heaven. And (as present on earth in the body of the sacrificer) they offer the Agnihotra oblations here in order to enjoy its results. And they sometimes attain to the office of Hotṛ priest in that realm, when the sacrificer experiences the fruits of performing the Agnihotra, at the time when those fruits come to maturity. They assume various different forms and are known as gods.

The liquid substances, too, which carry the merit arising from the Agnihotra ritual, and on earth are poured into the Āhavanīya fire, (94) are swallowed up by that fire and assume a subtle invisible form and proceed to the other world with the sacrificer, going *via* the smoke, etc., up into the sky until they eventually enter the world of heaven (dyu-loka) from there. These subtle liquid substances, which are the results of offering oblations and form part of the Agnihotra, are now called "Faith" and enter the world of heaven in company with the sacrificer in order to construct a body for him in the sphere of the moon. In doing this they are said to be "offered as an oblation." There they enter the world of heaven and set up a body for the sacrificer in the sphere of the moon. That is why the present text says, "The gods offer the oblation of Faith. From their offering emerges Soma the King (the moon). For the Veda says, "Faith, verily, is water." (95)

The question previously raised was, "Do you know after how many times of being offered as an oblation water becomes a human voice and rises up and speaks?" (96) And by way of an answer it was said, "That world is fire." This shows that the liquid forming part of the rituals is what is called "Faith", and sets up a body for the sacrificer (in the sphere of the moon). It is said that *water* acquires a human voice because water preponderates (in the sacrificer's body on the moon), but not because the other elements are absent.

And the construction of the body proceeds as a result of the merit of performing the Agnihotra, while the liquid substances are a part of it. Hence the liquid substances are the predominating factor in the construction of the body, and this is why it is said, "Water acquires a human voice." For it is only one who performs ritual who can get a human birth (in which one acquires a voice).(97)

* * * * *

19. How can the substance called milk be the support of everything? Because it can be taken as the cause of everything. It is the cause because it is invariably involved in such rituals as that of the Agnihotra. And there are hundreds of texts in the Veda and the derivative literature to show that the whole universe is but a transformation (pariṇāma) of the oblations offered in the Agnihotra and other rituals. (98)

* * * * *

20. When the particular portion of ritualistic merit through which such sacrificers attained to the moon is exhausted through enjoyment, the watery body that has been instituted for this enjoyment on the moon melts away under the heat of the fire of their grief at seeing the prospect of their enjoyment coming to an end, as snow and hail melt under the rays of the sun, or as the solidity of the sacrificial butter melts in the flames of the sacrificial fire.

Next the author of the Sūtras says, "When the deeds are exhausted." He means that when the merit arising through sacrifices and other rituals has been exhausted through enjoyment, then the souls re-descend "with a remnant." Why do we maintain this? Because of the testimony of the Veda and of the derivative literature, he says.

The Vedic texts themselves speak of this re-descent "with a remnant," as for instance when they say, "He whose conduct here is excellent attains an excellent rebirth, either as a Brahmin or as a Kṣatriya or as a Vaiśya; whereas he whose conduct here is vile attains a vile rebirth, either as a dog or a hog or a dog-eater." (99) The author will explain later (100) how the word "conduct" refers indirectly to the remnant. (101) Another circumstance pointing to the existence of such a remnant is the fact that all living beings are conditioned by the very situation of their birth to different grades of enjoyment. For this cannot be accidental, as we know in a general way from the Veda that our prosperity and adversity are conditioned by our past good and evil deeds.

The derivative literature (102) also shows that the re-descent is to the accompaniment of a remnant, by saying that those who belong to particular castes and stages of life, if they apply themselves to their religious duties as laid down, after proceeding to another world at death and experiencing there the fruits of their ritualistic acts, attain rebirth here on earth at a particular place, caste and family, and endowed with a particular degree of longevity, learning, wealth, joy and intelligence, and become engaged in a particular vocation as conditioned by their remnant of merit and demerit.

But what is this "remnant"? Some say that it is a remnant that still remains over from the ritualistic actions performed for the sake of heaven after their fruits have been enjoyed, left behind like the sticky traces of oil left in an empty oil-barrel. When an oil-barrel is emptied, it is never completely emptied. There are always some traces of oil left clinging to the body of the barrel, and the "remnant" is a remnant in this sense.

The people who argue thus are not to be put off by the criticism that traces of oil may very well cling to the body of a barrel, there being no *a priori* contradiction, but that there cannot be a remnant of occult force (adṛṣṭa) in the case of deeds of which the fruits have been consumed, because the consumption of the fruits logically implies the exhaustion of the occult force. For they maintain that we have no proof that the fruits of the ritualistic action that takes us to heaven are *totally* consumed. True, the souls proceed to the sphere of the moon to enjoy the fruits of those acts in their entirety. But when there is only a minute fraction of merit left they are unable to stay in the sphere of the moon any longer. It is like the case of some servant of the royal household, who first appeared before the royal family duly equipped with all the paraphernalia of royal service, but who gradually loses the greater part of it in the course of a long sojourn at court and eventually is left with nothing much more than his parasol and sandals, in which condition he finds it impossible to retain his position in court any longer. Similarly, the one who no longer has any more merit than the remnant is unable to retain his position in the sphere of the moon.

But there is something wrong with this reasoning. For there cannot really be any remnant in the case of meritorious deeds performed for the sake of heaven if the fruits have been consumed, this being a contradictory notion in the way already pointed out. True, you for your part maintained that the fruit of the deeds leading to heaven was not enjoyed in its totality. But this view is mistaken. For no one who takes his stand on the authority of the Veda can suppose that meritorious acts performed for the sake of heaven do not generate their full fruit for the sacrificer while he is in heaven, or that they generate a remnant of fruit for him when he has actually fallen from heaven. The clinging of a remnant of oil to the oil-barrel, on the other hand, is intelligible, as it is something we actually perceive. And the courtier's retention of the remnant of his courtly paraphernalia is also something we perceive. But in the case of descent from heaven, the retention of a remnant of the merit that led to heaven is not anything we can perceive; nor can we even conceive it either, as it would contradict the Vedic teaching that the fruit of such acts was heaven.

And the matter cannot really be understood in any other way except as we have explained it. It cannot be that a part of the sacrifices and other meritorious action performed as laid down for the attainment of heaven can remain with the sacrificer as a remnant after he has fallen from heaven, like the remnant of oil clinging to the empty barrel. For if what was conceived to cling to the sacrificers as the "remnant" was only a part of the sacrifices and other meritorious work whereby they had attained experience of heaven, then such a remnant could only be excellent and could not be anything vile. That, however, would contradict the Vedic text that introduced the distinction between "He whose conduct here is excellent" and "He whose conduct is vile." (103) Hence, when the merit derived from rituals leading to heaven has been exhausted, there must remain a modicum of merit and demerit derived from acts of a different kind, acts of which the fruit lies here below. This is the "remnant", and it is equipped with this that souls descend from heaven for rebirth here below.

It was said earlier by the opponent that the souls cannot descend with any remnant because consideration of the text "*Whatever* work" (104) showed that they only descended after they had exhausted *all* their merit through enjoyment. But this has been shown to have been wrong by the mere fact of our having demonstrated that there *is* a remnant. "Whatever work he did here" has to be taken to mean "Having exhausted whatever fruits were due to him *in the next world* through experiencing them by way of enjoyments resulting from rituals."

The opponent also tried to maintain that it was not possible to make the distinction "Fruits in heaven result from one kind of action, fruits on earth from another," on the ground that death brought out all fruits without exception that had not yet begun to manifest. But this thesis, too, has already been answered by our demonstration that a remnant must exist. Moreover, the opponent will have to explain why it is that we have to recognize that death brings out merit and demerit that has not yet begun to fructify. He might say that the unfolding of all other merit and demerit was obstructed by the merit and demerit that *had* begun to fructify, and that when the latter came to an end at death the unfolding could proceed. To this we reply as follows. Just as the unfolding of all other merit and demerit is obstructed before death by the merit and demerit that have begun to fructify, so,even at the time of death,is the unfolding of weaker merit and demerit obstructed by more powerful merit and demerit, as not all fruit can enter into manifestation at the same time. For one cannot maintain, merely on the ground that they all have the common characteristic that their fruits have not yet begun to manifest, that all the merit and demerit that are due to be experienced in all future births suddenly begin to manifest at once on the occasion of one particular death, and that they together constitute the beginning of a single new birth, as this would be in contradiction with the fact that quite separate (and often contradictory) fruits result from different acts. (105) Nor can it be said that some merit and demerit come into manifestation at death and that the rest are destroyed, for this would be in contradiction with the fact that fructification takes place with no exceptions. Merit and demerit cannot be suppressed and prevented from eventual fructification except through the special prescribed methods such as penances. The derivative literature, too, shows that one kind of merit and demerit may remain for a long time obstructed from fructification by another kind which has contradictory fruit, in such texts as, "Sometimes meritorious acts remain sterile (without fruit) until the one drowning in transmigratory life is released." (106)

Moreover, if all unfructified merit and demerit came into manifestation at one death and constituted the beginning of a single new birth, then, since merit and demerit cannot arise from acts performed in heaven or hell or animal births, there could not be any further merit or demerit for those who attained these regions, and they would never be reborn, for lack of any conceivable cause. And this would be in contradiction with the doctrine found in the derivative literature (107) that in the case of murder of a Brahmin and the like a single act could result in many births. And one cannot establish the existence of any other way of knowing the nature of merit and demerit, or their causes and results, than Vedic revelation. Moreover, this hypothesis that death is what brings to manifestation (all merit and demerit except that which is instituted during the present birth) cannot be stretched to make a universal rule, as some acts have visible fructification in the present birth, as for example the Rain Sacrifice (kārīrī)....

Finally, the objection that there could never be liberation if there were a remnant of merit and demerit overshoots the mark, as the Veda declares that *all* action and its results are destroyed through right-knowledge. So the doctrine that souls re-descend with a remnant of merit and demerit prevails.

And they descend, says the author of the Sūtras, "as they ascend, or otherwise." We know that they may descend along the same route as they ascended from the fact that smoke and ether, which are stages on the upward path to the ancestors (pitṛ) are found also in the account of the descent, as also from the words "by that course by which they came." (108) And we know that it may be "otherwise" from the fact that in one case "the night, etc.," are not mentioned (109) and clouds and other stages are introduced. (110)

* * * * *

21. Thus it is only those who have performed ritual sacrifices and not others who ascend to the moon. (111) As for the latter, they descend to the realm of Yama and experience torture appropriate to their evil deeds, and then ascend again to this world. How do we know that they descend and re-ascend again like this? Because it is mentioned in the Veda. A Vedic text placed into the mouth of Yama shows how those who die without having performed ritualistic sacrifices fall into the power of Yama, namely "The future world escapes the notice of the uncouth, the heedless, those who are deluded by the glamour of wealth. Whoever thinks

'there is nothing beyond this present world comes again and again into my power.' (112) And there are many other indications that those who do not sacrifice fall into the power of Yama, such as the text, "Vaivasvant (Yama), he to whom the sinful have to go." (113)

The great authors of the authoritative texts that derive from Vedic tradition, such as Manu, Vyāsa (114) and others, speak of the expiation of vile conduct as taking place in the City of Correction, (115) in stories such as that of Naciketas (116) and others. And again the authorities on the Purāṇa speak of the seven hells beginning with the Place of Bellowing (raurava) as places for experience of fruits of sinful acts. Those who do not perform sacrifices go to places such as these. How could they go to the moon? That is the meaning implied by the Sūtra. (117)

* * * * *

22. There is a Vedic text about death which runs, "The voice of a person merges in his mind when he dies, his mind in his Vital Energy, his Vital Energy into fire, fire into the supreme deity." (118) The question being newly taken up now is, "Is it the voice itself, associated with its function, that is said here to merge in the mind, or is it only the function that does so?"...

So the final explanation is that it is the function only that is withdrawn into the mind. It means that the function of speech is first withdrawn, while the function of the mind continues for a certain time. Why? Because, as the author of the Sūtras puts it, "this is what we find." We find that in actual fact the function of the mind is withdrawn first, while the mind itself lingers on. No one, however, perceives the voice itself, together with its function, being withdrawn into the mind.

(XII.1) ADOPTING THE PATH (TEXTS)

Well, but is not the the dissolution of voice into the mind guaranteed by the authority of the Vedic text in question? Not so, for voice is not made up of mind. Only that can dissolve into anything which has previously emerged from it, as a dish that has been shaped from clay dissolves back into clay. But there is no evidence to show that voice emerged from mind. On the other hand the rise and suppression of a function may come from something of a different nature from that in which the function inheres. Burning, the function of the element fire, originates from fuel (consisting of wood) springing from the element earth, while it is brought to an end when the fire is quenched by the element water.

But what, on this view, is the case with the text "Voice merges in mind"? The author says, "And also because of the text." He means that the text fits in with this view, as it can well speak of "voice" when it means the function, treating the function and what has the function figuratively as identical.

There is , however, another text in which it is said that all the sense-organs without exception merge in the mind: it runs, "Therefore he whose fire of life has ceased goes to rebirth with his sense-organs merged in his mind." (119) And so, says the author of the Sūtras, in that text also we have to take it that it is only the functions of the sense-organs that become merged in the mind. For it is seen that the eye and other sense-organs, no less than the voice, cease to function just before death, while the mind still continues to function on. And again, the organs themselves, as independent principles, could not dissolve in the mind, and the view that it is the functions only that dissolve in the mind is eminently compatible with the Vedic texts. Though all the (functions of) the organs are withdrawn into the mind without exception, the text "Voice merges in mind" just picks out voice by way of a convenient example....

The mind, too, having received into itself the functions of the outer organs, dissolves into the Vital Breath — but only with its function. This is the way we have to understand the last text. (120) For in the case of those just on the point of dreamless sleep or death the functions of the mind are found to cease, while that of the Vital Energy, consisting in vibratory movement, continues on for a time. And mind cannot dissolve into the Vital Energy with its essence (svarūpa) as it is not made up of the Vital Energy....

This Vital Energy of which we are speaking resides in the "overseer" (adhyakṣa), the "knowledge-self" (121) with its external adjunct comprising the impressions of his knowledge, secular and sacred, his ritualistic works, and his acquired skills and aptitudes. (122) This is to say, the functions of the Vital Energy serve it. How do we know this? The author of the Sūtras says, "Because of their 'gathering round him', etc." For there is another Vedic text which shows how all the organs without exception "gather round the overseer" (at the time of death) — namely, "Thus, at the time of death, when breathing has become short, all the organs gather round him (like the king's ministers round a dying king)." (123) And the text goes on to mention the Vital Energy specially, and say that it follows the overseer, in the words, "When he ascends (from the body), the Vital Energy ascends with him;" (124) and then the text goes on to say that the organs follow the Vital Energy, in the words "When the Vital Energy ascends from the body, all the organs ascend with it." (125) And when the text says, "He retains particular consciousness (vijñāna)" it means that the overseer has particular consciousness, and this implies that the other organs remain associated with him as well as with the Vital Energy....

But why does the author of the Sūtras speak (126) of the Vital Energy as merging in the elements including fire, when the Upanishad speaks only of fire and says "The Vital Energy merges in fire"? In regard to this, the author of the Sūtras says (127) "Not in the one principle only." That is, at the time of waiting to attain another body, the soul does not abide in the single principle of fire only, as we see that the body which it eventually attains to is an effect compounded of a variety of different substances. This is shown, for instance, by the question and answer concluding "Water attains a human voice," (128) and its implications have been set out in the Sūtra "But the body has a threefold nature, because water only *predominates*." (129) And the Veda and derivative literature both teach the same point. The Veda says, "Consisting of earth, consisting of water, consisting of wind, consisting of ether," (130) and the derivative literature says, "All this world takes birth in regular association with subtle indestructible particles of the five elements." (131)

Now, it might be objected that there is another Vedic passage which first asks, with reference to the time when speech and the other organs have become merged and the soul is waiting to attain another body, "Where is the soul then?" and afterwards declares that it rests in work (karma), in the words, "Those two (Yājñavalkya and Ārtabhāga) spoke together; what they spoke of was work, all that they praised was work." (132) To this, however, we reply that this "resting in work" refers to the continued activity of bondage in the form of experience of objects through the senses promoted by work, (133) denoted in that passage by the technical terms "graha" and "atigraha". But here, in the passage we are at present concerned with, the soul is said to rest in the elements because its new body will arise from the elements. Moreover, even in the passage speaking of the soul resting in work, the mention of "praise" shows that work was only being mentioned as an important factor and not in a way to allow the possibility of anything else apart from the elements being the resting-place of the soul at this time. (134)

Is this ascent of the soul different according to whether the sacrificer has or has not performed meditation on the symbolic significance of the sacrifices he has performed? Or is it the same in either case?... We reply that the ascent must be the same in the two cases "up to the beginning of the path of the gods." For the texts do not mention any difference. The one who has not performed meditation on the symbolic significance of the sacrifices that he has carried out rests in the subtle elements which are the seeds of his next body, and proceeds towards further transmigration, prompted to have the experience of taking yet another earthly body by his merit and demerit. But the one who has performed meditation (on the symbolic significance of the sacrifices) resorts to the subtle exit at the crown of the head, (135) which is lit with the light of knowledge. This is what the author of the Sūtras was referring to when he said that the ascent from the body must be the same in the case of both those sacrificers who had and those who had not meditated, but only "up to the beginning of the path of the gods."

One might ask, if the one who had performed meditation was going to attain immortality and would not be subject to another body, how it could be that he resorted to the elements or set out on a path. We reply that what we are saying now refers to the case where, in the words of the author of the Sūtras, "There has been no burning up." When the passions (kleśa) such as nescience (136) have not been completely burnt up, then the one who is waiting to attain conditional immortality through the lower knowledge (aparavidyā), based on meditation on the symbolic significance of the ritual, can set out on a path and rest in the elements. For the organs cannot attain to any new place without a vehicle. Hence there is nothing wrong with our position.

Taken in its context, the further text "Fire merges in the supreme deity" (137) means that the fire as there described, associated with the "overseer" (adhyakṣa), the Vital Energy, the group formed by the organs and the other subtle elements pertaining to the dead person, merge in the supreme deity.

What is the nature of this merging? One might initially suppose that it implied the complete dissolution of the merging entity, considered in its true essential nature. For, in the present case, this would agree with the fact that it originally arose from the supreme deity. It has already been established that the supreme deity is that from which all that has origination proceeds. So merging would involve becoming entirely identical with that into which the merging took place.

To this we reply that the subtle elements such as fire, which are the vehicle of hearing and other organs, remain in being, as the author puts it, "Until release from transmigration" – release from transmigration, that is, occasioned by right knowledge. For there are texts, the author of the Sūtras says, teaching transmigration, amongst which we might cite "Some embodied souls attain a new womb for further embodiment, while others descend to the level of plants, – each according to the work he has performed and according to the sacred learning he has acquired." (138) If it were not for this, every one would merge totally in the Absolute at the moment of death, since their external limiting adjunct (upādhi) would stand destroyed. But this is impossible, as it would imply the absurd conclusion that the Vedic injunctions and the Vedic metaphysical teaching were alike useless. But if (as on our view) bondage is conditioned by erroneous cognition, then one cannot escape from it except through right knowledge. Hence, even though everything proceeds from the supreme deity, this merging here taught implies an unresolved residue in the form of a seed of future empirical existence, just like the merging that occurs in dreamless sleep, and at the time of Cosmic Dissolution at the end of a world-period. (139)

* * * * *

23. And this fire, along with the other subtle elements that form the vehicle for the soul when it vacates the present body, must be of subtle (imperceptible) consistency, both from the point of view of its nature (intangible) and dimensions (minute). (140) For there are texts saying that it emerges from the body through the subtle physical canals (nāḍī), which show that it must be minute, since it could only pass along these if it were minute in size. It is on account of its intangibility that it knows no physical obstructions. Hence, also, the fact that the bystanders cannot perceive it when it issues forth from the body (at death). Hence, too, the fact that it is not destroyed when the gross body is destroyed by burning on the funeral pyre or otherwise.

Further, the warmth that people feel when they touch this gross body is the warmth of the subtle body alone. For at death, even though the gross body remains in being along with its properties, such as colour, heat is not perceived there, but only in the gross body in its living condition. Hence it follows that this heat must reside in something other than the familiar gross body,(i.e. in the subtle body, which must consequently exist). And the Veda confirms this idea in the text "It is warm as long as it lives, and cold when it dies." (141)

* * * * *

24. The description of the transmigratory process has already begun, and in that context we heard the words "There this Spirit (puruṣa), completely detaching himself from the parts of the body..." (142). With a view to describe the transmigratory process in detail, so as to make it clear when and how this detachment takes place, the text proceeds further, beginning with the words "Where this Self".

"This Self" means the Self that has already been discussed earlier in the present context. "When this Self has become weak," proceeds the text. Here it is the weakness of the body that is figuratively spoken of as the weakness of the Self, for the Self, being incorporeal, cannot intrinsically become weak. The same considerations apply when it is spoken of as becoming confused, as it were, and unable to tell things apart. It is not that it can really become either confused or unconfused, since it is the eternal and changeless light of pure Consciousness by very nature. Therefore the text says, "When it becomes confused *as it were*." At the time of the departure of the soul from the body at death there seems to ordinary worldly people to be a sort of dislocation in the soul caused by the merging of the organs within, and they express it by saying "He's passed into a coma, he's in a coma."...

So at this time the organs, speech and the rest, gather round this Self. Then there takes place the complete detachment of this embodied soul from the parts of the body. But how does this detachment take place? And in what sense do the organs gather round the Self? The text goes on: "This Self, gathering into itself these particles of light," by which it means the sense-organs such as the faculty of sight, spoken of as particles of light because they illuminate colour and the like. Gathering them in completely, receiving them directly into itself without a trace left over. The prefix "sam" is used to show that the process is different from what obtains in dream, where they are not gathered in completely so that no trace is left. In dream the Self just receives the organs without completely enfolding them, as is shown in such texts as "The faculty of speech has been received, the faculty of sight has been received," (143) "having taken with him a fragment of this all-inclusive world,"(144) and "taking the shining functions of the organs." (145)

"He proceeds down into the heart," that is, into the ether in the lotus of the heart. It means that his consciousness becomes manifest in the heart region, since all disturbance in the intellect and other faculties have subsided. It does not mean that the Self literally "goes" down into the heart or that it undergoes changes such as disturbance or subsidence, as such notions are precluded by the text, "He *seems* to think, he *seems* to move." (146) All change is attributed to it falsely on account of its external adjuncts such as the intellect.

But when does this "receiving of the particles of light" take place? To answer this question the Upanishad refers to the "spirit in the eye," (147) itself a ray of the sun, which remains assisting the function of the faculty of sight as long as the body continues, prompted to do so by the merit and demerit of the experiencing soul. But at the time of death it leaves its activity of assisting the faculty of sight and returns to its true self, the sun. (148) This is what was taught in the text "Where the voice of the dead man joins fire, his Vital Energy the wind, his power of sight the sun." (148) They gather again when he next takes a body. And the same thing happens when he goes into dreamless sleep and wakes up. (149)

(When a man is dying) all his organs become united with his subtle body. (150) The bystanders then say, "He cannot see." When the deity presiding over the sense of smell withdraws, the sense of smell becomes united with the subtle body, and they say "He cannot smell." And it is the same with the other organs. The deity presiding over the function of taste in the sun is either Soma or Varuṇa, and when it withdraws its support they say "He cannot taste." Similarly, they say "He cannot speak, he cannot hear, he cannot think, he cannot touch, he cannot understand." This implies both the withdrawal of the support of the presiding deity and the uniting of the organs (or faculties) with the subtle body in the heart.

Next a description is given of the internal activity that occurs after the organs have been withdrawn into the heart. When the text speaks of the heart it means the open orifice of the heart. By "the tip" it means the end of the subtle canal (nāḍī) which is the way of escape out from the heart. It is said that it shines because it shines with its own light, as in dream, the light coming partly from the particles of light that have been absorbed with the organs, and partly from the inherent light of the Self. The soul as knowledge-self (vijñānamaya), with the external limiting adjunct of the subtle body, vacates the gross body through the tip of the heart that has been lit with the inherent light of the Self. Compare the text of the Atharva Veda, "In what shall I ascend, when I ascend (from the body)? Supported in what shall I find support? And he created the Vital Energy (prāṇa)." (151)

The light of the Self as pure consciousness is always most evident in the subtle body. All the changes that appear to occur to the Self, such as birth and death, departure from the body and arrival in the body, etc., occur through this adjunct. For it is comprised of the group of twelve organs beginning with the intellect. (152) It is the thread (sūtra) on which all is strung, the source of life, the inner self in all that moves or is fixed. What route does it follow when it issues forth from the body with the help of the light at the tip of the heart?

To this question the text replies, "Either by the eye...." This is what occurs if there is knowledge or merit to warrant its proceeding to the world of the sun. "Or else by the top of the head." This is what occurs if there is warrant for it to attain to the world of Brahmā. (153) Or it may depart *via* other parts of the body, according to its merit and sacred knowledge. When this knowledge-self has risen up from the body and is proceeding towards another world, the Vital Energy rises up and follows it, like a great minister with all the seals following a king. And when the Vital Energy rises up, speech and all the organs rise up and follow it. Here the Vital Energy is said to "follow" the knowledge-self and the organs to "follow" the Vital Energy in the sense of conforming to a superior, not in the sense that one moves later than the other in time.

Then this knowledge-self has particular cognitions, under the power of merit and demerit, just as in dream, and not spontaneously. If it could have knowledge of whatever it wished, every one would have done all that requires to be done (at death). But the fact is otherwise. Hence Vyāsa has said, "(Whatever being he remembers when he leaves the body, to that being he goes, O son of Kuntī), since he has ever dwelt on that." (154) At the time of death everyone has particular cognitions in the form of impressions, where the mind assumes peculiar forms promoted by merit and demerit. And the knowledge-self proceeds to where-ever it has to go, under the light of these particular cognitions.

From this we should conclude that all those who have faith, who are not heedless, and who want to obtain a superior world should apply themselves to the discipline of yoga, (155) should practise mental recapitulation of the spiritual truths that they have been taught, (156) and should amass the best stock of merit they can in order to achieve independence at this time (of death). All the traditional teachings strongly emphasize the giving up of all wrong behaviour. For when death has come, there is nothing more that can be done, as no one is independent when once his actions become solely conditioned by merit and demerit. The Upanishad has already declared, "One becomes holy through holy acts, evil through evil acts." (157) And the Upanishads of all the different Vedic schools have the sole purpose of showing the way to put an end to this evil. There is no other way of securing the total cessation of this evil except through application of the means prescribed in these texts. Hence the final purport of the present section is to teach that we should make all the efforts we can to carry out the measures prescribed in the Upanishads while we are still here alive in the world.

It has been said that the soul goes forth from the body heavily loaded and creaking like a cart. But what is this provender it takes on its journey to the other world, like the load of a cart? And what is it that it enjoys when it arrives at the other world, which fashions a body for it and so forth? The Upanishad replies that it is knowledge of all kinds, prescribed and prohibited and non-prescribed and non-prohibited. (158) These accompany the soul on its journey. And also "knowledge derived from previous experiences (pūrva-prajñā) — that is to say, the (collective) impression (vāsanā) of one's experiences of the fruits of past deeds. This impression plays a necessary part in initiating fresh activity and in bringing to fruition the latent effects of past action. Hence it also accompanies the soul, for the latter could neither act nor enjoy the fruits of its action without it. The sense-organs are helpless in regard to anything of which they have no previous experience. But in the experience after death the senses are able to function even though they have no previous experience because they are prompted by the (collective) impression of the soul's previous experience. We find in the world that some people are gifted with talent for certain activities like painting from birth and without need for training, while others are absolutely unable to perform certain tasks, although they are very easy. Again, some are naturally apt for the enjoyment of the good things of the world, some not. The conditioning factor here is the revival or non-revival of the "knowledge derived from past experiences (pūrva-prajñā)". So without this "knowledge derived from past experiences" no one can have any progress either in action or in enjoying the fruits of his past actions. Hence these three, knowledge, action and "knowledge derived from past experiences" are what accompany the soul as its provender on the journey to the next world, like the load on a cart. Because these three are the means to the production of and to enjoyment of experience in another earthly body, one should confine oneself in this life to auspicious knowledge and action, that one may attain a desirable body and desirable experiences in one's next life on earth — that is the meaning of the section. (159)

2. THE INJUNCTION TO ADOPT THE PATH

Attention has been drawn earlier (160) to the presence of a problem of deciding how far or in what sense knowledge of the Self and the adoption of the path of knowledge of the Self could be the object of an injunction. Part of the difficulty has been succinctly expressed by Sureśvara. If knowledge of the Self depended on an injunction it would imply the absurd consequence that the Self was the object of some action, while if it was not dependent on an injunction the whole enterprise of seeking knowledge of the Self would lack Vedic sanction and would belong to the realm of mere fallible human speculation, like the spiritual discipline of the Buddhists. (161) The question is further complicated by the presence in the Vedic texts of injunctions not merely to adopt the path for knowledge of the Self, but also to know it – "The Self should be seen" (162) – and even to continue with affirmation of the Self even after it has been known. (163) However, as we have already seen in an earlier volume (Volume IV, p.7), the Advaitin is from one point of view unwilling to concede that the spiritual path to enlightenment is totally dependent on Vedic injunction. For if he did, it would be open to the Ritualist to claim that even the metaphysical texts of the Upanishads fell within the scope of his own rules of exegesis.

Śaṃkara is categorical in saying that knowledge of the Self cannot be the object of an injunction to act (Extracts 1-4). The injunctive element in the texts is an injunction, not to know the Self, but to control the mind – either positively in turning it towards the Self or negatively in turning it away from all else. Again, the kind of knowledge required for realization of the Self is not a form of action. The texts enjoining meditation on the Self do not bear on knowledge of the Self and make it into an act that has to be done (Extract 5).

But once knowledge of the Self has been acquired, is there or is there not an injunction to sustain this knowledge through remembrance? Śaṃkara replies that, in principle, there can be no injunction, as in this case remembrance is automatic. But what about such texts as, "Once the wise man has acquired knowledge of the Self alone he should practise repeated affirmation"?(164) In the case of an enlightened person, Advaita distinguishes between the infinite Self, which the enlightened person knows himself to be, and the mind-body complex which continues to function in the realm of nescience, and without which there could be no enlightened Teachers. Notwithstanding his conviction that he is the infinite Self, the enlightened person is also aware of his role and function in the world. (165) Though he is no longer deluded into accepting the realm of nescience as real, his body and mind are still subject, within that realm, to conditioning by the unexpended portion of the merit and demerit that originated his present body. From this standpoint he is subject to Vedic rules and injunctions, even though in his inmost conviction he knows he is the infinite Self beyond them.

Śaṃkara makes the technical point, however, that the injunction addressed to the enlightened man to practise repeated affirmation must be interpreted as a restrictive injunction (niyama-vidhi) and not an original injunction (apūrva-vidhi). Had it been an apūrva-vidhi, it would have been positive in character and obedience to it it would have resulted in the enlightened person being conditioned to have further experiences in future lives. But the enlightened person cannot be conditioned to undergo further reincarnation, even though he may elect to do so voluntarily. (166) A restrictive injunction (niyama-vidhi), since it merely restricts the choice amongst courses to which the enlightened person in his aspect as an individual is already prompted before he hears it, is negative in character, and obedience to it does not imply any positive result such as being conditioned to undergo further experience in future lives (Extracts 6 and 7).

TEXTS ON THE INJUNCTION TO ADOPT THE PATH

1. Knowledge of the ritualistic section of the Veda has for its aim temporary welfare in the after-life and in lives to come, and that depends on carrying out its instructions. Metaphysical knowledge of the Absolute has for its aim supreme

(and eternal) beatitude, and does not depend on carrying out any later course of action for the achievement of this. When one has to enquire into the karmic merit that would follow upon a particular action, that merit lies in the future. At the time one comes to hear of it from the Vedic text, it does not yet exist. For it depends for its existence on human activity. The prompting provided by the text is also different in the two cases. A text prompting to meritorious action 'enlightens' a person in the sense of urging him to carry out its content. A text prompting a person to acquire metaphysical knowledge of the Absolute itself grants him metaphysical enlightenment, without the need of anything further to be done. Since the enlightenment arises from the prompting itself, the person is not prompted to *do* anything for enlightenment. Such enlightenment arises automatically and without action, as in the case of perception of an object which comes within the range of the senses. (167)

* * * * *

2. But do not these supreme metaphysical texts of the Upanishads supply the subject-matter for obedience to injunctions such as 'The Self should be known'? No. For we have already explained that these supreme metaphysical texts leave nothing over that has to be done. Texts like 'That thou art', which communicate the true nature of the Self, cause vision of the Self at the very time they are heard. So one does not have to go on afterwards to obey an injunction to see the Self, as if this were a separate duty. We have already given this answer before. (168)

* * * * *

3. Nor is the text 'One should meditate only on "It is the Self"' an originating injunction

(utpatti-vidhi, (169) from active obedience to which a reward would follow). Why not? Because, apart from acquiring metaphysical knowledge from the texts that state the true nature of the Self and negate the not-self, there is nothing further that has to be done, either mentally or physically. But the Ritualists hold that an injunction has only performed its office when there is the idea of some human activity that has to be performed over and above the mere reception of knowledge from hearing the text containing the injunction. (170)

* * * * *

4. The idea of fire, when one is in the presence of that well known object, is not dependent on an injunction, nor is it a mere creation of the human mind. It is in fact a piece of *knowledge*, conditioned by the nature of the object perceived. It is not an act. And it is the same with all objects of the various means of knowledge (such as perception, inference, etc.). This being so, knowledge of the Self in its true form as the Absolute cannot be dependent on an injunction to act. Imperative and similar forms applied to it, even in Vedic texts, lose their imperative force and become blunted, as razors become blunted if used against hard objects like stones. For here the object to which they are applied is something not subject to rejection or acquisition. (171)

* * * * *

5. But what do these apparent injunctions mean — texts like 'The Self, verily, should be seen, heard about...' (Bṛhad. II.iv.5), which have the appearance of injunctions? Their purpose, we say, is to turn the hearer away from the objects of his natural instinctive activity. The extraverted

person, who thinks 'Let me have what is desirable and avoid what is not desirable', does not achieve life's highest goal. But when such a person comes to desire the supreme human goal, texts like 'The Self, verily, should be seen' and so on turn him away from the natural concern with his psycho-physical organism and its interests, and engage him in continuous remembrance of the inmost Self. Then finally the true principle, the Self, not subject to rejection or acquisition, is taught to such a person, when he is sincerely engaged in investigating the true nature of the Self. (172)

* * * * *

6. Perhaps you will say that something else to be done *is* implied after the mere knowledge arising from hearing the text, namely sustained remembrance of the knowledge of the Self that arose from the text. But this is wrong, as sustained remembrance is already implied as an automatic consequence. The moment that knowledge of the Self arises from the texts that proclaim the Self, it necessarily puts an end to all wrong notions about the Self. When wrong notions of the Self have ceased, the natural memories that arise from them and bear on various aspects of the not-self no longer arise.

Morever, everything other than the Self is then seen to be an evil. For when the Self has once been known, everything else is seen as evil. For all this realm of the non-self is transient and painful and impure, and has many other defects, while the Self, the reality, is the opposite. Hence memories based on experience of the non-Self cease when the Self is known. Sustained remembrance of the knowledge of one's identity with the Self of all must follow automatically as (when all other memories have been obliterated) this is the only alternative left. And because such remembrance follows implicitly, it cannot be the subject of an injunction.

Further, it is on account of this sustained automatic remembrance of the knowledge of the Self that the defect of pain arising from grief, delusion, fear and fatigue ceases in the case of the enlightened person. Defects like grief and delusion proceed from wrong knowledge. And in support of this we have such Vedic texts as "What delusion?" (Īśa 7), "He who knows the bliss of the Absolute experiences fear from no quarter" (Taitt.II.9), "O Janaka, verily you have attained the fearless state" (Bṛhad.IV.ii.4) and "The knot of the heart is broken".(173)

* * * * *

7. As for the opponent's earlier statement that texts like "Once the wise man has acquired knowledge of the Self alone, he should practise repeated affirmation" (Bṛhad.IV.iv.21) referred to acts of meditation over and above the mere understanding of the meaning of the words of the text, we agree that it is true. But such texts do not constitute original injunctions (cp.M.V. p.197). They only constitute restrictive injunctions, as they merely specify one already-known alternative.

Perhaps you will now ask how we can say that meditation is already known as one possible alternative among others, seeing that we have said earlier that sustained remembrance of the knowledge of the Self was regular, as it was the *only* alternative left. Quite right. But the merit and demerit that brought into being the body in which enlightenment was attained must nevertheless be fully worked out. Even after enlightenment has been attained, thought, word and deed inevitably continue. For merit and demerit that are already under way are more powerful (than knowledge), like an arrow that is already in flight and must run its course.

Therefore the stream of remembrance of knowledge of the Self is liable to be overpowered by the merit and demerit that occasioned the present life, and hence activity to strengthen it is already known as a positive alternative. Sustained remembrance of the knowledge of the Self gained from the Upanishadic texts, therefore, has to be supported by renunciation and dispassion and other characteristic disciplines of the spiritual life.

But this duty is not to be taken as resting on an original injunction, because it can be seen to be a duty without one. Therefore texts like 'Once the wise man has acquired knowledge of the Self alone, he should practise repeated affirmation' must be taken as restrictive injunctions, prompting one to adhere strictly to sustained remembrance of the knowledge of the Self which one has already gained. For no other way of interpreting the text is possible. (174)

3. PRELIMINARY QUALIFICATIONS FOR THE PATH

The teaching contained in the Extracts of the present section partly overlaps that found in the following section in so far as some of the Extracts speak of the purification of the mind through the cultivation of moral and spiritual qualities, which is the main topic of the section that follows. Moreover, the concluding Extracts in both sections point out that the virtues required culminate in renunciation and detachment. But the emphasis in the Extracts gathered in the present section is on the formal qualifications needed for entering on the practical path of Vedantic enquiry, whereas the shorter section that follows concentrates on the kind of spiritual qualities that have to be cultivated by one actually treading the path. Though the Extracts in the section that follows the present one speak of spiritual qualities in a general way, they do occasionally overlap with the first two sections of Chapter XV, to come in Volume VI, which deal in a more specialized way with certain particular aspects of the practical path.

Assuming that a person belongs to one of the three higher castes and has learned the requisite Vedic texts by heart, then the fundamental requirements are: "Discrimination of things eternal from things transitory, indifference to enjoyment of the benefits of this life or the next, the moral equipment of inner and outer control, etc., and desire for liberation." Nevertheless a number of further topics about qualifications for adopting the path are discussed, and Extracts are given in the following groups.

Group A (consisting of a single Extract)) discusses the problem of whether, and in what sense, Śūdras may follow the path of Vedanta, since the rule that they may not learn or even listen to the Vedas is accepted. It is noted that the teachings of the Epics and Purāṇas, including the Bhagavad Gītā, are available to them. And if certain Śūdras, like Vidura, are known from sacred tradition to have attained enlightenment, this is explained as being due to the fructification of the impressions of Vedic knowledge gained on account of meritorious deeds committed in past lives. The author of the Sūtras, as well as Śaṃkara and even Rāmānuja, have been accused, in this context, of treating knowledge of the Absolute as a kind of class-privilege and of failing (in contrast to the Buddhists) to protest against the cruel punishments assigned to the Śūdras for listening to the Veda. (175) Śaṃkara of course took his stand on the authority of the derivative literature, particularly of the Dharma Śāstras, such as those attributed to Manu, Gautama and Vasiṣṭha. It is difficult to know how rigidly the caste laws were applied in such matters. Śaṃkara quotes Manu's phrase "Whoever practises universal benevolence and friendliness is a Brahmin." (176) Perhaps the statement was not intended to include Śūdras: but it points to a tolerant rather than to an exclusive attitude to the interpretation of caste rules both on the part of Manu and Śaṃkara.

Group B establishes the existence of a spiritual path on the basis of the distinction between a "higher" and a "lower" knowledge found in the Vedic texts. Group C points out how the same rituals that lead to worldly and other-worldly rewards, if performed for the sake of those rewards, lead to purification of the mind if performed without the desire for rewards and are in this way a preparation for the path of knowledge. This idea has ancient roots, for Vācaspati quotes a passage from the Śatapatha Brāhmaṇa (177) which maintains that performance of ritual sacrifice for self-purification is better than performing it for material ends. The last two Extracts of the group extend the principle to rituals performed in association with meditation on their symbolic significance.

The Extracts of Group D enlarge on how the performance of one's caste duties in a disinterested spirit purifies the mind and promotes a *desire* to know the Self, and is in this way a *remote* auxiliary (ārād-upakāraka) to knowledge of the Self. The Extracts in Group E insist that he who wants knowledge of the Self must normally renounce action, ritual and family life. But Śaṃkara makes it clear in his Commentary to Brahma Sūtra I.iii.38 that he accepted that non-renunciates of low caste could attain enlightenment; he attributed this phenomenon to Vedic discipline performed in a previous life.

TEXTS ON THE QUALIFICATIONS FOR THE PATH: GROUP A

1. To this argumentation we reply that the Śūdra (178) is not eligible for the holy knowledge, as he is not allowed to learn the Vedas. Only one

who has learned the Vedas by heart and understands their meaning is eligible to secure the ends of which the Veda treats. The Śūdra cannot learn the Vedas, as no one can learn the Vedas by heart (from a Teacher who knows them) without first undergoing the upanayana ceremony (of initiation) and receiving the sacred thread, and this is the right of the three higher castes only. You may say that it is conceivable that a Śūdra should desire the holy knowledge. But mere desire for something cannot make one eligible for it unless one is actually able to acquire it. Nor does mere eligibility for something in the worldly sense make one really eligible for it. For in the case of anything to do with the traditional teaching, the question of eligibility has to be decided from the standpoint of the rules of the tradition. Judged from this standpoint, the Śūdra cannot acquire the holy knowledge because he is not allowed to learn the Vedas by heart (which is one of the preliminary qualifications)....

And there is another reason why the Śūdra is not eligible for the holy knowledge, namely the mention of investiture with the sacred thread (upanayana) and other ceremonies in the Vedic passages dealing with spiritual knowledge. "He initiated him as a pupil," (179) "'Teach me, holy one,' he said, approaching with reverence," (180) and "Devoted to the Absolute, intent on the Absolute, seeking for the Absolute in its supreme form, they approached holy Pippalāda with fuel in their hands, thinking he would tell them everything." (181) Even a text like "Without initiating them, he spoke to them as follows" (182) only shows that the people in question were already initiated before. That the Śūdra cannot undergo purifying ceremonies of any kind is declared in the text from the Smṛti which calls him "once-born" in the words, "The Śūdra, the fourth caste, is once-born," (183) and in other passages such as "The Śūdra can neither fall from caste nor undergo any purifying ceremony." (184)

And there is another reason why the Śūdra is not eligible for knowledge of the Absolute. Only when Satyakāma had shown that he was not a Śūdra by his truth-telling would Gautama proceed to initiate him and give him teaching. This is what is implied by his words "No one but a Brahmin would have admitted this. Heap the fuel, my dear one. I shall initiate you. You did not swerve from Truth." (185)

Again, one must notice the prohibitions found in the derivative literature against his hearing the Veda, learning the Veda by heart or learning its meaning. As regards his hearing the Veda, we have the text, "If a Śūdra listens in to recitations of the Veda, his ears shall be filled with molten metal and gum" (186) and "A Śūdra is a walking crematorium, so one should not recite the Veda in his presence." (187) This already implies a prohibition against learning the Veda by heart. How could anyone in whose presence the Veda may not be recited learn it by heart? He would never so much as hear it. Further, his tongue has to be cut out if he so much as pronounces the Veda, while his whole body has to be cut to pieces if he commit it to memory. (188) It follows from this that knowledge of the meaning of the Veda and fulfilment of its injunctions are prohibited, as is indeed openly stated in such texts as "The meaning should not be imparted to a Śūdra" (189) and "Learning the Veda, sacrifice and charity are for the twice-born (alone)." (190)

But in the case of those (Śūdras) like Vidura and Dharma-Vyādha (191) in whom knowledge of the Absolute arises through the power of the impressions of previous good deeds, nothing can prevent such knowledge from bearing its due fruit. For the fruit of knowledge arises inevitably and without exception. Moreover, the text from the Smṛti (192) "One may recite before all four castes" declares that all four castes have the right to instruction in the Epics and Purāṇas. But the principle that the Śūdra has no rights in relation to the Veda stands.(193)

TEXTS ON THE QUALIFICATIONS FOR THE PATH: GROUP B

2. Moreover, there are two different kinds of knowledge that have to be acquired here, the highest knowledge (paravidyā) and the lower knowledge (aparavidyā). The text first speaks of the lower knowledge as consisting of the Ṛg Veda, etc., and then goes on to mention "That highest knowledge through which the Imperishable (akṣara) is known." Here the Vedic teaching is that the Imperishable is the object of the higher knowledge. But if one were to assume another Imperishable, different from the supreme Lord and characterized by invisibility and other (negative) attributes, then this would not be the highest knowledge. For this distinction between highest and lower knowledge is made with reference to the fruit it yields, final beatitude in one case, temporary prosperity in this world and the next in the other. And no one claims that a knowledge of the principle of "Nature" (pradhāna) taught by the Sāṃkhya school leads to final beatitude.

Furthermore, on your view there ought to have been mention of three kinds of knowledge, if the supreme Self was to be set up as something different from and higher than the Imperishable, the latter being taken (in the manner of the Nature of the Sāṃkhyas) as the womb of all creatures. But the text actually speaks of only two kinds of knowledge that have to be acquired. Consider also the previous text, "What is that, holy Sir, on knowing which all this is known?" (194) Knowledge of all through knowledge of one is intelligible only if that one is the Absolute, the Self of all, not if it is Nature, the sphere of the non-conscious alone, nor if it is the mere enjoyer considered in abstraction from the objects of his enjoyment. (195)

Consider also the yet earlier text, "He taught knowledge of the Absolute (brahma-vidyā), the foundation of all knowledge, to his eldest son Atharvan." (196) This passage, which begins by mentioning knowledge of the Absolute as the supreme knowledge, proceeds then to distinguish between a supreme knowledge and a lower knowledge, and shows that knowledge of the Imperishable is the supreme knowledge and also that it is equivalent to knowledge of the Absolute. That knowledge, said to be equivalent to knowledge of the Absolute, would be contradicted if its object, the Imperishable (akṣara), were not the Absolute (brahman). The lower knowledge, consisting of the Ṛg Veda, etc., which is knowledge of ritual (karma), is mentioned as a preliminary to knowledge of the Absolute in order to eulogize the latter. For in other places (in the same Upanishad) knowledge of the ritual is decried, as in such texts as "Frail are these barques, consisting of sacrifices, eighteenfold, (197) which are called the lower form of ritual activity. (198) Those deluded ones who hail this as the best fall again into old age and death." (199) And having denounced the lower knowledge, it proceeds to show that the one who has become indifferent to it is a fit candidate for the highest knowledge, in the words, "When the Brahmin has surveyed the worlds accumulated through ritualistic action, let him acquire disgust for them. One cannot attain to that which is uncreate through anything made. (200) To know that transcendent principle one should betake oneself, fuel in hand, (201) to a Teacher who is learned in the Veda and himself established in the Absolute." (202)

* * * * *

3. Aṅgiras then spoke to Śaunaka, and this is what he said. Those skilled in the meaning of the Veda, (203) and possessed of direct vision of ultimate reality, say that the knowledge conveyed by the Veda is of two kinds, the higher (paravidyā)

and the lower (aparavidyā). The higher knowledge is knowledge of the supreme Self. The lower knowledge has for its sphere merit and demerit, and the means that lead to them and the results that flow from them.

Perhaps you will ask how it was that when Śaunaka asked, "What does one have to know in order to become omniscient?" Aṅgiras began talking about the two kinds of knowledge when he ought simply to have answered the question put before him. But there is nothing wrong here, for the answer is based upon the fact that things have to be known in a certain order. The lower knowledge is in fact nescience and has to be (ultimately) negated. For when one knows the lower knowledge in its entirety, one does not know anything as it really is. The procedure is analogous to that of commentators, who first refute the *prima facie* view before going on to state the conclusive view.

The lower knowledge, the Upanishad continues, consists of the four Vedas, (204) namely the Ṛg Veda, the Sāma Veda, the Yajur Veda and the Atharva Veda, as well as the six auxiliary Vedic sciences of pronunciation (of the Vedic texts), ritual, grammar, etymology, prosody and astrology. (205)

And now the higher knowledge is described, that through which one attains to the Imperishable, of which the definition is to be given below. When the root "gam" takes the prefix "adhi" it usually means "attain to". And in the case of the Supreme, "attaining to" and "knowing" are identical. For attainment of the Supreme means cessation of nescience and nothing else.

You might perhaps ask how any knowledge could be "higher" and be a means to liberation if it stood (higher than and therefore) "outside" the Ṛg Veda and the other body of texts mentioned. For we have the text from the derivative literature,

"All the (so-called)) derivative literature (smṛti) that is not properly based on the Veda, and all contentious rationalism, are held to be worse than useless for the after-life, as they are concerned exclusively with the realm of darkness." (206) Should we not therefore shun this (so-called) higher knowledge as mere contentious rationalism and therefore useless? Moreover, the text, (though itself part of an Upanishad), seems to exclude the Upanishads from the body of texts representing the Veda, or otherwise why would it have separated the higher knowledge from the lower knowledge, the latter consisting in the total body of the Vedic texts?

But the assumptions behind the question are wrong. For what the term "higher knowledge" here means concerns (not texts but) what is known and realized. The "higher knowledge" here means immediate awareness of that Imperishable Principle which is to be known of (in the first instance) from the Upanishadic texts. It does not mean mere committing to memory of the words of the Upanishads, whereas "knowledge of the Veda" always means mere knowledge of the series of words contained in the Vedic texts. But knowledge of the Imperishable Principle will never arise from a mere knowledge of the series of words contained in the Veda. There has to be the proper approach to a competent Teacher and the cultivation of detachment and other such further measures. That was why knowledge of the Absolute was mentioned separately from knowledge of the (words of the) Veda and called the higher knowledge.

In the case of the injunctions of the ritualistic part of the Veda there is some ritual like the Agnihotra which still has to be performed by an agent who has assembled various kinds of equipment after he has first understood the meaning of the injunctive text. But this is not the case with that "higher knowledge" here under consideration. The latter is complete at the very time of understanding the meaning of the text. For nothing remains but mere retention of the knowledge of a truth conveyed by words alone. (207)

* * * * *

4. It has been declared earlier that an ignorant man, identifying himself with a particular caste and stage of life, etc., forfeits his independence like a beast of burden through his duties to the gods and other beings, to which he submits under pressure of the spiritual law. (208) The text now goes on to explain what these acts are, the duty of which makes a man forfeit his independence like a beast of burden, and also to explain who these "gods and other beings" are whom he serves like a beast of burden by his deeds.

This householder already under discussion, this ignorant man condemned to action, this "individual" distinguished by the whole apparatus of body and senses – he it is who is referred to in the text by the word "self". This "self" is an "object of enjoyment" to all living beings from the gods down to the ants. For he serves all of them on account of acts enjoined on him on account of his caste and stage of life and for other reasons.

Sacrifice (yāga) means offering a portion of one's possessions to a deity (devatā). (209) When this includes placing the offering in a sacred fire, it is called an oblation (homa). The text here means that the individual sacrificer loses his independence and becomes like a beast of burden to the gods through the necessity of having to perform ritualistic action in the form of sacrifice and ritual.

He is a "beast of burden" to the Vedic seers (ṛṣi), says the text, in that he recites their hymns daily. He is a beast of burden to the ancestors (pitṛ) in that he offers them cakes and water and also in that he desires children and makes efforts to have them.... He is a "beast of burden" to men in that he puts them up in his house, gives them a place and water, and also gives them food, the latter whether they stay with him or not and whether they ask for it or not. He is a "beast of burden" to the beasts of burden themselves in that he arranges for their fodder and water. He is a "beast of burden" to the wild animals and birds and ants in that he supports them by throwing out crumbs for them and by offering them the refuse from washing-up etc.

Thus he (the householder) serves the gods and the rest by these various actions. Hence, as the text puts it, just as a person desires the health and continued existence of their own body, and feeds and protects it all round to secure this end, even so all creatures from the gods downwards wish for the health and safety of such a source of pleasure to themselves as the householder in question, who thinks he must repay all creatures as if he were their debtor. That is, they protect him all round, as householders themselves protect their livestock. As the text said earlier, "Therefore they (the gods) do not like it that men should know this." (210)...

The text now continues, "At the beginning this was the Self alone." If the knower of the Absolute is released from that beast-of-burden-like bondage to duties, what is it that makes one proceed as if helplessly to accept the bonds of ritualistic action, to the neglect of the pursuit of spiritual knowledge, which would release one from bondage?

We realize that it has been said that the gods "protect" such a person. But they only protect those who are qualified for ritualistic action and thus fall within their jurisdiction. Otherwise there would be transgression of the law that one receives the just results of one's meritorious acts and does not receive the fruits of acts one has not committed. The gods do not protect all men as such, irrespective of whether or not they are qualified to perform ritualistic action. Therefore there must be some compelling force which makes a man extraverted and turns him away from the Self, his own true home.

One might think that this force was nescience, since it is the one afflicted by nescience who becomes extraverted and plunges into action. But nescience is not exactly what prompts one to action. Its function, rather, is to conceal the true nature of the real. All we can say is that it clearly lies behind some other prompting cause, as darkness lies behind the immediate prompting cause which makes us fall into a ditch or the lake at night-time. So the immediate prompting cause of extraversion still remains to be stated. And it is stated now, in the following section, to be desire. The Kaṭha Upanishad speaks of the "immature souls," steeped in natural nescience, who "pursue desires for external things." (211) In the derivative literature we have such passages as "This is desire, this is passion." (212) In the Law Book of Manu (213) all prompting to action is traced to desire. And the same point is now made in the present text in detail from here right on till the end of the chapter.

"At the beginning this was the Self alone," says the text. The words "the Self alone" should be taken to refer to (the general subject of the topic in hand, i.e.) the naturally ignorant soul, the member of a caste identifying himself with the physical and subtle bodies and their appurtenances. "In the beginning" means before association with a wife in marriage. There was then (before marriage) no wife or the like, no desirable being associated with the future householder himself. He was "alone" means he was alone but associated with nescience, the source of all desires such as that for a wife. Overcome by the natural impression of nescience, which makes for the false connection of action and its factors, such as agency and result, etc., with the Self, he (the future householder) felt desire.

The form his desire assumed was: "Let me, agent of actions as I am, acquire a wife, which will qualify me for ritualistic action (as a householder). Let me have a wife to qualify me to perform rituals... and let me have a child (through her), let me be myself reborn as a child. Let me have wealth, too, in the form of cows and the like, for wealth is the means to sacrifice. And let me perform ritualistic sacrifices for prosperity here and welfare in the worlds to come. As I stand now I am a debtor (to the gods and other creatures). Let me perform those ritualistic sacrifices which will carry me to the worlds of the gods and other exalted beings, and also the optional rituals which lead to (benefits on earth such as) sons and wealth and also heaven and the like."

Desire, says the text, is "limited to this." The immediate objects of desire are wife, sons, wealth and ritualistic merit – that is to say, desire for the means to further ritualistic action. The "worlds", such as those of men, of the ancestors (pitṛ) and of the various gods, are the results for the sake of which the means are desired. Therefore the one real desire is the desire for "the worlds". Though one, it may be regarded as two-fold if separate account is taken of desire for the means. Hence the text will affirm later, "For both of these are but desires." (214)

All activity is undertaken for the sake of some result. Hence the text assumes that it will have been understood that its teaching about the presence of desire for the means implied the presence of desire for the "worlds" also. This must be taken into account in evaluating the statement "Desire is limited to such ends as these." When you have already spoken of eating, you do not make special separate mention of the satisfaction which follows it, as that was what the eating was for.

Desire, then, consists in this twin desire for ends and means, by which the ignorant one feels compelled to weave a cocoon round himself like a silk-worm. In this condition he abandons himself entirely to the path of ritualistic action (karma-mārga), (215) becomes extraverted and does not recognize his Self, his own true home, as the Taittirīya Brāhmaṇa points out in the words "Bemused by the fire and choked by its smoke, he does not recognize the Self, his own true home." (216)

But one might ask how desire could be said to be "limited to this," inasmuch as desires are infinite. Anticipating a query of this sort, the text proceeds to say that one cannot get more than this even if one wants it — more, that is to say, than ends and means. One cannot, in this world, acquire anything whatever, whether immediately visible or not, which is not either an end or a means. There can only be desire for what can actually be acquired. And since nothing can be acquired but ends and means, the text speaks of desire as "limited to this." The meaning behind it is that, as desire consists in the twin longing for visible and invisible things as ends or means, and as this is the special province of man afflicted by ignorance, it is something that the man of knowledge (i.e. the aspirant to knowledge) must give up. (217)

* * * * *

5. Nescience has been mentioned. In this connection it has been noted that the man afflicted by nescience will worship a deity as

other than himself in the conviction "He is one and I another." A man of this kind, it has been further said, identifies himself with a particular caste and stage of life. He feels that ritualistic action is actually a duty, and proceeds with ritual sacrifices under the impulse of desire. As he serves gods and other beings, he has been called "an object of enjoyment to all living beings." It was all these living beings, indeed, who had projected him as an object of enjoyment through their own ritualistic acts. And he, likewise, projected the whole world and all living beings as objects of his enjoyment through his oblations and five-fold ritualistic acts. (218) Every single individual is thus the enjoyer of and the one enjoyed by the whole world, according to the rituals and meditations he has performed. Everyone is both the cause and the effect of everything else. On the part played by symbolic meditations here we shall speak further in the section of the Bṛhadāraṇyaka Upanishad called the Madhu Vidyā. (219) There it will be explained how everything is the effect of everything else and so is "honey" (in that it is the end-product of the mingling of innumerable separate factors), and the explanation will show how in the end only the one Self exists.

The ignorant man has projected a universe for his own enjoyment through his five-fold optional ritualistic actions, beginning with oblation, and through his meditations on symbols. This universe is divided seven-fold as cause and effect. (220) And the seven parts are called seven foods because they are objects of enjoyment. Therefore he is called the father of those foods.

But in the realm of knowledge of the Absolute there cannot be desire, as all is one. This implies that the natural wisdom of this world and worldly heroism not based on obedience to the Veda lead to further world-projection. Action and thought of this kind can lead to evils even like descent into the world of plants. The text, however, is referring (not to secular ends and means but) to the ends and means suggested by Vedic revelation, and aims to inculcate indifference even to them, as a prelude to urging knowledge of the Absolute. For no one will seriously apply himself to the pursuit of knowledge of the Absolute unless he has already acquired the conviction that *all* this world of transmigration, manifest and non-manifest, consisting of means and ends, is impure and transient and painful and the realm of nescience — and has begun to feel complete indifference to it. (221)

TEXTS ON THE QUALIFICATIONS FOR THE PATH: GROUP C

6. Stated in brief, the goal to promote which this holy treatise called the Gītā (Gītā Śāstra) has been composed is supreme beatitude, characterized by the final cessation of transmigratory experience and its cause. And this consummation arises from the spiritual path of devotion to knowledge of the Self in association with renunciation of all ritualistic action. The Lord Himself declares that this is the spiritual path taught by the Gītā in such a text (from the Anu Gītā) as "This spiritual path is the most adequate for experiencing the state of the Absolute."(222) Also found there are the following texts, namely "(He attains to the Absolute) who neither practises good works nor bad works, who is neither respectable nor disreputable, who remains absorbed in the one support of all, silent, not thinking of anything" (223) and "Spiritual realization implies the renunciation of all works." (224) And at the end of the Gītā itself the Lord says to Arjuna, "Giving up all paths (of action), take refuge in Me alone." (225)

There is also the path of action, envisaging advantages in future lives, which is prescribed for those who belong to particular castes and stations of life, and which may, on occasion, be the cause of obtaining exalted positions such as that of a god. When this path is followed in a spirit of offering all one's deeds to the Lord and without any personal desires for oneself, it purifies the heart. And purification of the heart prepares the way for devotion to knowledge, and is thus indirectly a cause of supreme beatitude inasmuch as it is a factor in the rise of knowledge. It is to express this very idea that the Lord will say later, "Having committed all his actions to the Absolute" (226) and "Yogins perform action without attachment for the purification of their minds."(227)

* * * * *

7. O sinless one (Arjuna), I, the omniscient Lord, at the beginning of the present world-period, when I had first brought forth the creatures, brought to light once more the traditional teaching of the Veda as a means to their temporal prosperity and final release. I declare that the path of the three castes (Brahmins, Kṣatriyas and Vaiśyas), who had the right and duty of following the Vedic teaching, had two forms.

Then the Lord explains what the two forms of the path are. One form of the path I taught (He says) was that where knowledge itself is the discipline (yoga). It is for the Sāṃkhyas, (228) that is, those who have discriminative knowledge of the difference between the Self and the non-self, who have renounced the world straight from the stage of celibate student, (229) who have direct insight into the meaning of the Upanishadic texts, (230) who are houseless monks (parivrājaka) of the Paramahaṃsa order, and established in awareness of the Absolute. The other form concerns those "yogins", those men of action, for whom action itself is the path....

(XII.3) ADOPTING THE PATH (TEXTS)

The text says "One does not attain the actionless state (naiṣkarmya) simply by desisting from action." "Action" means ritualistic acts and the like (231) which, when performed in this or any other birth, are indirectly the means to devotion to knowledge, in that by destroying the load of accumulated sins they cause purity of mind and a resultant access to knowledge. This is confirmed by such passages from the derivative literature as "Knowledge arises in men through the destruction of (the impurity resulting from) their evil deeds."(232)

By the "actionless state" (naiṣkarmya) the text means the state of being beyond action, of being void of action, of being devoted to knowledge, of being established as the actionless Self in its true nature.

When the text says "One does not attain the actionless state simply by desisting from action" it is implied , that, on the contrary, one has to attain it through engaging in action. (233) If it be asked *why* one can not attain the actionless state without engaging in action, the reply is that engaging in action is the means of attaining the actionless state, and one cannot attain a particular end without resorting to the appropriate means. That the discipline of action (karma-yoga) is a means to the discipline of knowledge (jñāna-yoga) — which is itself nothing other than the actionless state — is taught both in the Veda and here in the Bhagavad Gītā. It is taught in the Veda, for instance, when the means for acquiring the desired knowledge of the "world of the Self" that is under discussion is proclaimed in the passage beginning "Brahmins develop the desire to know this ("world of the Self") through repetition of the Vedic texts and Vedic ritual sacrifice." (234) And the Lord will teach the same doctrine here in the Bhagavad Gītā in such passages as "But renunciation, O Mighty-armed One, is difficult to attain except through the discipline of action," (235) "Yogins perform action without attachment for the purification of their minds" (236) and "Sacrifice, charity and ascetic acts are what the wise resort to for purification." (237)

Here the objection might be raised that the text "He should promise to refrain from harming (sacrificing) any creature and resort to the actionless state" (238) shows that the actionless state can also be attained through the mere renunciation of prescribed ritual. The actionless state is moreover perfectly familiar to the world as that which supervenes when one does not not engage in any action. So why should one who wishes to attain the actionless state engage in action? To answer this objection the Lord replies, "Nor can one attain the goal (of the actionless state) through mere (formal) renunciation," that is, through merely desisting from action without having acquired spiritual knowledge. (239)

* * * * *

8. If a man gives up attachment and performs the obligatory daily ritual as a duty, without desire for advantage to himself, his mind, previously soiled by attachment to the fruits of action, is purified by the daily ritual and attains to clarity. When purified and clear it becomes capable of enquiry into the Self. The Lord now goes on to explain how one whose mind has been purified through the performance of the obligatory daily ritual gradually turns towards Self-knowledge.

Such a one does not detest the optional ritual, even though it no longer becomes him to perform it. He does not think, "This merely perpetuates transmigratory life by initiating new bodies, so what is the use of it?" Nor does he feel any special attachment to the daily obligatory ritual, even though it helps him spiritually. He does not think, "This will lead to liberation by causing me to adhere steadfastly to purification of the mind and through this to the search for spiritual knowledge." Even in regard to the daily obligatory ritual he looks for no personal advantage and develops no attachment or special liking for it. He is, in fact, as the text says, a renunciate (tyāgin), one who renounces the "fruits" of his actions and yet continues to perform the obligatory daily ritual. He is penetrated by the constituent "sattva", (240) which enables him to discriminate Self from not-self. He is wise, possessed of the wisdom of Self-knowledge. His doubts have been dispelled: those doubts which had been set up by nescience have been dispelled by the conviction "Realization of one's own Self is the means to the highest beatitude, and there is no other means whatever."

That man who acquires the requisite qualifications through performance of the daily obligatory ritual in the way just stated gradually purifies his mind and becomes awake to the fact that he himself *is* the actionless "Self (of all). Such a one attains to that devotion to knowledge which consists in going beyond the whole realm of action, and which is referred to in such texts as "Renouncing all actions through the mind" (241) and Seated... neither acting nor causing to act." (242)

* * * * *

9. You (243) claimed earlier (244) that the obligatory daily rituals produce a special effect (*viz.* liberation) when associated with meditation, just as poison associated with spells (245) does the body no harm and curds accompanied by sugar produce not fever but health. You are welcome to this contention, as we ourselves support it

and it involves no contradictions. There is no contradiction whatever in the supposition that ritualistic action associated with meditation and performed in a disinterested spirit should have a special effect. For we have Vedic texts to the effect that he who sacrifices to the Self is better than he who sacrifices to the gods, as in the passage beginning, "He who sacrifices to the Self is better than he who sacrifices to the gods" (246) and "The rituals performed in association with meditation... (become more powerful)." (247) And the meaning of the words "he who sacrifices to the Self" has been explained by Manu as referring to the supreme Self, when he speaks of "him who sacrifices to the Self" as "seeing the same in everything" (248) – unless it refers to his state immediately preceding this vision. (249) He who sacrifices to the Self performs the obligatory daily rituals to purify his soul, (250) as the text "This limb of mine is purified by this ritual" (251) indicates. The passage in Manu Smṛti beginning "Through the ritual prescribed for conception and the later stages of birth and development" (252) likewise shows that the obligatory rituals are concerned with the purification of the body, senses and mind. And when he who sacrifices to the Self has become purified by performance of the obligatory daily rituals in a disinterested spirit he becomes able to see the same one principle in all. Either in that or in some other birth he will later acquire vision of the Self. This is the meaning of the phrase. (253) "Seeing the same everywhere, he attains spiritual sovereignty." The phrase "He who sacrifices to the Self" really refers to his state immediately preceding vision of the Self, and is used to indicate that the obligatory daily rituals accompanied by symbolic meditations (on themes prescribed by the Veda) are a preliminary condition leading towards the ultimate acquisition of knowledge of the Self.

And there is a further point. We have the text (254) "The wise say that the highest realm of the constituent (guṇa) "sattva" (255) is constituted by Brahmā, the World-Projecting Ṛṣis, Dharma in embodied form, (256) and the deities presiding over the principles of Mahat (257) and the Unmanifest." But later the same work shows how those who proceed on the path of disinterested performance of the obligatory rituals (nivṛtti) (258) go beyond the state of equality with the gods evoked in the above-quoted verse, which is the highest point for those who travel on the path of optional rituals (pravṛtti), and become "eternally dissolved in the elements." As for those who read "Go beyond the elements" in this passage, they constitute no threat to our interpretation as they have little knowledge of the Vedic wisdom. (259)

Nor are the passages (quoted from the Śatapatha Brāhmaṇa) to be dismissed as mere eulogy. For the chapter in which they occur deals with the maturation of merit derived from ritualistic action to the point where it leads to identity with Brahmā. And it is well known that the Karma Kāṇḍa dealing with such subjects is continuous for purposes of interpretation with the Upanishads, which teach that knowledge of the Self lies beyond the whole empirical sphere. The fact that neglect of prescribed rituals and addiction to forbidden acts do have real effects on the fate of the individuals in question is shown by the presence in the world of (low degrees of life such as) plants and dogs and pigs, (260) not to mention the fact that people do in fact see ghouls like the "vomit-eaters". (261) Nor could one conceive any acts apart from those enjoined or forbidden in the Veda and Smṛti which could be either perceived or inferred to result in birth as a ghoul or a dog or a pig or a plant, when neglected or perpetrated respectively. And no one supposes that these states are not the result of former actions. Therefore states like those of ghoul, animal or plant result from neglect of enjoined acts and resort to forbidden acts. And in just the same way, we conclude that the very high states culminating in identity with Brahmā, also, are the result of the maturation of merit derived from acts. Therefore the texts (from the Śatapatha Brāhmaṇa and Chāndogya Upanishad about rising higher than the realms of the gods through disinterested practice of ritual accompanied by meditation) are not untruths inserted by way of eulogy (arthavāda) in the manner of such texts as "He cut out his own omentum" and "He howled." (262)

Perhaps you will say that the passages about the omentum and the howling are not "eulogistic" but state historical facts. Let it be so, if you wish. This can do no harm to our own principle, nor can it in any way harm our position. Nor can you say that the positions of Brahmā or of the World-Projecting Ṛṣis can be reached through the performance of optional (self-interested) rituals, since the (highest) fruit of the latter had been declared to be no more than *kinship* with the gods. Therefore attaining the position of Brahmā or the World-Projecting Ṛṣis is the result of the performance of the obligatory daily rituals plus (certain powerful optional) rituals such as the Sarvamedha and the Aśvamedha (in a spirit of desire for the fruits). But in the case of those who perform the daily obligatory rituals (only) without any personal desire for fruit but only for the sake of self-purification, these rituals become for them a means to the rise of enlightenment. For we have the text from the derivative literature, "(Through repetition of the holy texts, through austerities, through oblations, through learning, through offerings to the ancestors, through sacrifices and through the five great sacrifices) (263) this body is made fit for the attainment of the Absolute." (264) Nor are we saying anything contradictory in connecting ritualistic action with liberation, since it is a remote auxiliary to the latter. How this is so, we shall explain below, at the end of the fourth

Chapter. (265)

* * * * *

10. We have seen from the preceding "topic" (Brahmā Sūtra IV.i.16-17) that when the obligatory daily ritual such as the Agnihotra is performed by one desirous of liberation, with liberation as the ultimate goal in mind, then it must be accounted as a cause of purity of mind, inasmuch as it extinguishes the demerit arising from past sins. And because it is a preliminary condition for knowledge of the Absolute as a means to liberation, it works together with knowledge of the Absolute for one and the same end.

Further, it is to be observed that obligatory daily rituals like the Agnihotra may either be performed blindly as mere ritualistic ceremonies, or else they may be performed to the accompaniment of knowledge of their secret significance. (266) For we have the formulae that imply their performance without knowledge. Fruits are promised, for instance, to "one who sacrifices knowing thus," to "one who offers an oblation knowing thus," to "one who intones a psalm, knowing thus," to "one who sings a hymn, knowing thus." We also have texts like "He should appoint as overseer of the sacrifice one who has this knowledge and not one who does not have it" (267) and "They perform rituals with the pronunciation of OM, both those who know the syllable OM to be as just described and those who do not." (268)

In this connection, the following doubt arises. When we say that, in the case of the seeker of liberation, obligatory daily rituals like the Agnihotra co-operate with knowledge of the Absolute to produce the same fruit of liberation, since they are an (indirect) cause of knowledge, (269) do we mean this only of such rituals performed in association with knowledge, or do we mean that it could also be true of some rituals performed without knowledge? Why does such a doubt arise? Because on the one hand we have such a text as "They desire to know this Self through sacrifice," (270) which declares that sacrifices and other practices are means to realization of the Self without specifying whether they have to be associated with knowledge or not. And on the other hand there are texts (271) which specify that the Agnihotra and other rituals must be performed in association with knowledge. From this our *prima facie* conclusion would be that it was only rituals associated with knowledge that played a part in the knowledge of the Self. For there are texts implying that what is associated with knowledge is superior to what is not, such as, "He who knows thus wards off repeated deaths the very day he offers a sacrifice." (272) And there are passages from the derivative literature to the same effect, such as "Hear it now according to the yoga-wisdom, possessed of which, O descendant of Pṛthu, you will cast off the bonds of action" (273) and "Action is far inferior to the yoga-wisdom, O Conqueror of Wealth (Arjuna)." (274)

To this the author of the Sūtras replies, "For we have the text, 'Whatever is done with knowledge'." (275) It is true that the daily obligatory ritual such as the Agnihotra performed with knowledge is superior to the same ritual performed without it, just as a learned Brahmin is superior to one who is not learned. (276) But the Agnihotra ritual and the like performed without knowledge is not altogether beneath notice. For we have the Vedic declaration, "They desire to know the Self through sacrifice," (277) which speaks of the Agnihotra and other ritual as being a cause of knowledge of the Self, without specifying whether such ritual must be accompanied or need not be accompanied by knowledge.

(XII.3) ADOPTING THE PATH (TEXTS)

You will say, perhaps, that it is known that the Agnihotra performed by one in possession of knowledge is superior to such ritual performed without knowledge. And from this you might conclude that the Agnihotra and other such ritual performed without knowledge was of no account as a cause of knowledge of the Self. But the truth is otherwise. It is correct to assume that, as a cause of knowledge of the Self, ritual such as the Agnihotra performed with knowledge has greater potentiality on account of the presence of knowledge, and therefore produces greater results. But the text "They desire to know this Self through sacrifice" (278) says that the Agnihotra and the rest have a part to play in the knowledge of the Self whether they are performed accompanied by knowledge or not....

Hence we must conclude that every performance of the Agnihotra and other obligatory daily ritual before the rise of knowledge, whether in association with knowledge or not, and whether in this birth or a previous one, is, each according to its own perculiar capacity, instrumental in extinguishing that demerit arising from past sins which obstructs knowledge of the Absolute. It must therefore all be accepted as a "cause" of knowledge of the Absolute. Hence our original position that performance of such ritual co-operates with knowledge of the Absolute for the one end of liberation stands. It must be remembered, however, that in order to have this function, it depends entirely on the support of the inner discipline of hearing the metaphysical texts of the Upanishads, cogitating over them and meditating on them persistently, along with faith, singleness of purpose and other necessary psychological qualities. (279)

* * * * *

(XII.3) ADOPTING THE PATH (TEXTS)

11. All this programme of ritualistic activity and symbolic meditations on factors in the ritual serves, in the case of the desireless seeker of liberation, merely for the purification of the mind. In the case, however, of one who has not performed symbolic meditations and who is activated by desire, the rituals laid down in the Veda and the derivative literature serve for the attainment of the Southern Path (280) and eventual return to the world. On the other hand mere natural activity as prompted by the instincts and pursued without regard to Vedic injunctions leads to a descent into the animal and vegetable realms. For there is the Upanishadic text, "But these oft-returning tiny creatures, to whom it is (continually) being said 'Be born!' and 'Die!' do not belong to either of these paths. This is a third state." (281) And there is also the Vedic text "Three (kinds of) creatures left the path." (282)

But he whose mind has been purified and who is without desire feels no inclination for what is external, transient, associated with ends and means, and proceeding from impressions of acts in this and former lives. In him desire to know the inmost Self takes root. And this is the subject that is expounded in the Kena Upanishad by the method of questions and answers, beginning with the question "At whose (kena) will?" (283) In the Kaṭha Upanishad it is said, "The Creator pierced the apertures of the senses outwards. Hence one sees what is without, not the Self within. A certain wise man, desiring immortality, turning his sight inwards, beheld the inmost Self." (284) And in the Atharva Veda we find, "When the Brahmin has surveyed the worlds accumulated through ritualistic action, let him acquire disgust for them. One cannot attain to that which is uncreate (the Absolute) through anything made. (284) To know that transcendent principle one should betake oneself, fuel in hand, (285) to a Teacher who is learned in the Veda and himself established in the Absolute." (287) This is the only way in which the one who has acquired indifference to worldly means and ends can come to hear of, think over and finally acquire immediate experience of the inmost Self. (288)

* * * * *

12. "Those who worship Hiraṇyagarbha enter blind darkness." (289) This text, by denying the reality of Hiraṇyagarbha, denies the reality of the whole world of effects. If Hiraṇyagarbha really existed, objection would not have been raised against his worship.

Perhaps it will be contended that the objection against worship of Hiraṇyagarbha is only made in order to enjoin meditation on Hiraṇyagarbha in company with the performance of ritualistic action, as is suggested by the text "They enter blind darkness who practise mere ritual." (290)

It is, indeed, perfectly true that the (exclusive) worship of Hiraṇyagarbha is decried in order to make way for a conjunction of meditation on Hiraṇyagarbha as a deity with ritualistic action. The ultimate purpose of ritualistic action, however, is to take the practitioner beyond the realm of death, understood as the natural urges to action prompted by nescience. And, in the same way, the conjunction of meditation on the deities with ritualistic action, designed to purify the heart of the meditator, is also to take the practitioner beyond the realm of death, understood again as the urge towards action based on attachment to results, consisting in the longing to accomplish various ends and the consequent longing for the necessary means. (291) Indeed, a purified (saṃskṛta) man is precisely one who is free from the impurity of death in the form of this twin longing. Hence that brand of nescience which consists of meditation on deities in conjunction with ritualistic action is for the sake of going beyong death in that form.

Hence we must conclude that the one who has gone beyond death, understood as nescience in the form of the twin desire for ends and means, and who is equipped with dispassion and who is intent on studying the Upanishad teaching, is already on the brink of the achievement of knowledge of the sole reality of the supreme Self. In comparison with his earlier nescience, (292) his present knowledge of the Absolute (brahma-vidyā), which is the means to immortality, is regarded as "later". (293) And this knowledge is spoken of as being "conjoined" with nescience in the sense that both are possessed by one and the same man (though at different times). Worship of Hiraṇyagarbha, therefore, is (in one sense) decried in real earnest because it does not directly lead to the same result as knowledge of the Absolute, the means to immortality. Though it is a cause of the removal of impurities, it does not directly lead to liberation in the full sense.

Since the worship of Hiraṇyagarbha is decried, it follows that Hiraṇyagarbha has only relative or conditional existence. His off-spring, the world, called "the immortal", is thus denied reality in comparison to the Self, the only reality properly so called. (294)

TEXTS ON THE QUALIFICATIONS FOR THE PATH: GROUP D

13. Now, it was said earlier that a man achieves the state of spiritual sovereignty through knowledge alone. As this might lead one to suppose that, on this view, the actions enjoined in the Veda and the derivative literature were useless, an account of how action can be of service to man's genuine ends is here given to ward off such a suspicion.

We have already explained the term "ṛta" in the text (to mean duties rightly comprehended exactly as they are laid down in the Veda). (295) "Svādhyāya" refers to private recitation of the Vedic texts on one's own. "Giving out" means teaching the holy texts, which one has oneself learned by heart, to others, and is known as "the Brahman sacrifice". (296) We have to supply the idea that these activities such as "ṛta", etc., "have to be carried out." "Truth" means truth-speaking, or else truth in the sense explained above (of truth put into practice in speech and deeds). (297) Tapas means voluntary acts of self-denial such as fasting. (298) Dama means restraint of the external senses. Śama means restraint of the internal organ (antaḥkaraṇa or mind). The sacrificial fires must be tended. The Agnihotra must be offered (daily). Guests must be served with reverence. "What concerns one as a man" means worldly dealings and duties, and they must be attended to faithfully as they crop up. A family must be reared. Procreation implies approaching one's wife in season. Preservation of the line means seeing that there are grand-children, which involves getting one's sons married.

It has to be understood that even the person who is carrying out all these actions (karma) has to carry on resolutely with his private recitation of the Vedic texts and his teaching of them to others. Each one of them has to be understood as being accompanied by private recitation and teaching of the Vedic texts. For knowledge of the meaning of the texts depends on (their being kept alive in people's memory through) private recitation (svādhyāya), and man's highest good depends on knowledge of their meaning. Teaching them to others serves to prevent them passing out of living memory and occasions special merit. So private recitation and teaching of the texts should not be neglected. (299)

* * * * *

14. Perhaps you will say that as the rise of knowledge is (in some sense) dependent on (the purifying force of previous) action, there can only be one stage of life. (300) Because actions are enjoined for one in the householder state only, there is the doctrine that there is only one stage of life, (301) and this agrees very well with the Vedic texts enjoining "life-long" action. (302)

But this is not so. For action is of various kinds. It is not only rituals like the Agnihotra that constitute action. There are other courses of action pertaining to other stages of life (where no fire is maintained for ritual) that are recognized as promoting the rise of knowledge, such as continence, voluntary self-denial (tapas), truth-speaking, restraint of the mind (śama), restraint of the external senses (dama) and harmlessness. These and also others, such as meditation (dhyāna) and prolonged abstraction (dhāraṇā), are especially helpful in promoting spiritual knowledge in other stages of life as they can be practised there in a highly concentrated form. The present text will say later, "Seek to know the Absolute through austerity (here = concentration)." (303)

And again, spiritual knowledge can arise before one enters on the householder's state, on account of (purifying) actions performed in previous births. (304) And since one enters the householder's state in order to be able to carry out (prescribed Vedic right) action, and since the ultimate goal of action is spiritual knowledge, then if one were already in possession of spiritual knowledge entry into the state of a householder would be useless. Sons, too, are begotten for the sake of attaining to "worlds". And how could one whose desire for "this world" or "the world of the ancestors (pitṛ)" or "the world or the gods (deva)" had ceased, and who beheld "the world of the Self" (305) ever established as eternal, find any (306) purpose in action? And so how could he ever engage in it? Even one who had already entered into the householder state,and who experienced the rise of spiritual knowledge in that state through the maturation of his earlier knowledge,would see no further purpose in actions and would desist from them. And this is made clear by such Vedic texts as "Behold, I am about to leave this (householder's) condition." (307)

Nor can it be argued that this is wrong on account of the great lengths to which the Veda goes in describing actions. One cannot, for instance, argue that the Veda lays great stress on certain ritualistic actions like performance of the Agnihotra, that ritualistic actions involve one in great expenditure of energy and effort since the Agnihotra and other sacrifices imply the assembling of all sorts of materials, that austerity and continence and the like can be performed in the householder's state as well as in the other ones, that the other stages of life involve small equipment — and then, after all this, go on to conclude that the householder's state cannot be considered as just another alternative on the same footing as the other states.

For this whole position is contradicted by the fact that one can receive benefit from what one has done in earlier lives. (308) What was said about there being so much emphasis on action in the Veda does not damage our position either. For action performed in previous lives, whether ritualistic action like performance of the Agnihotra sacrifice,or whether of the nature of restraint like observance of continence, etc., can promote the rise of spiritual knowledge. This is why some people are dispassionate from their very birth whereas others plunge into a life of action and are passionate and enemies of culture. And from this we must further conclude that when the dispassionate ones enter states of life other than that of the householder it is on account of impressions and impulses derived from (good actions in) former births.

And there is another reason why such a large proportion of the Veda is taken up with action. The results of action are legion! The things that can be obtained through action defy enumeration, including, as they do, sins, heaven, sanctity and all the rest. And human desires for all these results are legion too. And it is to serve these desires that the Veda devotes such a large proportion of its space to enjoining actions. Everyone knows how numerous desires are – "Let me have this, let me have that."

And there is another reason for the emphasis laid on action. It is also a means to the rise of knowledge. As we have already said, (309) actions are a means to knowledge. And the immediate emphasis is always on the means, not the end.

Well then, are we to say that if knowledge arises through action, then if one wants knowledge, it would be useless to apply oneself to anything else? Are we to say that knowledge arises from actions only, because they consume the obstacles to its manifestation, namely previously accumulated demerit? Are we to say that efforts made to pursue hearing, cogitation and sustained meditation apart from the path of works are useless? No, because there is no universal law to prove such a view. There is no universal law that knowledge invariably arises through the annihiliation of some obstacle to its rise and not through efforts directed towards meditation, austerity and earning the grace of the Lord. (310) Disciplines not taught in the path of works, too, such as continence and harmlessness, contribute to the rise of knowledge. (311) And its *direct* causes are hearing, cogitation and sustained meditation. (312)

So it remains true that there are also other stages of life besides that of the householder, and also that *everyone* has a right to spiritual knowledge (313) and that the highest end of man arises from knowledge alone. (314)

* * * * *

15. The fact that the text here in the passage "having taught the Veda" begins with a section on practical duties means that the duties laid down in the Vedic texts and Smṛti have to be performed regularly before realization of the Absolute. And the present parting instruction is added for the purification of the human mind. A cultured and purified man can triumph easily over all obstacles to the knowledge of the Self. For we read in the Smṛti "One overcomes impurity through austerity and attains immortality through knowledge," (315) and the present text itself will say later, "Seek to know the Absolute through austerity." (316)

Duties, therefore, have to be performed as an aid to the rise of knowledge, as is shown by the word "instruction" in "He (the Teacher) gives parting instruction." It is wrong not to carry out instructions. And another reason showing that duties have to be performed as an aid to the rise of knowledge is that (in the present Upanishad) duties are taught first, and are set out before the topic of knowledge of the Absolute is taken up in its pure and unmixed form. Later, in such texts as "When one finds fearlessness as one's support in Him" and "He fears nothing from any quarter" and "(He does not then think) 'Why did I not do what was right?'" (317) the Upanishad will show that once knowledge has arisen there is nothing more action can do. From this also we conclude that the function of action is to aid the rise of knowledge through consuming the effects of previously accumulated demerit. And also because a Vedic text actually says this in the words "Having crossed over death through ignorance (= action), one attains immortality through knowledge." (318)

The earlier teaching of "ṛta" etc. (319) was simply to show that these things were not useless. But here the idea is that there is a regular rule that the duties mentioned have to be performed as a means to the rise of knowledge.

Having taught the Veda, the Teacher (ācārya) gives the pupil subsequent instruction after the latter had learned the texts by heart. That is, he then instructs him in its meaning. From this we should conclude that the pupil should not return home from the house of his Guru (guru-kula) (320) immediately after learning the Vedic texts by rote without first enquiring into the practical teachings (dharma-jijñāsā). And the same is taught in the Smṛti in the text, "Having gained his knowledge first, he should proceed with his duties." (321)

Well, but what exactly are the Teacher's subsequent instructions? Speak the truth. That is, say what has to be said as a result of properly gained knowledge. Likewise practise "dharma". Here "dharma" means in quite a general way all duties that have to be performed, as the text mentions individually the particular duties envisaged when it talks about "speaking the truth", etc. Do not neglect your private recitations of the Veda (svādhyāya). Bring choice gifts and offer them to the Teacher as a return for the knowledge he has given you. (322) With the permission of your Teacher, take a wife and see that your line is not cut off. Even if a son does not come, proceed with the rituals that lead to one, as the mention of son, grand-son and procreation (323) shows that this is what is meant. For if only physical measures had been meant, the text would have just said "procreation".

Do not be careless about truth, or you will become involved in untruth. The word "careless" shows that one must not speak untruth even through forgetfulness, otherwise the text would just have prohibited the speaking of untruths (and left it at that).

Do not be careless about duty. Because duty means what has to be done, careless here means not doing it. And this must be avoided. Duty must at all costs be done, that is the meaning. In the same way, you must not be careless about action to safeguard your own legitimate worldly interests. Nor should you be careless over actions required for your own prosperity and good name. Nor should you be neglectful of your own private recitations of the Veda or of your duty to teach it to others, as both these duties have to be done on a regular (daily) basis.

One must not be careless about one's duties to the gods and ancestors. Your mother is a deity. Be one to whom his mother is a deity. Similarly, your father is a deity, your Teacher (324) is a deity, your guest is a deity. It means that all of these (are not literally deities but) must be worshipped like a deity.

And you must fulfil all such other duties as are commended by the learned. One should neither neglect these nor indulge in discreditable activities, even though learned persons may be found indulging them. And you must apply yourself, for the sake of secret grace, to imitate whatever good deeds not in conflict with the Vedic teaching that the Teacher may perform. But you should never perform other deeds (such as are bad and in conflict with the Veda), even if they are performed by the Teacher.

And those Brahmins — Kshatriyas and the others are not meant in this context — who are Teachers or who have similar qualities and who are superior to ourselves in rank must be given seats and treated hospitably, and you must seek in every way to allay their fatigue. Or else (i.e. if the word 'not' has been left our of the received text), it means that when such revered people are assembled for conversation you should not so much as breathe audibly but should bend all your efforts to catching the drift of their discourse.

Further, whatever proper donations you have to give should be given in deepest reverence. No improper donations should be given, nor should proper donations be given with insolence. Whatever has to be given should be given with good grace, with modesty, with awe and yet in a friendly spirit. (325)

* * * * *

16. The whole realm of transmigratory life, characterized by action, its factors and results, which is of the nature of the three constituents, sattva, rajas and tamas, all imagined through nescience, has been declared to be an evil, together with nescience, its root. And it has been described under the allegorical figure of a tree in the verse beginning, "With roots above," and of this tree it has been said, "Having cut down this tree with the sword of non-attachment, one must seek out that abode (of Viṣṇu)." (326)

Now, all transmigratory life falls within the realm of the three constituents, so that one is faced with the question of how one can bring transmigratory life to an end if one cannot bring its cause to an end. And the text here proceeds, in the passage beginning "The duties of Brahmins, warriors and cultivators (vaiśya)," to recapitulate the whole teaching of the Gītā in brief, and to define the ultimate purport of the Veda and the Smṛti, considered in their entirety, and to say exactly what has to be done by those who desire to attain the true goal of human life.

The Brahmins, warriors and cultivators are all brought together in one compound word, while the labourers (śūdra) are excluded from it because they are "once-born" and hence do not have the right to learn the Veda. (327) Inner restraint and the other duties (to be mentioned below) are apportioned to these various castes according to their natural qualities, issuing from Nature (prakṛti), the Divine Creative Power (māyā) of the Lord, composed of the three constituents. (328)

Or the compound could be broken down differently to mean that the constituent called sattva was the source of the nature of the Brahmin, the constituent rajas tinged with sattva that of the nature of the warrior, the constituent rajas tinged with tamas that of the nature of the cultivator, the constituent tamas tinged with rajas that of the labourer. For we see that Brahmins, warriors, cultivators and labourers are characterized by peace, habit of command, enterprise and mental dullness respectively.

Or the compound might equally be taken to mean that a person's nature (disposition) in this life is determined by latent tendencies acquired from deeds in previous births which now manifest and prompt him towards his peculiar caste-duties. And the reference to "qualities" (guṇa) in the text is (not to the "constituents" but) to the qualities (guṇa) arising from these innate dispositions. The disposition is said (loosely) to be "a cause" because a quality cannot arise without a cause....

But is it not a fact that inner restraint and the like are ordained for Brahmins, and other qualities for other castes, by the Veda? And, if so, how can the text say that they are "conditioned by the 'constituents'"? But there is no difficulty here. The Veda ordains inner restraint and other qualities *in accordance with* the presence of the "constituents" in such and such a proportion in each class of persons on whom the pursuit of particular qualities is enjoined. (329)

What are these duties? The natural duties of the Brahminical caste are inner and outer restraint as already explained: (330) bodily, mental and vocal austerity as previously explained, (331) purity as explained, (332) forbearance, moral rectitude, knowledge theoretical and practical, faith in the revealed teachings.... The natural duties enjoined on warriors are heroism, fire, fortitude, dexterity and ability to deal unerringly with sudden emergences, refusal to turn one's back on the enemy in battle, open-handed liberality, lordly bearing in the presence of inferiors. The natural duties enjoined on cultivators are tillage, care of cows and trade.

The natural reward for the proper performance of these enjoined caste-duties is attainment of heaven (svarga). For there are such texts from the Smṛti as "The members of the various castes and stages of life who have applied themselves to their special duties enjoy the fruits of their deeds after death and then are reborn in favourable circumstances in regard to birth-place, caste, family, opportunity for spiritual merit (dharma), length of life, learning, career, wealth, happiness and intellect." (333) And in the Purāṇas, too, we find that different "worlds" and different other rewards are specified for the members of different castes and stages of life (whose duties have been well performed).

But when the duties are performed for a different reason different results follow, and these are now going to be explained. A man who is of a particular caste and has undergone the requisite sacraments and who is intent on the different duties of his caste and stage of life loses thereby his impurities of body, senses and mind. He then becomes fit for devotion to the path of knowledge. (334) ... Man only attains "success" in the form of becoming fit for devotion to the path of knowledge if he worships the Lord by performance of the duties of his caste in the way described. All action proceeds from the Lord as Inner Controller of every living being,and this whole world is pervaded by Him.

One's own duty, therefore, even if it is intrinsically humble, is better than the duty of another, even if one performs that duty well. No one commits sin if he performs the work dictated by his nature, as an insect that is born in a poisonous substance comes to no harm from that substance.... But the duty of another brings danger, and he who does not know the Self cannot cease from action even for an instant.

One should never, therefore, give up the duties to which one was born, even if they are from some points of view objectionable. For all acts are in some way objectionable, from the very fact of coming within the realm of the three constituents, just as the purity of fire is invariably tainted by smoke. No one can escape from having this objectionable element in his acts by giving up his own natural duty, even if he manages to perform the duty of another. And no one who is ignorant of the spiritual truth can entirely give up action. Hence one should not give up one's natural duty even though it include objectionable elements. (335)

* * * * *

17. The problem we now consider is whether spiritual knowledge is something pursued altogether independently of the ritualistic and other duties of one's caste and "stage of life", (336) or whether it is pursued in dependence on them. And one might initially suppose that knowledge was in no way dependent on them, as it has just been said (337) "Therefore, in

encompassing its own end, knowledge is not dependent on duties of caste and stage of life, such as the (householder's) lighting and tending of the household fire."

To modify this notion, the author of the Sūtras now begins a new Sūtra with the words, "And there is dependence on all of them." It means that knowledge does depend in some sense on all duties of caste and stage of life: it is not *altogether* independent of them. This is not the contradiction one might suppose, for while spiritual knowledge is not dependent on anything for the realization of its own end as knowledge, it is dependent on other things for its *rise*. (338) We know this, says the author of the Sūtras, from the Vedic texts mentioning ritualistic sacrifice and other such matters. That ritualistic sacrifices are instrumental in the attainment of spiritual knowledge is shown by the text "The Brahmins seek knowledge of this Self through repetition of their Veda, through ritual, through charity, through austerity and fasting." (339) Because they are connected here with *seeking* knowledge, it is clear that ritual sacrifice and the rest are only a means to the *rise* of knowledge.

Consider also the text "What is here called ritual sacrifice is really the life of the celibate student." (340) Here the life of the celibate student, which is a means to spiritual knowledge, is eulogized by being called ritual sacrifice, long ritual sacrifice (sattrāyaṇa) (341) and fasting,(342) and this implies that ritual sacrifice and the rest are themselves means to knowledge. And there is another Vedic passage which implies that the duties of caste and stage of life are a means to knowledge, namely that which begins "I will tell thee briefly of that state which is declared by all the Vedas, for the sake of which austerities are performed, and for the sake of which people follow the life of celibate studentship." (343) The derivative literature, too, says "Meritorious actions dispose of the taint of sins. When the taint of sins has first been removed by acts of merit, then knowledge has scope." (344)

The author's use of the words "like a horse" (345) is to indicate propriety. Propriety ordains that a horse should not be made to draw a plough (like an ox) but should be harnessed to a chariot. In the same way the duties of caste and stage of life play no part in spiritual knowledge's encompassing its own end (of beatitude), but they do play a part in giving rise to (the *desire* for) spiritual knowledge.

On this question one might take the following line. One might suppose that ritual sacrifice and the rest cannot really be means to the attainment of knowledge at all, and this is because there is no injunction (vidhi) for them. Vedic statements like "They seek knowledge through ritual," (346) which merely state facts,are intended to eulogize knowledge, not to enjoin ritual as a means to attaining knowledge. They simply mean "So great a thing is spiritual knowledge that people try to attain it through short sacrifices and long sacrifices and fasts."

Against such a position the author of the Sūtras says, "Nevertheless the seeker of knowledge should be equipped with internal and external restraint and the other preliminary qualities." (347) For these qualities *have* been enjoined as means to spiritual knowledge in the passage, "Therefore, becoming restrained within and restrained without, leaving off all action for personal ends, toughening himself up with resistance to discomfort and concentrating his mind, he sees the Self in the Self within." (348) And what has been enjoined, the author continues, must necessarily be carried out.

You will say that even here it is only

said that when he is equipped with internal restraint and the other qualities he does *in fact* see, which is a description of fact and not an injunction. Not so, we reply. For as the sentence in question begins with the word "therefore" it must refer back to the phrase "One should know the nature of that alone" occurring in a previous sentence, and be part of that injunction. The text in the Mādhyandina recension clearly envisages an injunction, as it says "He *should* see." (349) So it follows that even if spiritual knowledge did not have to depend on ritualistic sacrifice and the like, it would still have to depend on internal restraint and the rest. But as a matter of fact we know that spiritual knowledge *does* depend on ritual sacrifice and the like, on account of the text specifying ritual. (350)

Perhaps you will say that this text only says that Brahmins *do* seek knowledge of the Self through ritual, and that no actual injunction in this matter is found. This is true. But the author of the Sūtras proceeds with the word "nevertheless". Nevertheless, he means, because the connection between desire for knowledge of the Self and ritual has never been mentioned before, an injunction must be assumed to be *implied*. For if there had been no previous suggestion of this connection between ritual sacrifices, etc., and knowledge of the Self, the text could not be a mere recapitulation of anything already familiar. Moreover there are other texts such as "Pūṣan, without teeth, receives the crushed portion," (351) in which no injunction occurs overtly, and where the absence of any restatement of anything already familiar (352) forces one to assume an injunction, as argued in the Pūrva Mīmāṃsā Sūtra "Pūṣan and crushing must be taken to occur in subsidiaries, as they are not mentioned in connection with the main sacrifice." (353) And the author of our present Sūtras has already said "Or it is an injunction, as in the case of holding (sacrificial fuel)."(354)

Moreover, it has been explained in Smṛti texts such as the Bhagavad Gītā, too, how ritual sacrifices and the like, if performed without desire for individual gain, are (indirect) means to knowledge of the Self for those desirous of liberation. (355) Hence the rise of knowledge of the Self does depend (in some sense) on ritual sacrifice and the like, and also on internal and external restraint and on all duties of caste and stage of life. A distinction between the two classes of activity can, however, be drawn. Internal and external restraint and the like are more proximate causes, because they are directly connected with knowledge of the Self by the phrase "Whoever knows thus." (356) Ritual sacrifices, on the other hand, are only connected with promoting the *desire* to know, and hence are to be regarded as more distant aids....

Indeed, the mere fact that the duties of caste and stage of life have been enjoined at all shows that they must be auxiliaries to the acquisition of knowledge of the Self. Injunctions occur at such texts as "The Brahmins seek knowledge of this Self through repetition of their Veda, (through ritual, through charity, through austerity and fasting.)"(357) Hence the author of the Sūtras said, "And knowledge of the Self is (in some sense) dependent on all the duties of caste and stage of life, on account of the text (358) enjoining ritual and the rest as aids to knowledge of the Self, but with due distinction of function according to propriety, as in the case of a horse." (359)

But the statement that duties of caste and stage of life are auxiliaries to knowledge of the Self must not be understood to mean that they contribute to the power of knowledge of the Self to bring about its own peculiar benefits to the one possessing it, in the way, for instance, that the preliminary rituals help the actual rituals in securing their benefits to the performer. For knowledge is not subject to injunction, and the benefits of knowledge do not have to be sought by any active means. Ritual such as the New Moon or Full Moon Sacrifice, which is enjoined and hence must be a means to an end, may well depend on other auxiliaries (such as preliminary rituals) if it is to produce its fruit of attainment of heaven. But this is not the case with knowledge (which can never be enjoined in the first place). It is in this sense that the author of the Sūtras said, "Therefore, in the encompassing of its own end, knowledge is not dependent on duties and stage of life, such as the (householder's) lighting and tending of the household fire." ((360) Hence the statement that ritual and the like were auxiliaries was only meant to say that they were auxiliaries in regard to the *rise* of knowledge (by promoting desire for it).

Nor should one complain that on this basis there will be a contradiction, inasmuch as the relation of the injunction to the sacrificer will be both constant and impermanent. (361) For different injunctions bearing on one and the same ritualistic act may stand in a different kind of relation (as to permanence or impermanence) with the sacrificer. There is a permanent relation with ritual arising from the injunction assumed in the case of such texts as "(He offers the Agnihotra) as long as he lives," (361) but this does not have knowledge of the Self as its beneficial result. And there is another, impermanent, relation with the injunction assumed in the case of the text "The Brahmins seek knowledge of this Self through repetition of their Veda, through charity, through austerity and fasting," (363) and this injunction *does* promise knowledge of the Self as its fruit. It is like the order to have a sacrificial post of hard acacia wood. On account of having an injunction having permanent connection with the sacrificer, it serves the purpose of sacrifice. And on account of an injunction not permanently connected with the sacrificer (but only for a particular end) it serves the sacrificer's immediate personal ends. (364)....

Consider the case, also, of widowers and other people who are not married householders, and who are consequently bereft of the wherewithal to offer sacrifices, and who do not belong to any of the official stages of life and are thus banished to an "intermediate stage". (365) Are they or are they not entitled to knowledge of the Self? And here one might initially suppose they were not, since performance of the duties of caste and stage of life has been given as one of the causes of knowledge of the Self. And these they are not able to perform.

Against this the author of the Sūtras remarks, "And even those in an intermediate stage." Such a person is entitled to knowledge of the Self even though he is not in any of the stages of life because, as the author of the Sūtras puts it, we find examples of such a thing in the Veda. We learn from the Veda that Raikva (366) and Gārgī (367) and others who were not married householders possessed knowledge of the Absolute. And the Smṛti, too, confirms this. For we learn from the Mahābhārata that Saṃvarta ((368) and others were great yogins, even though they went about naked and paid no attention to the duties of caste and stages of life.

Well, you will say, you have given us hints from the Veda and the Smṛti. But what conclusion do you draw from them? To this question the author of the Sūtras replies with the word "Grace". Even in the case of the widower and the rest, the *grace* of knowledge of the Self can be earned through particular meritorious acts of repetition (japa), (369) fasting and worship of deities which can be carried out by all human beings as such. And the derivative literature, too, show that even he who carries out the duties assigned to the various stages of life has the right to the repetition of formulae in the verse "The Brahmin can gain his end (of liberation) by repetition alone, (370) whether he does anything else (e.g. ritual) or not. Whoever practises universal benevolence and friendliness is a Brahmin." (371) Moreover, the grace of knowledge can descend on account of duties pertaining to caste and stage of life that have been performed in former births. And in the text "He attains perfection after many lives and then goes to the supreme abode" (372) the derivative literature, too, shows how the particular latent impressions (saṃskāra) that have been amassed from previous lives can also bring on knowledge of the Self through their "grace". And because knowledge has an immediately perceptible result, (373) the one who desires knowledge has the automatic right to hear teaching and to benefit from other means of knowledge, provided only that there is no obstacle. (374) So there is no contradiction if widowers and others at some "intermediate stage" are said to have the right to acquire knowledge of the Self.

But the author of the Sūtras then reiterates that membership of one of the stages of life in the regular caste system is better, as a means to knowledge of the Self, than belonging to an "intermediate stage", as this clearly transpires from the Veda and derivative literature. And the Veda also leaves an indication on the point in the text "By this path the knower of the Absolute, who does meritorious works and shines with light." (375)... And there is an indication in the derivative literature, too, namely "The Brahmin should not remain a single day without performance of the duties of his stage of life. If he remain so for a year he must perform a 'kṛcchra' penance."(376)

* * * * *

18. The passage from "On beholding the army of the Pāṇḍavas" to "And saying to Govinda 'I shall not fight' he held his peace" (377) should be taken as intended to point out the reason for the rise of grief and delusion and other states which bring on further experiences in the realm of transmigratory life. The passage beginning "'How can I fight against Bhīṣma in battle with arrows?'" (378) show the grief and delusion (attachment) felt by Arjuna and the attachment for the kingdom to which he belonged, for his elders and Teachers and sons and dear ones and relatives and dependants, for whom he cherished the sentiment "I belong to them and they to me." His grief and delusion arose from his affectionate feelings for and dread of separation from these people, and were based on erroneous self-identification with them. For his power of discrimination was overwhelmed by these feelings, and, as a result, he withdrew from his warrior's duty of battle in the midst of a war in which he was already engaged, and proposed to engage in a mendicant's life, which is not the duty of his caste.

The implication is that all living beings tend naturally to give up their own duty and follow another line of duty when their minds become subject to such defects as grief and delusion. Even if they keep to their own line of duty in thought, word and deed, yet they do so with desire for fruits and with egoistic feeling. In these circumstances, transmigratory life in the form of further pleasure and pain from higher and lower re-incarnations arising from further merit and demerit proceeds on uninterrupted. It is in this sense that grief and delusion were made responsible (earlier) for bringing on further experiences in transmigratory life. Hence the Lord (Vāsudeva Kṛṣṇa) begins His teaching to Arjuna "Thou hast felt pity where pity was not in place," (379) making Arjuna the occasion for an act of compassion to the whole world, and having the intention to teach the whole world that there is no other way out of grief and delusion except knowledge of the Self in association with renunciation from all duty. (380)

* * * * *

19. One could not imagine even in a dream that a knower of Self should resort to the yoga-of-action (karma-yoga), (381) for the latter springs from wrong knowledge and is opposed to right knowledge. (382) Hence it is the renunciation-of-action and the yoga-of-action of the one who does *not* know the Self which are spoken of here as leading to the highest good. This renunciation-of-action on the part of one who does not know the Self is different from the earlier-mentioned *total* renunciation of action effected by the one who does know the Self. It is only a partial renunciation of action, because it is coupled with the continued sense of agency. Because it is associated with such disciplines as the general and special laws of restraint (yama and niyama) (383) it is troublesome to carry out. That is why the yoga-of-action is said to be preferable to it, because easier....

The yoga-of-action in the Vedic tradition is only figuratively spoken of as a "yoga" or as "renunciation" (saṃnyāsa) because it exists as a preliminary to these two. In what sense it does so is indicated by the Lord in the following verse. (384) Renunciation in the true sense (pāramārthika), says the Lord, is hard to attain without previous practice of yoga. "That sage who is equipped with yoga soon attains the Absolute."

By "yoga" is here meant the yoga-of-action (karma-yoga) of the Vedic tradition. It means dedicating one's action to the Lord without caring for personal advantage. A sage (muni) is so called because he dwells long on (practises "manana" on) the form of the Lord. "Attains the Absolute" here means "attains renunciation in the full sense," as renunciation in the full sense is characterized by knowledge of the highest Self, and there is the Vedic text "Renunciation is Brahmā, Brahmā is the supreme." (385) Such a sage will soon attain to the Absolute, to renunciation in the full sense, meaning establishment in unbroken knowledge of the supreme Self. (386)

TEXTS ON THE QUALIFICATIONS FOR THE PATH:GROUP E

20. Because of the specification "desiring this world (of the Self) *alone*," we gather that those who want the three external "worlds" (387) have no right to renounce the world and become wandering monks. An inhabitant of Kāśī (Benares) who wants to go to Gaṅgādvāra (Hardwar) will not set off for the East! The instruments for those who want the external "worlds" consist in acquisition of sons and in rituals and meditation on the Absolute in its lower aspect (i.e. under limited forms). For we have the Vedic text "This world is to be attained through acquiring a son and not through any other act." (388) Hence those who want this world should not abandon the special means for attaining it, such as the acquisition of a son, and take up the life of a wandering monk, for monkhood is not the means to obtaining this world.

The text is thus justified in saying "Those who want this Self *alone* " take up the life of a wandering monk."Obtaining the world of the Self" means remaining established in the Self when one's nescience has been destroyed. Therefore, if a person should desire the Self for his "world", his chief means of attaining it will be the inward-directed one of refraining from all action, just as acquisition of a son and the like are the chief means for obtaining the external "worlds". But actions like acquisition of a son and the like are not the means to obtaining the Self for one's "world". And we have already explained how action of any kind is contradictory to having the Self for one's world, as the two cannot logically be combined. (389) Hence those who want the Self for their world must definitely renounce the world as wandering monks. It means they must renounce all activity. And just as appropriate means such as acquisition of a son and the like are laid down and enjoined for the one who wants the three external "worlds", so are refrainment from all desires and leaving home as a wandering monk definitely prescribed for the one who wants the Self for his world, the (future) knower of the Absolute. (390)

* * * * *

21. There are some who hold that even the knower of the Absolute has desires. It is clear that they do not know the Bṛhadāraṇyaka Upanishad, as it says that desires for sons and the like belong to the realm of the spiritually ignorant. (391) And they do not know the distinction that that text makes between that realm and the realm of enlightenment, in the passage "What shall we do with progeny, we for whom this Self is our world?" (392) Nor do they understand the contradiction, amounting to mutual incompatibility, between enlightenment — which implies the obliteration of all action, its factors and results — and nescience and its effects. Nor do they know the statement of Vyāsa (on the subject). (393)

Action and knowledge, as ignorance and knowledge respectively, are mutually contradictory. So in the Mahābhārata Vyāsa raises the question "In the Veda there are two commands, perform work and abstain from work. What do people achieve through knowledge and what do they achieve through work? I wish to hear the answer to this problem and beg you to explain it to me. It seems that the two paths run counter to one another. And he showed the contradiction in the two paths by his answer in which he said, "All creatures are bound through action and released through knowledge. Hence those ascetics who have direct knowledge of supreme Reality do not perform action." (394)

Hence knowledge of the Absolute serves the ends of man alone and without the co-operation of any other factor, as otherwise everything would be a contradiction. It is a means to the realization of man's ends in itself and independently of any other auxiliary. Hence wandering forth from one's house as a homeless monk (pārivrājya), being the renunciation of all means to (ritualistic) action, is implicitly enjoined as part of the discipline. For at the end of the Fourth Book of the Bṛhadāraṇyaka Upanishad (395) it is laid down "This *only* is the means to immortality." And the text also provides an inferential sign in that Yājñavalkya, who was a ritualist, decided to abandon his house and wander off as a homeless monk. (396)

* * * * *

22. In whatever way, with whatever desires for personal ends, men approach Me I grant their desires, as such people do not desire liberation. For one cannot have desires for personal ends and desire for liberation at the same time. Those who have desires for personal ends, I reward with the granting of those ends. Those others, however, who desire liberation, and carry out the behests of the Veda punctiliously and without desire for personal ends, I reward with the gift of spiritual knowledge (jñāna). Those who already have spiritual

knowledge and who have renounced the world, and who desire liberation, I reward with the gift of liberation. Similarly, those who resort to Me in distress I relieve of their distress. (397)

* * * * *

23. If an objector should claim that (pain was natural to the soul despite what was said in the Upanishads to the contrary because) sensations of pain and other kinds of unpleasantness were a matter of constant direct perception, (398) we deny it. We say that such so-called "direct" experiences are of the same class as "I am declining," "I was born," "I am old," "I am fair," "I am dark" and "My end has come" which refer in fact to something that is not declining, born, old, fair, dark or subject to termination. If you say that all these perceptual judgements are true, we reply that the real truth is not easy to comprehend, as Indra himself, the king of the gods, persisted in his error even after the immortality of the soul had been explained to him with the aid of the illustration of a dish of water, (399) and later remarked, "It has gone to destruction." (400) And the extremely intelligent Virocana, son of Prajāpati himself, regarded the body as the Self.

The Buddhist Nihilistis, too, are all drowned in the sea of this fear of Indra's that the soul must be mortal. The Sāṃkhyas, too, admitted (401) a witnessing consciousness (sākṣin) over and above the body, mind and sense-organs, but abandoned the authority of the Veda (which teaches that the Self is one) and so, in their philosophy of duality, remained in the realm of death. Others, such as the followers of Kaṇāda (the Vaiśeṣikas, followed on this point by the Naiyāyikas,) make efforts tc cleanse the Self, regarded by them as the "soul-substance" associated with its nine alleged "qualities", (402) as one might cleanse a garment by the application of soda. (403) Then there are the devotees of ritual (the Mīmāṃsakas) who accept the authority of the Vedas and withdraw their minds from interest in external objects as well. And yet, just like Indra, they take one's experience of one's identity with the Self, the ultimate reality, as a state seeming like destruction. (404) They go (in their metaphysical ignorance) revolving helplessly up and down from birth to birth like a bucket mounted on a machine at a well. And if this (ignorance about the true nature of the Self) is the case with these men of intellect and discipline, how will it be with other lesser beings, indiscriminating by nature and given over to objects of sense?

Therefore this doctrine of Prajāpati set out in the Eighth Book of the Chāndogya Upanishad, sections seven to twelve, can only be intuitively savoured by those exceedingly venerable wandering monks of the Paramahaṃsa order who have given up all desires for anything external, who depend on nothing outside their own Self, who have risen above the whole system of caste and stages of life, who are intent on acquiring the knowledge proclaimed in the Upanishads and who follow this traditional teaching (sampradāya) that one can rise above the body and its pleasures and pain. Even today, it is only such souls who teach this doctrine and verily no one else. (405)

* * * * *

24. It has been said above (406) "This Self hidden in all beings is not manifest, but can be seen through the sharp intelligence (of certain subtle observers)." But what is that impediment which can overcome even a sharp intellect (407) and prevent the Self from being seen? The present section (Vallī) of the Upanishad is begun to explain what it is that prevents the Self from being seen. For one can

only make efforts to remove an impediment when one actually knows what it is.

The sense-organs like the ears are called the "apertures" in the text and are said to be turned outwards, to proceed outwards. It is as turned outwards that they apprehend their various objects such as sound. Outward turned as they were, He pierced them. Who was "He"? The Self-existent One, that is, the highest Lord. He is ever independent and never therefore under the control of another. Therefore what one perceives is the external object composed of sound and the other elements, all of which are not-self. One does not perceive the Self within.

This is the nature of the people of the world in general. Nevertheless, a certain wise man, a man of discrimination, saw the Self within. It was like swimming against the current of a river! He saw "That which is within" and "That which is within is the Self" — that is the meaning of the term "pratyag-ātman" occurring in the text. In popular speech the word "ātman" is used for the inmost nature of something only. And the following text of the Smṛti shows that the word "ātman" has the same meaning from the etymological point of view, the text, namely, "It is called "ātman" because it is what obtains (āpnoti), receives (ādatte) and consumes (atti) objects here in the world, and also because it is continuously (santato) present." (408) He saw the Self (ātman) within, says the text under comment, his own true nature.

Here "saw" means "sees" by Vedic licence. He sees by turning his gaze around. It means he does the same with his ears and all his other sense-organs. He who has in this sense "averted his gaze" from all objects, he who has performed this purifying discipline, sees the Self within.

(XII.3) ADOPTING THE PATH (TEXTS)

Why should a wise man be prepared to go to such great lengths in restraining the natural tendencies of the sense-organs in order to see the Self? The reply given is "Desiring immortality." That is to say, desiring to be beyond death, desiring to enjoy the natural condition of the Self.

This our present natural outward-turned vision which sees the not-self, which is the impediment which obstructs vision of the Self, is called ignorance or nescience, because it is what opposes knowledge. Now the text proceeds to outline the condition of those whose vision is obstructed both by nescience and by thirst (tṛṣṇā) for the external objects, visible and invisible, which nescience conjures into existence.

Fools follow after external joys. They are caught in the all-pervading net of death, that is, in the complex of nescience, desire and desire-prompted action, in the net of transmigration, the net of repeated acquisition and loss of a body and organs, relatives, home etc. That is to say, they undergo a whole host of evils like birth, death, decrepitude and disease. This being so, the wise, the discriminating ones, who have realized their identity with the Self within, know perfect immortality, not just that figurative bodily "immortality" (meaning a long bodily existence in another world) which comes to an end. For the state of identity with the Self within "is neither increased nor diminished by action." (409)

Having known this immutable (kūṭastha), ineradicable immortality, these knowers of the Absolute do not desire anything whatever in this almost wholly evil world of transmigration, amongst these transient objects. For to do so would run counter to vision of the Self within. It means that they rise above all desires for sons, wealth or a "world" built up by ritualistic acts. (410)

* * * * *

25. This being so, if we consider the comparative efficacy for promoting Self-knowledge of the various different kinds of activity enjoined for those in the several stages of life, we find that the practice of humility and the other virtues recommended at Bhagavad Gītā XIII.6-11 is helpful, along with self-control (yama),(411) which is especially important, and mental virtues like meditation, learning, dispassion and others, practised concurrently. In other forms of activity, injury to others, along with attachment and aversion, etc., enter to a very large extent, and a largely passionate form of action results, for which reason the wise prescribe renunciation and adoption of the life of a wandering monk for those who desire liberation. "In the end, what is required is renunciation of the acts that have been prescribed. This external renunciation leads eventually to true dispassion" and "O Brahmin, what have you to do with wealth, relatives and wife — you who will one day die? Enter the cave within and seek out the Self. Where has your father gone and where are your ancestors?" (412)

In the Sāṃkhya and Yoga treatises, too, renunciation of household life is said to be conducive to knowledge. And renunciation of household life has the further advantage of not being associated with action for the promotion of desired ends. The treatises of all the spiritual schools agree that action for promoting desired ends is inimical to spiritual knowledge. Hence the proposition (413) that the one who is desirous of liberation and possessed of dispassion should wander forth as a houseless monk direct from the state of pupil-student, even though he has not yet acquired knowledge of the Self, is reasonable. (414)

4. SPIRITUAL QUALITIES TO BE CULTIVATED ON THE PATH

The topics discussed in this section do not need any preliminary introduction. He who treads the Path must pursue purity of mind, abjure desire, cultivate the qualities mentioned at the opening of Chapter XIII of the Bhagavad Gītā. Stress is also laid on "austerity" (tapas) as the key to mastery over concentration of the mind. Also stressed are faith (śraddhā), continuity of effort and the purity of mind that results from the avoidance of all deceit. This group of Extracts, like the last, ends with some entries declaring that spiritual discipline culminates in renunciation.

TEXTS ON SPIRITUAL QUALITIES TO BE CULTIVATED ON THE PATH

1. Now the text goes on to teach that purification is the means leading to the clear manifestation of the above-mentioned knowledge, as cleaning of the mirror is the means leading to the clear appearance of the face. The text says, "When nourishment is pure." "Nourishment" means "what is taken in." Knowledge of the material objects is taken in by the experiencer for his experience. His "purity" of nourishment means the purity of his knowledge in the sense of his perception of material objects. It means perception of objects that is not accompanied by the defects of attachment, aversion or infatuation. When this is achieved, there is purity of the mind (sattva-śuddhi). (415) When this latter is achieved, there follows a firm, unbroken recollection of the Self as the Infinite (bhūman), which has already been directly apprehended. With this there follows the loosening of all the ties, of all the thongs of evil set up by nescience, of the knots in the heart drawn tight by the deposit of the experiences of many births. Because purification of one's (perceptual) "nourishment" leads to all this, one should pursue it diligently.

The text has now unfolded (in the course of this seventh Chapter of the Chāndogya Upanishad) the entire content of the Vedic teaching, and with this it brings the little framework story it has composed to an end. It says that he, Sanatkumāra, showed Nārada the final reality beyond darkness, meaning beyond nescience. For Nārada had scraped off the impurity of his mind, the resinous exudations of attachment and aversion and the like, with the soda or knowledge and the practice of dispassion, and had rendered himself fit for the reception of the teaching. (416)

* * * * *

2. Every living being, the man of knowledge and even more the fool, acts according to his "nature" (prakṛti). His "nature" is the complex of impressions and acts of merit and demerit that he has performed in previous births which is manifesting in the present birth. What, then, will restraint either on my own part or that of another avail?

But if every living being acted in accordance with his own peculiar "nature" alone, then, since no one is without a peculiar "nature", would it not follow that the Veda was useless, since (it contains mostly injunctions and) it would not be possible to obey them by independent acts of will? To this the text replies: "Desire and aversion concern the objects of the various senses. One should not come under their grip, for they are the obstacles that beset a person's path."

The objects of the various senses are the objects of the world consisting of sound and the other elements. There is "desire" when they are wanted, "aversion" when they are not wanted. In this sense, desire and aversion for objects are inevitable.

But here the text proceeds to indicate the scope for independent human activity and for (the commands and prohibitions of) the Veda. Whoever is engaged in fulfilling the dictates of the Veda must, as a preliminary step, avoid the *grip* of desire and aversion. A man's nature in the above-mentioned sense, associated with desire and aversion, will impel him to act according to its own dictates, and this will lead him to abandon his own proper duty and assume that of another. But desire and aversion can be controlled by cultivation of their opposites. And when a man follows this course he begins to see the world from the Vedic standpoint and no longer falls under the grip of desire and aversion.

Therefore the text says "One should not come under the grip of desire and aversion." They are "The obstacles that beset a person's path" in the sense of being obstacles to the person travelling the path to the highest good, like highwaymen ambushing the road. (417)

* * * * *

3. The knower of the Self is worthy of worship. For he knows the Absolute in its supreme form, the supreme abode, the repository of all desires. (418) The whole universe lies in the Absolute. The latter "shines clear" because whatever shines by its own light shines clear. Those seekers of liberation who are desireless and free even from noble desires and who worship and serve a knower of the Self just like the supreme Deity — those wise souls go beyond human seed, they do not ever again have to enter a womb. For the Vedic text says, "He does not again take his pleasure anywhere." So the meaning of the verse is that one should worship a knower of the Self.

(XII.4) ADOPTING THE PATH (TEXTS)

In the next verse the Upanishad explains how the main discipline of the seeker of liberation is renunciation of desires. Whoever dwells on seen or unseen objects with desire, pondering on their qualities, is later reborn along with those desires, which constitute tendencies towards action, in circumstances where he may be able to realize them.

But the case with one whose desires are already fulfilled by his knowledge of the supreme metaphysical reality is different. His Self has been withdrawn from its lower form, of the nature of nescience, and "restored" to its true form. In the case of such a one, whose Self has been "restored", all urges to good or bad action are already dissolved and destroyed even while the body yet remains alive. Desires no longer arise in him, as their cause, nescience, has been destroyed.

If all this is so, then the gaining of the Self in its true form must be greater than any other gain, (419) and one might suppose that much repetition of Vedic texts (pravacana) and other such means should be resorted to to gain it. To obviate this idea, the text argues as follows.

This Self which we have just explained, the highest goal of man, is not to be attained by much repetition of Vedic texts. Nor is it to be attained through scholarship or ability to understand the meaning of books. Nor by much learning.

Then how is it attained? The man of knowledge who wishes to obtain the Self obtains the Self through that wish and not through any other means. For he is already "fully attained" by nature.

Next the text proceeds to describe the nature of that "attainment" of the Self which the enlightened man achieves. He "illumines" his own "body", that is to say his own nature as the supreme Self. (420) The meaning is that when a person obtains enlightenment the Self manifests like a pot or other object brought into light. So the gist of the verse is that the sole means to obtaining the Self is a praying and longing for the Self to the exclusion of all other desires.

Next the text declares that strength, diligence and ascetic practices, associated with renunciation of the world are needed as auxiliaries to praying and begging for the Self. For (as the verse puts it) the Self cannot be obtained by one who has not the strength that comes from devotion to the Self. Nor can it be obtained by one whose diligent concentration on the Self is undermined by attachment to such worldly objects as children and possessions (literally cattle) and the like. Nor can it be obtained by acts of severe self-discipline (tapas) performed outside the framework of renunciation. The word "tapas" in fact here means knowledge. (421) So the real meaning of the phrase is that the Self is not to be obtained through knowledge without renunciation of the world. Whatever man of discrimination or knower of the Self struggles for knowledge through these means, namely strength, diligence, renunciation of the world and knowledge arising through severe self-discipline, his soul enters the abode of the Absolute.

How does it enter the Absolute? The "ṛṣis" or men of direct vision, having known this Self, feel perfect happiness and contentment in this knowledge, and not in external means of satisfaction such as pampering the body. They have attained the supreme Self in its true form. They are without attachment and other such psychological defects and their sense-organs are controlled and at rest.

They are identified with the non-dual Absolute, which is all-pervading like the ether, and not merely identified with it in its conditional and limited form. They are "wise" in the sense of having perfect discrimination and self-control, being ever collected and concentrated by nature. They enter into the Absolute totally on the death of the body, as the ether apparently enclosed within the pot (ghaṭākāśa) throws off the appearance of limitation by its external adjunct (the pot) when the pot is broken. It is in this way that knowers of the Absolute enter the Absolute. (422)

* * * * *

4. Absence of self-praise, absence of ostentation, non-injury to living creatures, not being put out of countenance when wronged by another, uprightness and absence of crooked dealing, service of and obedience to the Teacher (ācārya) who teaches the means to liberation, cleanliness, both of the body through washing it with earth and water and also of the mind by removing such impurities as attachment by meditating on their opposites, firm adherence to the path of liberation, restraint of the lower self so that it keeps to the right path, indifference to the prospect of enjoyment of material objects now or in the future, clear appreciation of the evils attendant upon birth, death, old-age and disease and the pain involved in life – these and other qualities to be mentioned later are called "knowledge" for the reason to be explained below. In regard to the present verse, we may add that old age brings such evils as loss of intellectual power and physical vigour and exposure to contempt and ridicule. Diseases means those involving headaches and the like. And it has to be remembered that evils are of three kinds according to whether they arise in one's own organism (illness, etc.) or are inflicted by another living being or are the work of elemental forces (earthquake, famine, etc.).

The verse can also be explained as saying that birth, death, old-age and disease *are* pain, and the quality in question is that which enables one to see the evil in unnecessarily submitting to this pain. Even this only means that birth and the rest are called pain because they bring pain, not because they *are* pain literally. It is from the constant perception of pain and evil in birth and the rest that there arises indifference to the enjoyment of the objects of the senses and of bodily enjoyment. It is then that the senses and mind turn to the Self within, with a view to know that Self.

Amongst the further qualities called "knowledge" are absence of love for attractive objects, absence of feeling of deep intimacy in which you identify your very being with that of another, as when one feels happy or sad according to whether another person is happy or sad, or feels that one is alive or no longer alive according to whether he is alive or dead. This, says, the text, applies to children, wife, home and the like, and also to other close people such as one's family and servants. Because absence of love for attractive objects and absence of feelings of deep intimacy are to be pursued for the sake of knowledge, they are called knowledge.

A further quality here called "knowledge" is constant equimindedness at the advent of the pleasant or the unpleasant, where one does not feel elated at the arrival of the pleasant or angry when faced with the unpleasant.

Another such quality is the undeviating conviction in regard to Me, the Lord, held with unbroken concentration, that no one higher than the Lord Vāsudeva exists, so He alone is my refuge. Such unbroken concentration is devotion, and such devotion is knowledge (in the sense described above).

Resort to solitary places is also called knowledge in this sense. "Solitary" means either naturally solitary or artificially rendered so by removal of filth and measures to obstruct the entry of dangerous animals such as tigers or snakes. And "solitary place" means a solitary spot in the forest, or by a river, or on a sand-bank or in a temple. And "resort" to places means *habitual* resort to them. And this is called "knowledge" because in solitary places the mind feels calm, so that it is here that truly productive meditations on the Self and other themes takes place.

A further instance of "knowledge" in the above sense is dislike for the society of men. It means only dislike of the society of ordinary, uncultured, undisciplined men, not the society of the cultured and the disciplined, as this is an aid towards knowledge.

Again, constancy in knowledge-remembrance of the Self is called "knowledge". And so, lastly, is dwelling on the good results of true metaphysical knowledge, for it is from this that application to the means for acquiring such knowledge proceeds. The means are the absence of self-praise and the rest just detailed. Metaphysical knowledge of the truth arises when these means are matured through meditation on the Self. The purpose and result of metaphysical knowledge of the Self is liberation, which means cessation of transmigratory life. The qualities of absence of self-praise and the rest are called "knowledge" at the end (of the series of Gītā verses in which they are enumerated) because they are for the sake of knowledge. And what is other than these is ignorance, indulgence in crooked dealings and so forth. One must realize this well so as to get rid of them. For they are the cause of the continuation of transmigratory life. (423)

* * * * *

5. A divine nature (daivī prakṛti) leads to liberation from transmigratory life, and the two kinds of demoniac nature lead to bondage. So the Lord proceeds to describe the divine nature, to promote pursuit of it, and that of the two demoniac natures, that they might be avoided.

The divine spiritual equipment (daivī sampat) consists of the following qualities. Absence of all timidity. Purity of mind expressed in absence of deceit in all human dealings. Acquisition of information on spiritual and metaphysical topics such as the nature of the Self, etc., from the Veda and the Teacher, and assimilation of what has thus been learned through one-pointed concentration on it till it becomes a matter of direct experience. Devotion to this work of assimilation of knowledge is the chief item in the divine or virtuous equipment. On whatever course a man is qualified for, possession of any of the qualities here mentioned betokens a virtuous nature.

Charity means distribution of food and the like to the best of one's ability. Outer restraint (dama) (424) means suppression of the activity of the outer senses, for He will refer later to the suppression of the activity of the inner organ (mind) as "peace". (425)

Ritualistic sacrifice – which means such sacrifices as are enjoined in the Veda. Going through one's own Veda (svādhyāya), which means reciting the Ṛg or other Veda as the case may be. Self-discipline (tapas), which means the self-discipline of body, speech and mind to be mentioned below. (426) Uprightness and simplicity are to be maintained all the time.

Harmlessness, which means causing injury to no living beings. Truth-speaking, which means speech which avoids *both* the untrue *and* the unpleasant. Control of anger, which means self-control even when insulted or struck by others. Peace, which means bringing to a halt the operations of the mind. Absence of all back-biting. Compassion for all creatures in pain. Control of the senses in the presence of desirable objects, gentleness and absence of all cruelty, modesty, not being fidgety, which means absence of all unnecessary movement of the organs of action – these qualities, also are part of the equipment.

Fire (tejas), which means here "resolution" and not "brilliance of complexion"; forbearance, which means not allowing feelings of anger to arise even when one is insulted or struck; this is different from the "control of anger" mentioned before, which meant control of feelings of anger once they had arisen; buoyancy, which is a certain cast of mind that overcomes fatigue when it assails the body and senses and keeps them active; cleanliness, which is of two kinds: external cleanliness, which is effected with earth and water, and internal cleanliness, which consists in purity of mind as exemplified by absence of deceit and attachment; inoffensiveness; absence of excessive self-esteem. These are the qualities making up the divine spiritual equipment. "Divine" means "belonging to those who are born for a divine lot and are destined for an auspicious future".

Next the Lord describes the characteristics of one of demoniac nature. Ostentation, or advertizing your own spirituality; pride, or intolerable conceit over your wealth or connections; excessive self-esteem; anger; sarcasm, like telling a blind man he can see splendidly or an ugly person that he looks handsome or a man of low birth that he is an aristrocrat; ignorance, meaning wrong ideas, arising from absence of discrimination on the subject of what ought not to be done – all these are the characteristics of one born to undergo a demoniac life....

Such men do not know what to do to promote their own real interests or what to avoid doing so as to avoid harm to themselves. They lack inner and outer cleanliness, good manners and truth-speaking. They look upon the world in a spirit of cynicism. They deny that there is any basis for a moral law. They deny that there is any God to control the world in the light of a moral law. They affirm that the whole world comes into being through sex-union alone. They do not admit any other productive or guiding force to cause the existence of the world, such as the merit and demerit arising out of actions in former births and the like. The only cause they admit for the presence of living creatures is lust. This is the crude materialist view....

They are afflicted by egoism, which means that they attribute distinction to themselves and all manner of virtues which they may or may not really possess. Egoism in this form is called spiritual ignorance (avidyā) and is the worst of all vices and the root of all evil behaviour. They resort to force to overcome their enemies, prompted by desire and attachment. They also suffer from pride, that mental illness which inevitably causes people to transgress the spiritual law. They feel longing for women and other objects of enjoyment, and anger at unpleasant events. The demoniac souls suffer from these and many more vices.

Moreover, they feel hatred against Me, the Lord, present within their own body and the bodies of others and witnessing the activity of their minds. They hate Me and transgress My commands, and cannot tolerate the virtues of those on the true path (whom they attack and criticize in every way they can). (427)

* * * * *

6. (Now, says the text, we shall mention the defects that living beings must destroy. Of these) anger is that disturbed state of mind, marked by sweating and trembling of the body, that occurs when one is struck or abused. Elation is the opposite mental state, caused by the attainment of something deeply desired and marked by tears and the tingling of the body with joy. Rage is a peculiar contortion undergone by the mind in the face of something unpleasant. Greed, or the desire to get hold of the possessions of others, includes avarice, the refusal to part with one's own riches on proper occasions. Confusion (moha) is the inability to see what has to be done and what has not to be done. Hypocrisy is the display of one's own righteousness. Aggression is the desire to harm others. False-speaking is lying. Also mentioned are over-eating, back-biting and jealousy or inability to tolerate the advantages of others, as well as lust and anger, understood as desire for physical intercourse with women and objection to what prevents it. Finally there is mention of absence of self-control. These characteristics are called "non-yoga" (ayoga), for they represent distracted states of mind where it does not attain concentration. Their eradication is based on yoga.

What are called "yoga" in this sense? The text specifies absence of anger and elation and the rest, namely the opposites of the various non-yogas. They are called so many "yogas" because their nature is mental concentration. The text further specifies generosity, especially the sharing of one's goods with those who request it. By "renunciation" (tyāga) the text means the emphatic rejection of all pleasures in this world or the next, along with the means to attain them. Rectitude means uprightness and absence of all trickery in thought, word and deed. Gentleness means being gentle, "Śama" means strict control of the mind, "dama" means strict control of the senses.

Next another general definition of yoga is given, namely "Absence of conflict with any living being". For conflict occasions pain for living creatures, and there is no pain without conflict. Where no creature suffers, there, verily, yoga reigns.

Next the text speaks of nobility (ārya). It means absence of meanness and the bearing of a noble one (an ārya). Also mentioned is absence of cruelty, coupled with contentment. Contentment implies that the mind is just as light when one does not obtain what is needed as when one does.

Now, complete absence of conflict with all living beings is possible only in the case of a wandering ascetic (parivrājaka). Therefore the word "iti" is inserted to show that the three virtues beginning with nobility, as well as the others mentioned before, are not incompatible with life in any stage and are prescribed for persons in all stages. They apply to, and must be practised in, all stages of life in common. Whoever practises them "Penetrates everywhere through his knowledge," which means he becomes liberated. (428)

* * * * *

7. Now the three-fold self-discipline (tapas) is explained, self-discipline of body, speech and mind. Bodily self-discipline consists of honouring deities, Brahmins, elders and sages: also in absence of duplicity, continence and harmlessness. These are called the bodily austerity because they are acts carried out by the body with its organs. For the Lord will say later, "Whatever act is done through these five factors of action...". (429)

(XII.4) ADOPTING THE PATH (TEXTS)

The self-discipline of speech is as follows. Speech here means speech which is true and pleasant and ministers to the hearer's real interests in this world and the next, without awakening anxiety. If one communicates with another and all or any of these specifications are lacking, one is not practising self-discipline of speech. Even if what one says is true, and one or more of the other characteristics are lacking, one is not practising self-discipline of speech. The same holds true if what one says is pleasant, without one or more of the other characteristics. And the same is also true if what one says to the hearer's interest but one or more of the other characteristics is lacking.

But it is a very high degree of self-discipline in speech when what one says is calm and useful and avoids evoking dismay. An example of such speech would be, "Be calm, my child. Apply thyself to repetition of thy Veda and to the practice of yoga and all will be well with thee." Repetition of one's Veda according to the traditional rules is also a part of the self-discipline of speech.

Self-discipline of mind is as follows. There should be peace of mind, calm of mind bringing purity. There should be cheerfulness, a certain state of mind that comes out in a radiant expression on the face. There should be silence which means control of the mind. For control of speech depends on control of the mind, and the effect is here used by a figure of speech to mean the cause. If the text then goes on to add "control of mind", this means control of mind in general, while silence only meant control of mind in so far as it affects speech.

Also required for mental self-discipline is purity of intention, meaning absence of deception when dealing with others. (430)

* * * * *

8. And so we conclude that the father had an additional discipline in mind as an aid to knowledge of the Absolute. And he taught a form of self-discipline (tapas) because self-discipline is the most potent aid of all. Of all regular means to definite ends, it is recognized in the world that self-discipline is the most important. That was why Bhṛgu accepted self-discipline as a means to knowledge, even though his father had given him no special instruction about it.

And that self-discipline was the concentration of the senses and mind, for that is the means to apprehension of the Absolute. The Smṛti says: "The supreme form of self-discipline is the one-pointed concentration of mind and senses. It is better than all other spiritual duties and is called the supreme spiritual duty." (431)

* * * * *

9. Now the text lays down the measures that aid the renunciate in his pursuit of right knowledge, such as truthfulness and the like. They are predominantly virtues associated with withdrawal from worldly life (nivṛtti).

This Self is attained through truthfulness, through giving up deceit, and also by self-discipline (tapas), which means one-pointed concentration of senses and mind, undertaken on the principle "The supreme form of self-discipline is the one-pointed concentration of mind and senses." (432) This, and not the rigour of severe fasting and the like, is the highest and most useful form of self-discipline, because it is directed towards vision of the Self. (433)

This Self, then, is attainable through efforts towards right vision, associated with brahmacarya, which here means abstention from all preoccupation with sex. The word "constant" has to be applied to truthfulness, self-discipline and efforts towards right knowledge severally, on the analogy of a lamp which, placed in the centre of a room, lights up everything in the room. (434) And the text will later say, "In those in whom there is neither crookedness nor deceit nor cheating...". (435)

What is the Self to be obtained with the aid of these measures? There is a pure golden-coloured light in the ether of the lotus-shaped heart within the body which can be seen by the renunciates (yati) who strive with effort (yatana) and have rid their minds of anger and other defects. That is the Self, and it is obtained by the renunciates who *constantly* practise truthfulness and the other measures enumerated above, and not by those who only practise them intermittently. (436)

* * * * *

10. The means for understanding this Upanishad (the Kena) dealing with the Absolute (proceeds the Teacher speaking in the Upanishad text) are self-discipline, etc. Self-discipline (tapas) is control of the body, senses and mind. By restraint (dama) the text means cessation of all unbridled activity. By ritualistic action (karma) it means the Agnihotra and the like. For it is found that direct vision of the truth (tattva-dṛṣṭi) accrues through purity of mind, and only to one who has been purified by such practices. In the case of one whose impurities have not been removed by such practices, on the other

hand, it is seen that either no knowledge of the Absolute arises or else wrong knowledge arises even after they have been properly taught, as in the case of Indra and Virocana and others. (437)

Knowledge, therefore, arises through self-discipline and other practices performed either in the present life or in many previous ones, as is implied in such a text as, "The things taught here become evident only to that great soul who has supreme devotion to God and the same devotion to the Teacher as he has to God." (438) And we also have the following text from the derivative literature, namely, "Men acquire knowledge through the exhaustion of (the effects of) their evil acts." (439)

* * * * *

11. Now the text proceeds to outline what one has to do to achieve devotion to knowledge in its highest form. One must be equipped with a pure intellect, void of all deceit. One must keep the body and mind firmly under control. One must abandon the pursuit of sense-objects, which evidently means one must avoid all objects of pleasure and make use only of those objects which enable one to maintain the body in existence, and even in regard to these one must give up attachment and aversion.

The next stage involves resort to solitary places such as forests, rivers, sand-banks and caves, along with great moderation in eating. These measures are an insurance against sleep and other obstructions (at the time of long meditations) and hence contribute to lightness of mind. There must also be strict control over the activity of speech, body and mind, by which the text means to imply that all the senses and faculties of action must be reduced to their minimum activity. There must also be "dhyāna" and "yoga", where "dhyāna" means protracted dwelling on the pure essence of the Self and "yoga" means making one's whole life concentrated on meditation on the Self alone. By specifying that "dhyāna" and "yoga" must be "constant", the text seems to imply that no other duties are to be carried out, such as repetition of mantras (440) or the like. And the mention of "dispassion" (vairāgya) means constant indifference to and absence of thirst for present or future objects.

"Ego-sense" (ahaṃkāra), meaning identification of the Self with the body, senses and mind, must also be abandoned, likewise physical force, if associated with lust, attachment and other passions. The text cannot mean the abandonment of bodily strength as such, as this is inseparable from the body, and so one cannot abandon it. One must also abandon pride, which follows close upon elation and leads one to transgress the spiritual law, as the Smṛti points out when it says, "He who feels elated becomes proud, and after becoming proud transgresses the spiritual law." (441) Also to be rejected are desire and aversion. And even when all the typical failings that afflict the senses and mind have been overcome this is not the end. One must also give up the habit of receiving anything from anyone else, either to help maintain the body or to help carry out spiritual tasks.

Such a person is without any sense of possession. He is a renunciate of the (highest) paramahaṃsa order, not even personally concerned with the maintenance of the body, and hence a man of peace. He is an ascetic (yati) who has withdrawn from all personal endeavour and is devoted to knowledge. He is fit to "become the Absolute." (442)

Having "become the Absolute" he attains the serenity of the Spirit within. By his very nature he is incapable of any grief or desire. One cannot suppose that the one who is awake to his own nature as the Absolute feels desire for an object he does not possess....

He sees all creatures "the same as himself," that is, he sympathizes with their pleasures and pains as if they were *his* pleasures and pains. The phrase does not mean that he sees all other creatures *as* himself, as this characteristic will be mentioned in the following verse when the text says, "He knows Me through devotion." Thus devoted to knowledge, he acquires supreme devotion to Me. This "supreme devotion to Me" is none other than knowledge, this being the characteristic of the fourth kind of devotee of the Lord, as explained earlier in the words "Four kinds of people worship Me." (443)

Through this knowledge, here spoken of as devotion, he knows Me. That is, he knows the supreme Spirit, both under all the distinctions and variety set up by external adjuncts, and also in its true nature without them, pure like the ether. He knows Me, that is, in My pure form, as non-dual, as pure homogeneous Consciousness, birthless, deathless beyond decay, beyond fear, beyond destruction. Having known Me rightly, he enters Me forthwith. Not that the Lord means that the knowing and the entering are anything different, since the "entry" consists in no more than the certainty that the final goal of knowledge is nothing other than this, as is implicit in the text "Know Me as the knower of the body in all bodies." (444)

Here you might object and suggest that there was a contradiction. For when anyone knows anything, he knows it once and for all: he does not need to *devote* himself to knowledge of it. On your view (i.e. on the Advaitin's view), such an objector might complain, the text does not mean that he became aware of the Lord through knowledge, but only through *devotion* to knowledge.

But this objection does not apply. For the word "devotion" (in "devotion to knowledge") here refers to the fact that spiritual knowledge, when associated with the right conditions for its maturation and rise, and free from obstructing influences, invariably results in the permanent conviction that one is immediately aware of one's own Self in its true nature. "Devotion to knowledge " refers to that state of knowing where one has immediate awareness of one's own Self, and knows that the knower in the body is none other than the supreme Self. (445) Such a state is naturally accompanied by the renunciation of all action, since action depends on the notion of a distinction between the action, its factors and results. And the spiritual state above referred to depends on purity of mind, absence of pride and other auxiliary factors (446) which help to mature the knowledge that has arisen from the teachings of the Vedic texts and the Teacher.

It has already been explained how this devotion to knowledge (jñāna-niṣṭhā) is the fourth kind of devotion (bhakti) and superior to the other three others. (447) It is through this supreme form of devotion (parabhakti) that one knows the Lord as He really is, and immediately afterwards one loses all sense of difference between the knower of the body (kṣetra-jña) and the Lord. So there is no contradiction when it is said "He becomes aware of Me through devotion (bhakti) in the form of devotion to knowledge."

It is this aspect of Gītā teaching that confirms the teaching of the Upanishads, Epics and Purāṇas and all the derivative literature, inasmuch as they all teach renunciation of action as the final doctrine. We have such texts as "When they have attained knowledge, they leave home and take up the life of a wandering mendicant," (448) "Wherefore renunciation is said to be the greatest of the acts of self-discipline," (449) "Renunciation is superior to everything." (450) Here in the Gītā (451) "renunciation" means "renunciation of action." There are also other texts from the Smṛti such as "Having renounced this world and the world to come and the Vedas" (452) and "Giving up both the spiritual path and what is against the spiritual path." (453) And we have explained how there are other texts here in the Gītā which have the same meaning. (454)

You cannot claim that these texts (coming from such respectable sources) are meaningless. Nor can you say that they are merely eulogistic passages, for they appear in passages specifically dealing with their own subject (*viz.* renunciation).

Further, liberation means absorption in the true nature of one's own inmost Self, beyond all modification and change. One who wishes to go to the eastern sea cannot do the exact opposite and associate with someone going to the western sea. Devotion to knowledge means a determined effort to keep up the thought of the inmost Self in a continuous stream. To try to combine that with action would be a contradiction, like going towards the western sea when your goal was the eastern sea. Those who know the truth about the various means of knowledge (pramāṇa) are convinced that there is a contradiction between knowledge and action: they stand as far apart as a mountain and a grain of mustard-seed. Hence it stands proved that devotion to knowledge is only possible if there is complete renunciation of action. (455)

* * * * *

12. The Lord says, "This," meaning "this knowledge of the Absolute which is going to be expounded in the present chapter and which has already been taught in earlier chapters too." He refers to it as "this" so as to evoke it in

the hearer's mind. The word "but" marks this kind of knowledge off as special.

This right-knowledge is the direct means to liberation, as is shown by such texts as "Vāsudeva is all," (456) "All this is the Self," (457) "One only without a second," (458) "But they who think otherwise (and do not attain to spiritual sovereignty will find their fate decreed by another and will attain only a 'perishable world'." (459) I will teach unto you this most secret knowledge (proceeds the Lord), unto you who do not cavil. It is knowledge associated with direct experience, and having achieved it you will have been liberated from evil.

It is called the "King of Sciences" because it is the most brilliant. Knowledge of the Absolute outshines all other sciences. It is also the "King of Secrets". It is likewise the "Purifier of all Purifications". Its power of purification is beyond all description, since it reduces to ashes at a stroke all the merit and demerit arising from many thousands of births. It is said to be *direct* knowledge because it is immediate, like knowledge of pleasure and the like. (460) Some things which are valuable in some respects are found to be in conflict with the spiritual law (dharma), but this self-knowledge of the Self is not in conflict with the spiritual law. With all this it might be thought hard of attainment, so the Lord says it is something easy to learn like discrimination of jewels. And to prevent the supposition that it will bring no lasting benefits, because easy activities requiring requiring little effort usually bring little reward and great rewards require great efforts, the Lord adds that its reward is everlasting. Hence one should make sincere efforts to acquire knowledge of the Self. (461)

But, says the Lord, those who do not have faith in this knowledge of the Self, who deny both its existence and its rewards, those sinful beings who believe the demoniac principle that the physical body is all and who live to satisfy their vital instincts alone, (462) they could never be supposed to attain to Me, the highest Lord, even in a dream. That is, they could not even attain to mere devotion (bhakti), one of the subordinate phases of the path leading to Me. (463) Such persons certainly have to return. Where do they return? To further transmigratory life associated with death, the path which includes experiences in hell and in animal bodies. (464)

* * * * *

13. Those who worship Me thus with devotion (bhakti), with all desires for external objects restrained, not desirous of any gain but filled with love — to them I grant insight into My true nature, whereby they realize Me, the Lord, as their own Self. Who are these people? Those whose minds and senses are focussed on Me.

Then the Lord proceeds to answer the question, "Why do you give Your devotee right insight into Your true nature? To destroy what obstructions?" I think compassionately of their true welfare, He says. Seated in the heart of their personality, their inner organ (mind), I destroy their darkness of delusion, which consists in false cognition (mithyā-pratyaya) proceeding from non-discrimination. This I do by "the lamp of wisdom" in the form of discriminating knowledge.

This "lamp of wisdom" is filled with the clear oil of devotion(bhakti), is fanned by the breeze of ardent longing for Me, has intelligence purified by celibacy and other observances for its wick, has a dispassionate mind for its base, is protected by the chimney of an imagination that is withdrawn from sense-objects and unstained by attachment and aversion, and is shining with the right-insight that arises from constant one-pointed meditation. (465)

* * * * *

14. Which group understands yoga best? Those who are constantly engaged in action for the sake of the Lord in full concentration and as mentioned in verse 55 of Chapter Eleven of the Gītā, and who meditate on the Universal Form (of the Lord), resorting to nothing else? Or those others who give up all desires and renounce all action and meditate on the Absolute as characterized above, that is, without any external adjuncts and beyond the reach of senses and mind? The word "manifest" (vyakta) is generally used to mean "falling within the range of the senses and mind", this being the implication of the root "añj" (from which the word "vyakta" is derived). But the Absolute as the Imperishable (akṣara) is the opposite of this and not accessible to the senses and mind. The reference is to those who meditate upon it as already characterized, and its nature will be explained further below. (466) Which of the two classes are better versed in yoga?

In His reply, the Lord postpones His remarks about those who worship the Absolute in its unmanifest form for the following verse, and speaks for the present of those devotees (bhakta) who concentrate their minds on Himself, the supreme Lord in the form of the whole universe, (467) the Lord and sovereign Master over all lesser masters and powers, the Omniscient One whose vision is unclouded by the darkness of attachment and other passions. If any members of the latter class are ever concentrated in the manner described in the 55th verse of the

Eleventh Chapter of the Bhagavad Gītā, and if they worship Him with supreme faith, then He values them highest of all. They pass their time day and night with their minds fixed on Him without a break, so that it is but right to say that He values them highest.

Are the others, then, not valued so high? Listen to what is said in their case. These are the ones who are in every way devoted to that which is beyond the range of speech because it is not subject to determination by any of the means of knowledge.

Devotion (upāsanā) is defined as approaching near (upa) something laid down in the Veda as an object of worship by making it the object of one's thought, and remaining (āsana) (468) a long time in its proximity through a stream of identical images that flows continuously like a stream of oil....

Those (who practise meditation on the Absolute in its unmanifest form) attain to Him, intent on the good of all living beings. They practise true withdrawal of the senses, and are equiminded in the face of the pleasant and the unpleasant. It hardly needs to be said that they reach Him, as He has already said, "I deem the enlightened man to be My very Self." (469) You cannot say that those who are the Lord Himself are "valued highest" or "not valued highest".

Still, even though the difficulties of those who live intent on performing action for the sake of the Lord are great, the difficulties of those others are greater. Here the reference is to those who acquire a vision of the supreme Self and identify themselves with the Absolute or the Imperishable Principle (akṣara), their minds having acquired a taste for meditation on something unmanifest. Their difficulties arise from the need (on their path) to rise above self-identification with the body. (470)

* * * * *

15. The phrase "My devotee" means one who has made over his whole being to Me, the Lord the Omniscient One, the supreme Teacher, Vāsudeva. My devotee is one whose intellect is possessed by the idea that everything he sees, everything he hears, everything he touches, everything whatever, is nothing but the Lord Vāsudeva. Possessed of right knowledge in this way, he becomes fit for obtaining knowledge of the supreme Self, that is, My nature. In short, he attains liberation. (471)

* * * * *

16. "If you want concrete perception of this, (472) bring over a fig from that great bunyan tree." He did it, saying as he showed it, "Here it is, I have brought it, holy Sir." Uddālaka said to him: "Cut it up." "It is cut," replied the other. Then the father said, "What do you see?" Śvetaketu replied, "I see seeds that seem as small as could be." "Take one of them, my dear son, and cut it again." "It is cut." "All right, you've cut it. What do you see?" "I do not see anything at all, holy Sir."

Then the father said, "My dearest son, when the seed of the fig-tree was cut, you did not see the heart of that seed. And yet, my dearest, it is apparently from this subtle heart of the seed that the great bunyan tree proceeds as effect, standing there with its great thick trunk and myriads of branches and blossoms....

"Therefore have faith, my dear one." It is from the subtle (invisible) principle of Being that this whole gross universe of name, form and action proceeds. What has been ascertained on the basis of reason and revelation together is usually rightly comprehended. But a mind that is attached to the external objects and given over to the natural instincts and inclinations will find extremely subtle points impossible to understand without very strong faith. That is why the Teacher says, "Have faith." When there is faith, the mind can be concentrated on the point one wishes to know about, and this enables one eventually to know it. Compare such texts as "My mind was elsewhere." (473)

NOTES TO CHAPTER XII

(1) Gonda, I. p.362 (2) Cp. above, Vol.III p.41 f. (3) Cp. Ś.B. XI.i.viii.6, quoted Silburn, p.70 (4) See below p.51. (5) Ātmānanda p.91 (6) See below, p.12, line 2. (7) In Advaita these are not directly qualities of the soul as such, as they are in Vaiśeṣika teaching, but qualities of the mind-body complex with which the soul is falsely identified. (8) When the body is tired, the agent and experiencer feels tired: when the mind is agitated *he* feels agitated. (9) To qualify as an act in the full sense, a piece of activity has to be consciously directed to an end, and this end will be either in line with or against the Vedic injunctions and prohibitions. Trivial bodily movements of which we are hardly conscious do not count as action. (10) Bh.G.Bh. XVIII.14-16 (11) T.S. VI.iii.10.5 (12) Bṛhad. I.iv.16. Cp. Śaṃkara's Commentary to this passage below, p.73 (13) *Ibid.* (14) This is only explicable if actions produce regular results. (15) Bṛhad. III.ii.13 (16) Bṛhad. Bh. I.iv.10 (17) See above, Vol.III, p.5 f. (18) Bh.G.Bh. XVIII.18 (19) Bh.G.Bh. XVIII.67 (introduction) (20) Bṛhad. Bh. I.v.2 (21) Śaṃkara derives the word vṛkṣa (tree) legitimately from the root vraśc, "be felled". (22) Cp. Muṇḍ. Bh. I.i.8, above, Vol.II p.163 (23) Cp. Bh.G.Bh. XV.3 (24) "aśvattha" is taken as "a" (not) +"śva" (tomorrow) + "ttha" (stand). (25) Brahman from the root bṛh or bṛṃh, to swell, etc. (26) Kaṭha Bh. II.iii.1 (27) Yama, the god of death, is speaking. (28) The majority of people think in this way. Just a few pursue the means to the attainment of a higher world after death. As for efforts towards knowledge of the Self, they are rare indeed — that is the meaning. Sac. The Extract is from Kaṭha Bh. I.ii.5 and 6. (29) *Viz.* the Veda and Smṛti.

(30) To be understood in a technical sense, not a popular sense. The reference is to the performance of rituals as enjoined in the Veda to the accompaniment of prescribed meditations of various kinds relevant to the rituals in question. (31) On this latter path, cp. Chapter XIV section 2 below. (32) Ś.B. XI.xii.6.13 (33) Cp. Manu Smṛti XII.88. (34) Bṛhad. Bh. I.i.1 (introduction) (35) Kaṭha II.iii.1, cp. above p.9 (36) So far untraced. (37) Cp. Note 24 above. (38) The Bh.G. was apparently composed at a time when only three Vedas were recognized (Bh.G. IX.17). Śaṃkara conforms to the Bh.G. view here, though elsewhere he accepts the Atharva Veda as canonical. (39) Omniscience means, for Śaṃkara, not knowledge of all the details of this illusory saṃsāra, but knowledge of the Self which underlies it, the only reality. (40) Reading brahmaṇo viśva-sṛjo dhāma with D.V. Gokhale. (41) I.e. in the previous verse, Bh.G.XV.1. (42) I.e. their efforts pertain to the human sphere, not to the divine realms above the earth or to the sub-human life on the earth or in the realms beneath the earth. (43) Except through liberation, of course. (44) In practice, Śaṃkara identified the abode of Viṣṇu with the Absolute. Cp. Kaṭha Bh. I.iii.9. (45) Bh.G.Bh. XV.1-4 (46) Modern philology derives the word "asura" from the root "as" to breathe in harmony with the first alternative. (47) Bṛhad. Bh. I.iii.1 (48) Bṛhad. Bh. I.iv.10. (49) This applies directly to man in the three higher castes, Brāhmaṇa, Kṣatriya and Vaiśya, but only with qualifications to others. The Śūdra may acquire spiritual knowledge through the Purāṇas and Epics but may not study the Vedic texts or perform Vedic ritual. Cp. below, pp.66 ff. What about the foreigner standing outside the Hindu pale altogether? Even he is not excluded from all forms of traditional teaching. Cp. below p.109 f., where it is explained how "all human beings as such" can earn knowledge of the Self. (50) Reading Īpsati with Sac. for the Īkṣati of the G.P. Ed. (51) Aitareya Āraṇyaka II.iii.2.5 The Extract is from Taitt. Bh. II.i.1 (52) Cp. Praśna I.7 and I.8 (53) Muṇḍ. I.ii.10 (54) Praśna Bh. I.9 (55) When the older texts of the Upanishads were composed there were hardly any towns in India (cp. Frauwallner G.I.P. I. p.47), so householders in villages stood for householders in general. Because towns had grown up in the meantime,

Śaṃkara had to explain to his readers that the phrase was not intended to exclude householders living in towns. (56) Originally the idea was that when the moon waxed it was being filled with "nectar" (amṛta, the immortalizing beverage consumed by the gods), and when it waned this was because the nectar in it was being consumed by the gods. (57) Chānd. V.iv.2 (58) Cp. B.S.Bh. III.i.6, below p.36 f. (59) Absurd because it would make the Veda expound more difficult methods for the highest goal, liberation, when easier ones would have sufficed (60) At B.S.Bh. III.i.8 Deussen quotes Ā.D.S.II.ii.2-3 in this connection.Cp.p.39 below and Note 102. (61) On this theory, one's deeds in life 'a' condition one's circumstances (but not one's deeds) in life 'b', our deeds in life 'b' in turn condition our circumstances (but not our deeds) in life 'c'. (62) Bṛhad. IV.iv.2. I.e. the acquired aptitude and skills that accompany a man to his new birth are not limited to one birth only. (63) The sky is assumed to form a kind of roof. The space from the earth to that roof is the antarikṣa. Beyond the roof, and consequently invisible, is svarga or heaven. (64) Here Śaṃkara is simply following his text. (65) Lit. "By the maxim of the crow and the palmyra fruit." A crow alighted on a palmyra tree, and by a rare unlucky chance the fruit fell and killed it. So the meaning is, "By an extremely rare chance." Jacob, Handful, p.11. (66) Ait. II.i.1 (67) Bṛhad. IV.iv.2. See Śaṃkara's Commentary on this passage, below pp.52 ff. (68) Compare the case in modern times of professional boxers, who have been known to carry on a large proportion of their contest in total oblivion of their surroundings. (69) Chānd. VIII.xv.1 (70) The Brahmins, Kṣatriyas and Vaiśyas, the three higher castes, constitute the twice-born. (71) I.e. through meditation on the Five Fires or on other prescribed themes connected with the ritual. (72) Chānd. Bh. V.x.3-9, with omissions. (73) Chānd. V.x.8 (74) Cp. Bṛhad. Bh. IV.iv.2, trans. Mādhavānanda p.706 f. The reading in the present B.S.Bh. passage should be vidyā-karma, not avidyā-karma, cp. Hacker, Texte p.114, footnote 3. (75) Bṛhad. IV.iv.1-4 (76) Bṛhad. IV.iv.1 (77) Chānd. V.iii.3. The various stages of the cyclic passage of the soul borne aloft to the moon in watery smoke and redescending to earth in rain are symbolized as "oblations". The "fifth oblation of water" is the man's seed, derived from food into which rain has at one stage entered, passing into woman at the time of conception. It "comes to have a voice" when born as a baby. (78) Bṛhad. IV.iv.3 (79) Not caterpillar (80) Truth, knowable through the Veda and crowned by direct experience, is one and invariable. Human conjecture implies alternative views and hence falsity. Here, as so often in Śaṇkara, the alternative views of human conjecture are grouped in contradictory pairs. The Sāṃkhyas explain transmigration on the view that the organs and the soul are all-pervading, that neither of them require to be displaced for the sake of the new embodiment, that the soul does not act and that only the senses begin to act anew in a new body through the prompting of merit and demerit arising from past action. The Buddhist takes the opposite view that neither the soul nor the body are all-pervading — both are atomic in the temporal as well as the spatial dimension — and that it is the soul and not the senses which acts. Similarly, the Vaiśeṣika and Jaina, while both contradictory to the Sāṃkhyas and Buddhists in believing that transmigration involves the passage of a finite entity from one already existent body to another, adopt positions that contradict one another mutually. The Vaiśeṣika holds that it is the *mind* that moves from one body to the other, while the all-pervading soul, being motionless, does not. The Jaina, who does not admit mind as a separate category, makes the soul limited to the size of the body and supposes that it is the *soul* that moves to the new body in re-incarnation. The Extract is from B.S.Bh. III.i.1. (81) Immediately after the end of the passage from B.S.Bh. III.i.1 translated in the immediately preceding Extract, the Commentary introduces an objector who claims that the soul must leave the body enshrouded by the subtle elements but not by water. The passage in question, Chānd. V.iii.3, however, mentions water but not subtle elements. (82) Cp. above, Vol.II p.150 (83) Chānd. VI.iii.2 (84) Chānd. V.iii.3, V.ix.1. (85) B.S. III.i.6, Śaṃkara's Commentary on which appears in the immediately following Extract. (86) B.S.Bh. III.i.2 (87) The only continuous ritual fire maintained by the householder was the Gāharpatya. For Soma offerings, and larger sacrifices generally, other fires were lit from the Gāharpatya. Of these, the Āhavanīya was square in form and placed to the east. It was the fire into which libations cooked in the Gāharpatya were poured. Renou and Filliozat, Tome 1, Sect. 703 (88) It is the faith (śraddhā) with which the sacrificer performs the ritual that endows it with the power to bring about future effects. (89) Chānd. V.iv.2. The Vital Energies of the sacrificer offer the libation of the "water" of his past sacrifices into the "fire" of the "other world", as a result of which the sacrificer acquires a vaporous body on the moon. (90) Ś.B. XI.vi.2.6 (91) B.S.Bh. III.i.6 (92) For the Five Fires, cp. Chapter XIV section 3 below. (93) The Northern Path (cp. Bh.G. VIII.24) is the Path of the Flame, for which see Vol.VI Chapter XIV section 3 below. (94) For the Āhavanīya fire, cp. Note 87 above. (95) T.S. I.vi.8.1. (96) Bṛhad. VI.ii.2 (97) Bṛhad. Bh. VI.ii.9 (98) Ānandagiri quotes from the Veda "te vā ete āhutī hute utkrāmatas te antarikṣam āviśataḥ", a text which means that the oblations go to the atmosphere and thence into rain, then down into crops and finally through food into the embryo. He quotes Manu III.76 "Oblations duly offered into the fire reach up to the sun. Rain proceeds from the sun. From rain comes food and from food living creatures." The Extract is from Bṛhad. Bh. I.v.2. (99) Chānd. V.x.7. (100) B.S.III.i.9, Gambhīrānanda p.571 f. (101) Deussen (System, Chapter XXXIII) maintains one could find a distinction in Śaṃkara between moral conduct, which conditions one's next life on earth, and ritual, which conditions life in other worlds. Certainly, when the opponent appears to deny this he is contradicted, below p.42. Cp. also Note 159 below. (102) Cp. Ā.D.S. II.ii.2-3 (103) Chānd. VI.vii.10 (104) Bṛhad. IV.iv.6 (105) A man's total stock of unfructified merit and demerit might include both heaven and hell. It follows that all his merit and demerit could not begin to fructify at the same time. Govindānanda. (106) M.Bh. XII.290.18 (107) Cp. Manu Smṛti XII.55 (108) Chānd. V.x.5. (109) As they are at Chānd. V.x.3 (110) At Chānd. V.x.6. The Extract is from B.S.Bh. III.i.8 (111) The ascent to the moon is for the particular purpose of enjoying the fruits of sacrifices there. (112) Kaṭha II.6 (or I.ii.6) (113) R.V. X.xiv.1, as explained by Sāyana. (114) As usual in the B.S.Bh., Śaṃkara distinguishes Bādarāyaṇa from Vyāsa. Here he attributes to the author of the Sūtras (identified by him with Bādarāyaṇa) a reference to Vyāsa, whom he regarded as a separate person and the author of the M.Bh. and the Purāṇas. As S. Mayeda has shown (U.S. English trans. *ad loc.*) U.S. XVI.67 probably should not be taken as implying that the "Vedānta Sūtras" were composed by Vyāsa. That verse probably refers to the Upanishads (Vedanta) on the one hand and to the M.Bh. and Purāṇas composed by Vyāsa on the other. (115) Samyamana Pura, the abode of Yama. (116) Kaṭha I.i.1 ff. (117) B.S.Bh. III.i.13-15 (118) Chānd. VI.viii.6 (119) Praśna III.9 (120)"Mind (dissolves) into the Vital Energy," Chānd. VI.viii.6 (121)Vijñānātman — a name for the core of the individual soul that undergoes transmigration. It hardly seems to differ from the soul in the "subtle body" as described at B.S.Bh. IV.ii.8, with which the present Extract concludes. (122) Reading vidyā-karma, cp. Note 74 above. (123) Bṛhad. IV.iii.38 (124) Bṛhad. IV.iv.2 (125) *Ibid.* (126) At B.S. IV.ii.5 (127) B.S. IV.ii.6 (128) Chānd. V.iii.3 (129) B.S.III.i.2, cp. above, p.33. (130) Bṛhad. IV.iv.5 (131) Manu Smṛti I.27 (132) Bṛhad. III.ii.13. Here the conception of karma is widened to include other actions as well as ritual. It has been claimed (Silburn p.119) that this is the earliest example of "karma" being used in this sense in all the ritualistic teaching. (133) I.e. by the merit and demerit arising from past work. (134) If work was eulogized, the statements about it should not be taken literally. (135) Reading mūrdha-nāḍī with Govindānanda's Ratnaprabhā, cp. B.S.Bh. IV.ii.17. Hence the splitting of the skull required to be performed on the funeral pyre, as attested by the mediaeval poet Sūra Dāsa, Sūra Sāgara, ed. Vājapeyī, Pada 86. (136) Notice that nescience (avidyā) is here subsumed under the wider concept of "passion" (kleśa). This is a usage belonging to the school of Patañjali rather than Advaita, and its presence here in the B.S.Bh. can be seen as support for those who accept the "Vivaraṇa" sub-commentary on the Yoga Sūtras attributed to Śaṃkara as genuine. (137) Chānd. VI.viii.6 (138) Kaṭha II.ii.7. Śaṃkara is thinking of the power of the last thought before death to determine one's next life, as mentioned at Bh.G.VIII.6. See Sac's ṭīkā to Kaṭha Bh.II.ii.7 and Bṛhad Bh.IV.iv.2. For the latter passage, see below, p.55. (139) B.S.Bh. IV.ii.1-8 (selected passages) (140) Reading parimāṇataśca (141) Ś.B. VIII.vii.2.11. The Extract is from B.S.Bh. IV.ii.9-11

NOTES TO CHAPTER XII

(142) Bṛhad. IV.iii.36 (143) Bṛhad.II.i.17 (144) Bṛhad. IV.iii.9 (145) Bṛhad.IV.iii.11 (146) Bṛhad.IV.iii.7 (147) On this conception and its meaning in the Bṛhad., cp. Frauwallner, G.I.P., I. pp.63-65. Śaṃkara interprets it here as meaning the deity that presides over the organ of sight. (148) Bṛhad. III.ii.13. But Śaṃkara interprets this to mean that it is the presiding deities, not the actual organs, that are meant here. Cp. the following passage from his commentary *ad loc.*: "In every case the words 'voice' etc. refer to their presiding deities; the organs themselves to not depart before liberation." (149) I.e. the presiding deities depart and return on waking. (150) They withdraw from their seats at the extremities of the body, and unite with the subtle body in the heart. (151) Praśna VI.3-4 (152) Presumably the five organs of perception,the five organs of action and the mind and intellect. (153) On the world of Brahmā, cp. Vol.VI Chapter XIV section 2 below. (154) Bh.G. VIII.6 (155) According to Ānandagiri it means pursuit of the discipline laid down at Y.S. II.29-30: harmlessness, truth-telling, non-stealing, continence, non-hoarding of possessions, cleanliness, contentment, asceticism, assiduous recitation of the Veda (or repetition of OM) and worship of the Lord. (156) Parisaṃkhyāna. Śaṃkara gives an example of what this means at U.S. (prose) paras 112-116. (157) Bṛhad. III.ii.13 (158) Ānandagiri explains the meaning as follows: Prescribed knowledge is meditation, etc. Prohibited knowledge is the sight of naked women, etc. Non-prescribed knowledge is that of pots, etc, Non-prohibited knowledge is that of grass beneath one's feet, etc. Prescribed action means ritual sacrifices, etc. Prohibited action means the killing of Brahmins, etc. Non-prescribed action is ordinary going about, etc. Non-prohibited action is blinking, etc. Professor Hacker takes the second item (sight of naked women) to be ritualistic in character and quotes a parallel passage from B.S.Bh. III.iv.11 as evidence that Śaṃkara knew of and disapproved of "Vāmacāra" Tāntrika cults, Texte p.114, footnote 3. His conjecture may be confirmed from Madhusūdana Sarasvatī's Comm. to Sarvajñātman S.Ś. III.18, where he refers to "improper cults" in discussing this passage. (159) That is, good worldly deeds promote better conditions for one's next birth on earth, whereas

rituals are the governing factor in experience of heavenly joys, which cannot be everlasting. The Extract is from Bṛhad. Bh. IV.iv.1-2 (160) Above, Vol.IV p.6 f. (161) N.Sid. III.126 (162) Bṛhad. II.iv.5 (163) Bṛhad. IV.iv.21 (164) *Ibid.* (165) B.S. Bh. IV.i.15, cp. above, Vol.I p.47 (166) See below, Vol.VI Chapter XVI. (167) B.S. Bh.I.i.1 (168) Bṛhad. Bh. I.iv.7 (169) An originating injunction (utpatti-vidhi), contrasted with an injunction of application (viniyoga-vidhi), is the general injunction to perform a big ritual, for which big ritual there may be subordinate injunctions implying subordinate rituals which also carry stated rewards. Both these classes of injunction are, rather confusingly, called *original* injunctions (apūrva-vidhi), obedience to which brings a reward. The exception is those specifying injunctions which merely specify which course a ritualist should take *out of several to which he has already been prompted before hearing the present specifying injunction*. These are called restrictive injunctions (niyama-vidhi). They are regarded as a kind of prohibition, and no reward is promised for their observance, though failure to observe them would spoil the ritual. (170) Bṛhad. Bh. I.iv.7 (171) B.S. Bh. I.i.4 (172) *Ibid.* (173) Bṛhad. Bh. I.iv.7 (174) *Ibid.* (175) Rāhula Sāṃkṛtyāyana, p.689 f. (176) B.S. Bh. III.iv.38 (177) Ś.B. XI.ii.6.13, quoted at Vācaspati, Bhāmatī, Catuḥsūtrī, Eng. trans. p.84, with Note 71. (178) The fourth and menial caste. (179) Ś.B. XI.v.3.13 (180) Chānd. VII.i.1 (181) Praśna I.1 (182) Chānd. V.xi.7 (183) Manu Smṛti X.4 (184) *Ibid.* X.126 (185) Chānd. IV.iv.5 (186) Gautama Dharma Sūtra XII.4 (187) Swāmī Gambhīrānanda gives the reference Vāsiṣṭha 18. Śaṃkara is required by his B.S. text to cite the Smṛtis debarring the Śūdra from hearing the Veda, and cites them as they stand. But later he adds texts showing that the Śūdras may hear the Epics and Purāṇas and that some of them attained enlightenment, which he was not explicitly required by his text to do. (188) Gautama Dharma Sūtra XII.4 (189) Manu Smṛti IV.80 (190) Gautama Dharma Sūtra IX.1 (191) Vidura, counsellor especially to the Kauravas, was the son of a slave-girl, but known as "the wisest of the wise". Dharma-Vyādha, a flesh-selling huntsman, was accounted "learned in the Vedas and in all the knowledge of a

Brahmin," which knowledge was assumed to have been attained in a previous birth. (192) M.Bh. XII.327.49, G.P. Ed. Vol.III p.689. Bards and muscians and actors of the Śūdra caste were present at the great royal sacrifices to give recitations from portions of the Epics and Purāṇas that they themselves had composed. See Jośī, T.L., p.47 (193) B.S. Bh. I.iii.34,36-8 (194) Muṇḍ.I.i.3 (195) This would refer to the soul as conceived by the Sāṃkhya philosophers. (196) Muṇḍ.I.i.1 (197) The sacrificer and his wife and the sixteen priests required for an elaborate sacrifice, which must have been a rather costly affair. (198) I.e. mere ritual without symbolic meditation on the instruments and factors of the ritualistic act. Cp. Muṇḍ. Bh. I.11.7. (199) Muṇḍ.I.ii.7 (200) I.e. through attaining any world that one will have oneself created through sacrificial action in the way laid down at Ś.B. VI.ii.2.27. Cp. Silburn p.70 (201) As a symbol of willingness to serve. (202) Muṇḍ. I.ii.12. The Extract is from B.S. Bh. I.ii.21. (203) This is how Śaṃkara glosses the "brahma-vid" of the Upanishad, here taking "brahma" (the form that "brahman" assumes in a compound word) to mean the Veda. (204) Muṇḍ.I.i.5, here under comment, mentions all four Vedas, including the Atharva Veda to which it itself belongs. Does that mean that the Muṇḍaka Upanishad is a later work than the Bh.G., which recognizes only three Vedas, (cp.Bh.G. IX.17)? (205) The last is the science of determining the Vedic calendar and fixing the most auspicious dates for sacrifices. (206) Manu Smṛti XII.95 (207) Cp.below, p.194. The Extract is from Muṇḍ.Bh. I.i.4-5. (208) The immediate reference is to earlier words in the text under comment, *viz*. Bṛhad. I.iv.16. But cp. also above,p.5 (209) Sureśvara (B.B.V. I.iv.1795) connects "yāga" with "tyāga" (renunciation). The reference here and in the following sentence is to Pūrva Mīmāṃsā Sūtras IV.ii.27-28, which distinguish between sacrifice (yāga,yajña) oblations (homa) and giving in charity (dāna). (210) Bṛhad. I.iv.10. The gods do not like it that any man should "become all this universe," for then he "becomes" their own Self and they cannot prevail against him. (211) Kaṭha II.i.2 (212) Bh.G. III.37 (213) Manu Smṛti II.4 (214) Bṛhad IV.iv.22 (215) In Śaṃkara, the path of ritualistic action (karma mārga) is precisely what does *not* lead to liberation. It is contrasted with the path of liberation (mokṣa mārga) as mentioned at Bh.G.Bh.II.21. (216) Taittirīya Brāhmaṇa III.xi.i. Cp.Sureśvara,N.Sid. I.22. What is required is right vision, but the ritualist befogs himself with the smoke from his own sacrifices. (217) Bṛhad. Bh. I.iv.16 and 17. (218) At Ait. Bh. I.i.1 (introduction) Ānandagiri explains the "five-fold optional rituals" as so called because they involve wife, son, meditation, wealth (to pay for the materials and the gifts to the priests) and physical performance of the ritual. Cp. Eng. Trans. Gambhīrānanda, p.11, footnote. (219) Bṛhad. II.v.1 ff. (220) For more information on "seven-fold", consult Mādhavānanda, pp.198 ff. (221) Selected from Bṛhad. Bh. I.v.1 and 2 (222) M.Bh. XIV.16,12, G.P. Ed. Vol. IV. p.291 (223) *Ibid.* XIV.19.7 and 1, p.294 (224) *Ibid.*, XIV.43.26 (225) Bh.G XVIII.66. (226) Bh.G. V.10 (227) *Ibid.* V.11. The Extract is from Bh.G.Bh. I.1 (introduction) (228) In the polemical parts of his writing Śaṃkara uses the word Sāṃkhya to stand for the followers of the philosophical school of that name. But long before that school arose there was an earlier stage of the Sāṃkhya philosophy in which monistic intuition of the Upanishadic sages had not been abandoned, and Sāṃkhya and Yoga were simply names for different methods of spiritual enquiry. The Bh.G. belongs to that stage, and the "Sāṃkhya" of the Bh.G. is an Advaitin and not a dualist. (229) I.e. who have never married or entered the householder's state. (230) Echoes Muṇḍ. III.ii.6. (231) The "like" probably means all action apart from ritual performed on account of injunctions in the Vedic texts or Smṛti. Charity,acts of asceticism, fulfilment of special vows, fasting, etc., would be examples. (232) M.Bh. XII.204.8, G.P. Ed. Vol.III. p.539. (233) Cp. Meister Eckhart, "One should run into peace, but not begin in peace", Walshe, Vol.II p.187 (234) Bṛhad. IV.iv.22 (235) Bh.G. V.6 (236) Bh.G.V.11 (237) Bh.G.XVIII.5 (238) Gokhale quotes M.Bh. Aśvamedha Parva 46.18 (239) In the following verse the Lord avers that the reason for this is that "No one can ever remain a moment without acting, for everyone is necessarily prompted to act by the 'constituents' born of Nature." Only those who discriminate the Self from the "constituents" through knowledge attain to actionlessness. The Extract is from Bh.G. Bh. III.3 and 4. (240) Ānandagiri glosses "sattva" here not as a "constituent" but as the power to apprehend things as they truly are. (241) Bh. G. V.13 (242) *Ibid.* The Extract is from Bh.G.Bh. XVIII.10 (243) A pre-Śaṃkara Vedantin is being addressed. (244) See above, Vol.IV p.56 f. (245) The action of the spells and the sugar is to suppress some properties (śakti) of the substance in question and introduce others in their place, cp. Sureśvara, B.B.V. III.iii.30-31. (246) Ś.B. XI.ii.6.13 (247) Chānd.I.i.10 (248) Manu Smṛti XII.91 (249) Self-knowledge cannot, for Śaṃkara, be a *direct* result of action. (250) Purification (or preparation) is one of the four "fruits" admitted even by the Mīmāṃsakas as possible results of action, the others being production, attainment and transformation, cp. above, Vol.IV. p.49. (251) Ś.B. XI.ii.6.13 (252) Manu Smṛti II.17 ff. (253) At Manu Smṛti XII.91 (254) Manu Smṛti XII.50 (255) On the three "constituents", cp. above, Vol.II pp.74 ff. (256) Yama. (257) Lit. Mahat and Avyakta, but Kullūka's Comm. on Manu explains that the reference is to the two deities presiding over these principles, one of which must surely be Hiraṇyagarbha. (258) Note that Manu Smṛti XII.90 gives an interpretation of the terms "pravṛtti" and "nivṛtti" in which "nivṛtti" does not mean "cessation from action"(as it normally does in Śaṃkara) but "the disinterested performance of ritual associated with meditation." (259) Kullūka (thirteenth century A.D.) reproduces the view that Śaṃkara here dismisses. (260) So that descriptions of the results of evil deeds are not mere lurid fantasies designed to frighten people onto the right path (arthavāda) but are authoritative statements of fact. (261) Which can only be human souls in a fallen condition. (262) T.S. II.i.1.4 and I.v.1.1. (263) Manu Smṛti III.69 and 70 explain how the sacrifice to Brahman is the giving of metaphysical teaching, the sacrifice to the departed ancestors is laying down offerings for them, the sacrifice to gods is through libations in the sacred fire, the sacrifice to the "unshriven dead" (i.e. those who have died without due ceremony and who consequently haunt the earth like ghosts) is through offerings laid out at night on the ground, the sacrifice to men is through hospitality to guests. These are the five great sacrifices incumbent on the twice-born householder. (264) Manu Smṛti II.28

(265) I.e. at Bṛhad. Bh. IV.iv.22, especially the passage trans. Mādhavānanda p.754 f. The Extract is from Bṛhad. Bh. III.iii.i, introduction. (266) The word vidyā (knowledge) in this context means knowledge of the hidden symbolic significance of the ritual and of its relation to presiding deities, allied to meditation on that knowledge. (267) Chānd. IV.xvii.10 (268) Chānd. I.i.10. Chānd. I.i.1 ff. treats of OM. (269) They are a pre-condition in that they purify the mind. (270) From Bṛhad. IV.iv.22 (271) Such as Chānd. I.i.10, quoted above. (272) Bṛhad. I.v.2. In Śaṃkara's Commentary on this passage he makes ritual performed with "knowledge" in the sense of "knowledge of a piece of sacred lore" superior to ritual performed with "knowledge" in the sense of "merit from meditation on the symbolic significance of factors in the ritual." He mentions, in particular, the meditation on each of the 360 bricks of the fire-altar — one each day separately for all the days in a year — where each brick is taken as constituting a "day" in the "year" which makes up Prajāpati. This brings "immortality" (= freedom from rebirth on earth), but takes a year to perform. Hence the performance of the Agnihotra with knowledge of the secret lore about the milk in it is superior, as it brings the same result when only done once. On the secret lore about milk, cp. above p.38 (273) Bh.G. II.39 (274) The "yoga-wisdom" in these Gītā verses means that "knowledge" which gives the power to engage in action without the feelings of self-interest which bind the agent to the result of his action. (275) Chānd. I.i.10 (276) The Brahmins of classical India hardly used books. Even in the late Nineteenth Century Deussen noted with amazement that Pt. Rāma Miśra Śāstrī of Benares taught Vācaspati's Tattva Kaumudī Commentary on the Sāṃkhya Kārikās (133 pages in English translation) without the services of a written text. Deussen, Erinnerungen p.139. The traditional wisdom was in classical times *kept in being* only through putting into practice texts which had been *learned by heart* and so transmitted from generation to generation. It was in this sense that the learned Brahmin, who took part in this process of oral transmission, was superior to the Brahmin who was not "learned" and did not. (277) Bṛhad. IV.iv.22

(278) *Ibid.* (279) B.S.Bh. IV.i.18 (280) Cp. above,p.19 (281) Chānd. V.x.8 (282) Aitareya Āraṇyaka II.i.1 (283) The Kena, like the Īśa Upanishad, derives its name from the first word of its text, in this case "kena", lit. "by whom?" (284) Kaṭha II.i.1 (285) Anything attained through action belongs to the time-space world and is impermanent. The Absolute is attainable ultimately only through the knowledge that it is your own true nature. (286) Cp. Note 201 above. (287) Muṇḍ. I.ii.12 (288) Vijñāna means "immediate personal experience" here. Cp. Bh.G.Bh. VII.2, vijñāna-sahitam svānuhbava-yuktam. The Extract is from Kena Bh. I.i. (Introduction) (289) Īśa 12 (290) Īśa 9 (291) In particular, the longing to attain a higher world, and the longing for sons as a means to perform the necessary ritual to secure it. (292) That is, in comparison with his meditation on deities conjoined with ritualistic action, as mentioned above. Sac, M.R.V. p.270. (293) This interpretation explains how Īśa 11 can attribute both Avidyā (nescience) and Vidyā (knowledge) to the same person without self-contradiction. It does so through regarding them, from the nescience-standpoint of time, space and causation, as successive states. Sac, *ibid.* (294) G.K.Bh. III.25 (295) Taitt. Bh. I.1 (296) The term "Brahman" in early times meant the Vedic texts as repositories of divine power or the actual divine power resident in the texts. If "svādhyāya" keeps the texts alive in one's own memory, "giving out" creates the condition for them being available to mankind in the next generation. (297) Taitt. Bh. I.1, trans. Gambhīrānanda Vol.I. p.239. (298) The "kṛcchra" or "troublesome" form of fast is specified. On this, Cp. Note 376 below. (299) Taitt. Bh. I.9 (300) I.e. that of a householder in which a fire is maintained and rituals with libations to the gods are possible. The Advaitin rejects this view and finds a place for other stages of life besides that of a householder, according to the traditional teachings, *viz.* student, retired forest-dweller and wandering mendicant. (301) I.e. the householder's — this doctrine is referred to in Gautama's Dharma Sūtra I.iii.35. (302) E.g. Īśa 2. (303) Taitt. III.2 (304) So that there is no absolute dependence on being in the householder's state for purifying one's mind for spiritual knowledge. (305) Cp. Bṛhad. I.iv.15 (306) Refers to Vāmadeva and others

who attained knowledge of the Self at a tender age, cp. Bṛhad. I. iv.10, Ait. II.i.5. (307) Bṛhad. IV.v.2, where the great authority on sacrifice and ritual, Yājñavalkya, finds that he has realized the Self and tells his wife Maitreyī that he is about to renounce the life of action and ritual. (308) Just mentioned above. When this leads to the rise of spiritual knowledge before or during the householder's state people just break off action then and there. And this shows that there can be no rule "Spiritual knowledge *must* arise in the householder state." (309) Cp. above, Vol.IV p.55. The point is made even more emphatically above, Vol.V p.84. Action is a remote, not a direct, cause of knowledge. (310) On the grace of the Lord as the invariable antecedent of knowledge, cp. Bh.G.Bh. X.11. The doctrine that Śaṃkara is here combating ignored grace and maintained that knowledge arose as an almost mechanical result of the rigid adherence to a particular line of action. (311) A shrewdly aimed blow, as the ritualist's path of works cannot include continence, since it is concerned with sons, or harmlessness, since it is concerned with the sacrifice of animals. (312) Sac refers to other texts on the hierarchy of the means to knowledge: Bṛhad. Bh. I.iv.2; Bh.G.Bh. X.10,X.11, XVIII.45; B.S.Bh. III.iv.51, IV.i.18. (313 On this important and interesting point Sac quotes B.S.Bh. III.iv.20, Muṇḍ. Bh. I.i.1, introduction; Bh.G.Bh. XVIII.45; cp. above, Notes 187, 191. (314) Taitt. Bh.I.11 (315) Manu Smṛti XII.104 (316) A phrase occurring in the text under comment, *viz.* Taitt. I.11. In his Commentary to the passage in question, Śaṃkara identifies "tapas" with "concentration". The passage is mentioned here because concentration can only be attained through preliminary purification of the mind through performance of duty. (317) Taitt. II.7 and II.9 (318) Īśa 11 (319) Taitt.I.9. Cp. above p.92 f. (320) In this passage Śaṃkara uses the terms ācārya and guru synoymously. But in general guru is the wider term. Every ācārya is a guru, but not every guru is an ācārya. The term "guru" can be applied to any deeply respected elder or teacher: but an ācārya must have practical and theoretical mastery of a traditional science, such as grammar or philosophy, and be capable of imparting it to others. (321) Ā.D.S, II.xxi.5 (Gambhīrānanda) (322) I.e. knowledge of the Vedic texts by rote. It is the ordinary pupil proceeding to a householder's life, not a sage who has received enlightenment, that the text has in mind here. (323) At Taitt. I.9 (324) The Teacher at whose house you live as a boy and from whom you learn the Vedic texts by heart. It does not necessarily mean the Teacher to whom you ultimately repair for spiritual instruction. (325) Taitt. Bh. I.11 (326) Cp. above pp.13 ff. (327) In particular, they are not eligible for the upanayana or initiation ceremony whereby the boys of the three higher castes are "taken over" (upanayana) by a guru, acquire their sacred thread and become eligible to learn the Veda by heart and so are "born anew". Cp. above p. 66 f. (328) On the "constituents", cp. above Vol.II pp.74 ff. (329) The objector's idea was that one could not obey an injunction to be restrained if one was already conditioned to be restrained by very nature. To this it is replied that conditioning through a particular proportion of the three "constituents", such as is found in each of the castes, is general in nature, supplying no more than a natural tendency *towards* the qualities to be cultivated. But the latter do not actually come to fruition without willed activity. (330) It is interesting to find śama and dama, inner and outer restraint, the first two qualities in the famous group of six qualities necessary for the Advaita path, mentioned together as early as the Gītā. At B.S.III.iv.27 (cp. p.105 below) they are already found mentioned as the opening qualities of a stereotyped series. The connecting together of this particular series of qualities goes back to Bṛhad. IV.iv.23, but not the actual names "śama" and "dama". (331) See below pp.133 ff. (332) *Ibid.* (333) The G.P. Ed. of the Gītā and the English translator A. Mahādeva Śāstrin refer to Āpastamba Dharma Sūtra II.ii.2-3, D.V. Gokhale to Gautama Dharma Sūtra XI.29 (334) Cp. above p.81 ff.(335) In particular, the message to Arjuna is that, as a born warrior, he should not desist from battle on account of the loss of life his fighting may cause. The Extract is from Bh.G.Bh. XVIII.41-48 (selected passages) (336) As celibate student, householder, retired forest-dweller or wandering monk. (337) In the previous Sūtra, *viz.* B.S. III.iv.25 (338) Because, as will appear below, disinterested ritualistic action and other forms of purifying action give rise to the *desire* for knowledge. (339) Bṛhad. IV.iv.22 (340) Chānd. VIII.v.1 (341) Chānd. VIII.v.2 (342) Chānd. VIII.v.3 (343) Kaṭha I.ii.15 (344) The text is untraced. (345) B.S.III.iv.26, the text at present under comment. (346) Bṛhad. IV.iv.22, quoted above. (347) On this group of qualities,cp. Note 330 to the present Chapter. (348) Bṛhad. IV.iv.23. Here the terms "śama" and "dama" are not yet found in their stereotyped form, but the text is clearly the source for the later Advaita doctrine of the "Six-fold Spiritual Wealth" which begins with those two qualities. (349) Śaṃkara's Commentary on the Bṛhad. follows the Kāṇva recension of that work. The fact that he quotes the Mādhyandina recension in the B.S.Bh. is part of the evidence suggesting that his B.S.Bh. was to a considerable extent based on earlier oral or written traditions of Brahma Sūtra interpretation. (350) Bṛhad. IV.iv.22, quoted above. (351) Taittirīya Saṃhitā (Black Yajur Veda) II.vi.8.5. (352) The statement occurs in a section devoted to the Darśapūrṇamāsa sacrifice in which neither Pūṣan nor crushed portions figure. (353) P.M. Sūtra III.iii.34. The Mīmāṃsaka rule was that a factual statement that could not be related to an injunction in the portion of the text where it was found had to be related to some other injunction, in this case to that at Bṛhad. II.iv.5. (354)B.S. III.iv.20 (355) Bh.G. XVII.25 (356) Bṛhad. IV.iv.23 (357) Bṛhad. IV.iv.22, already quoted above. (358) *Ibid.* (359) B.S. III.iv.26. Śaṃkara here recapitulates what he has said earlier in this section. Rituals awaken desire for knowledge: inner and outer restraint more directly promote the capacity for knowledge. (360) B.S. III.iv.25, already quoted. (361) The injunctions to perform ritual as they stand are permanent: but they will be rendered impermanent when knowledge of the Self supervenes, as the sacrificer will then pass beyond competence for ritualistic action. (362) Quoted P.M.Bhāṣya VI.iii.1. (363) Bṛhad. IV.iv.22 (364) The argument has taken a rather formal and theological turn. It is assumed at the beginning of the paragraph that a Mīmāṃsaka might object that the Advaitin's interpretation of the role of Vedic injunctions to ritualistic action would land him in the contradiction of taking such injunctions as permanently binding in some cases and not in others. Śaṃkara replies on the principle of *tu quoque* by showing that the Mīmāṃsakas themselves do the same. They take the injunction to have an acacia-wood sacrificial post as part of a permanent injunction to *all* ritualists "for the sake of being able to have a sacrifice at all" (kratvartha), but *also* as a specialized one to *some* ritualists for the particular personal end (purusārtha) of attaining valour. See B.S.Bh. III.iv.33, trans. Gambhīrānanda p.791, footnote, and also Govindānanda's Ratnaprabhā Commentary *ad loc.* (365) The presence of the sacrificer's wife at the sacrifice was of crucial importance in Vedic ritual, and thus the widower could not be said to qualify as a householder in the full sense. (366) Chānd. IV.i.1 ff. Raikva was a hermit who lived under a cart, scratching his sores, yet he possessed the divine knowledge and was prepared to communicate it to the rich and well-born on his own terms. (367) Bṛhad. III.vi.1 and III.viii.1 ff. Gārgī, daughter of Vacaknu, was a lady philosopher, apparently unmarried. Unlike her near-contemporary Thales, she was not content with the belief that water was the ultimate principle of all things, but asked "In what is water woven warp and woof?" (368) Mentioned in M.Bh. Aśvamedha Parva Chapter 7, G.P.Ed. Vol.IV. p.279 ff. (369) The term "japa" or "mantra-japa" does not usually refer to "taking the name of God" with a rosary in Śaṃkara's texts, but to repetition of Vedic verses (mantra). The latter meaning is excluded here, as there is reference to "all humans as such," which includes those who are not entitled to repeat the Veda. Hence, by exception, Śaṃkara probably had the idea of repetitions of such formulae as "oṃ namo bhagavate vāsudevāya" with a rosary in mind here, the repetition of which is recommended at Viṣṇu Purāṇa I.xi.54-55. Repetition of a short formula with a rosary is accounted a meritorious act by Kumārila (Jha p.227), but it is not mentioned elsewhere by Śaṃkara. When "japa" is mentioned at Y.S. I.28 the classical commentators, including Śaṃkara, refer only to the repetition of Vedic verses and hymns or Om. Cp. also Y.S. II.1, with commentaries, and Maṇḍana, B.Sid. p.156, with Abhipraya Prakāśikā Comm. of Citsukha, (Anantakṛṣṇa Śāstrī p.530) — praṇavasya mokṣa-śāstrāṇāṃ copaniṣat-prabhṛtīnāṃ japaḥ. (370) Repetition of OM, etc., says the thirteenth century commentator Kullūka. This is the formula used by those who regard japa as japa of OM or Vedic verses and hymns. (371) Manu Smṛti II.87 (372) Bh.G. VI.45 (373) Unlike the ritual sacrifices, for instance, where the "fruit" will not be seen until after death and which may therefore depend on conditions, such as eligibility to perform certain ritual, which only revealed teaching can lay down. (374) For example, the Vedic prohibitions would be an obstacle against the Śūdra learning the Vedas and performing rituals to purify his mind for knowledge. But there would be no obstacle to his acquiring knowledge through the study or repetition of a text from the derivative literature like the Gītā. (375) Bṛhad. IV.iv.9 (376) The quotation is untraced. The kṛcchra penance is a twelve day fast in which food is reduced each day, with no food at all on the last three days. The Extract is from B.S.Bh. III.iv.26-27, 33, 36-39 (selected passages) (377) I.e. Bh.G I.2 - II.9 (378) Bh.G. II.4 (379) Bh.G. II.11 (380) Arjuna's proposal to become a mendicant is interpreted as entering on the mendicant's way of life. This is not the same as renunciation of all duties, which results from the acquisition of a new standpoint, *viz.* "I am not the agent." The Extract is from Bh.G. Bh. II.11 (introduction) (381) Karma-yoga for Śaṃkara is performance of the duties prescribed in the Veda and derivative literature without attachment to any promised "fruits" and as an offering to the Lord with a view to purify one's mind. (382) It is a means to right knowledge, but is itself incompatible with right knowledge, as the very performance of yoga-of-action implies attributing agency to one's actionless Self. (383) Yoga Sūtra II.30 and 32. The general laws are non-injury, non-theft, truth-speaking, continence and non-acceptance of gifts. The special laws are cleanliness, contentment, self-discipline (tapas), repetition (of OM and Vedic texts and hymns) and offering of one's deeds to the Lord. (384) I.e. Bh.G. V.6 (385) It has survived in Mahānārāyaṇa Upanishad 78, but Ānandagiri calls it a "Taittirīya" text, which suggests that it may have been current in that school before being embodied in an Upanishad. Ānandagiri explains that though the masculine form "Brahmā", which normally means Hiraṇyagarbha, is used, it really has the meaning of the neuter term "Brahman" (= the Absolute). D.V. Gokhale's Ed. of the

Bh.G.Bh. retains the "Brahmā" of the Upanishadic text, other editions alter it to "Brahman". (386) The Extract is from Bh.G.Bh.V.1 (introduction) and V.6 (selected passages) (387) This world, the world of the ancestors (pitṛ) and the world of heaven (svarga), lying respectively on the surface of the earth, in the "atmosphere" (antarikṣa) between the earth and the "roof" of the sky and in the invisible realm beyond the roof of the sky. They are referred to as "Bhūr", "Bhuvaḥ", "Svaḥ" respectively in the three "āḥrtis" (invocations) prefixed to the daily Gāyatrī prayer. (388) Bṛhad. I. v.16 (389) See e.g. Bṛhad. Bh. II.iv.14, trans. Mādhavānanda p.375. Cp. also the following Extract.(390) Bṛhad. Bh.IV.iv.22 (391) Bṛhad. III.v.1 (392) Bṛhad. IV.iv.22, cp. the immediately preceding Extract. (393) To be given just below. (394) See M.Bh. XII.241.1-7, G.P.Ed. Vol. III p.585 f. (395) Bṛhad. IV.v.15 *ad fin.* (396) Bṛhad. Bh. II.iv.1 (397) Bh.G.Bh. IV.11 (398) Supposed by the objector to be an authority outweighing the indirect testimony of the Upanishads. (399) See Chānd. VIII.viii.1 ff. (400) Chānd. VIII.ix.2 (401) Note the use of the past tense which confirms the view suggested above (Vol.IV p.171 f.) that the Sāṃkhya was no longer a living creative school in Śaṃkara's day (402) Intellect (buddhi), happinness, pain, desire, aversion, effort, merit, demerit and latent tendency. This Vaiśeṣika theory of the qualities of the soul has already been stated and refuted above at Vol.IV pp.236 ff. (403) The sentence satirizes the Vaiśeṣikas who, having neglected the authority of the Upanishads and failed to realize the purity, unity and infinity of the Self in their own inner mystical experience, indulge in the farce of attributing purely imaginary "qualities" to the Self and then inventing an intellectual discipline for neutralizing them. If even such reputed intellectuals as the Vaiśeṣikas are at sea when it comes to the nature of the Self, it shows that it is a difficult subject to tackle without Upanishadic guidance, and one cannot just rely on one's own interpretation of one's perceptual experiences. That Buddhists, Vaiśeṣikas and Sāṃkhyas all differ in their theories of the Self is a further argument against those theories. (404) Kumārila (Ś.V. Ātmavāda verse 147) takes the soul as imperishable in liberation. But he refers to Yājñavalkya's famous statement "There is no consciousness after death" (Bṛhad. II.iv.12) to show that it "seems like destruction." Śaṃkara of course interprets Yājñavalka's phrase differently. (405) Chānd. Bh. VIII.xii.1. On the possible reference to Gauḍapāda in the last para, cp. above, Vol.I Chapter I Note 41. (406) Kaṭha I.iii.12 (407) Reading tad-abhibhavāt with Sac. (408) The Sanskrit words enclosed in brackets are traditionally held to be etymologically related to the word "Ātman". (409) Bṛhad. IV.iv.23 (410) Kaṭha Bh. II.i.1-2 (411) Non-injury, non-theft, continence, truth-speaking, not hoarding, Y.S. II.30. (412) M.Bh. XII.175.38, G.P. Ed. (413) Quoted earlier from Jābāla Upan. 4 (414) Bṛhad. Bh. IV.v.15 (415) In this ancient expression, occurring here in the Upanishad text itself, the word "sattva" means "antaḥ-karaṇa" (= internal organ or mind). (416) Chānd. Bh. VII.xxvi.2 (417) Bh.G.Bh. III.33-34 (418) All desires are imagination projected onto the Absolute, so when the Absolute is attained, they are attained. Sac. It does not mean that the enlightened person has whims that are all fulfilled. (419) Like Ā.D.S. I.xxii.2 (420) Such "illumination" consists in the mere removal of the darkness of nescience. Cp. Bh.G. Bh. X.11, below, p.143 f. (421) I.e. tapas (self-discipline) culminating in knowledge. Sac. (422) Muṇḍ. Bh. III.ii.1-5 (423) Bh.G. Bh. XIII.7-11 (424) The word "dama" is etymologically related to Latin dominus, domus, German zähmen, French dompter, English tame, dominate, domesticate. (425) The reference is to the next verse, Bh. G. XVI.2 (426) See the following Extract. (427) Bh. G.Bh. XVI.1-4: 7-8: 18 (selected passages) (428) Śaṃkara, Adhyātma Paṭala Vivaraṇa 12-14 (429) Bh.G XVIII.15. The five factors of action are the agent, his vehicle (the body), some organ of the body to serve as instrument of the act, the various activities of the Vital Energy and a divinity presiding over the activity of the bodily organ. On the deity presiding over the bodily organ, cp. above p.53 f. (430) Bh.G. Bh. XVII. 14-16 (431) M.Bh. XII.250.4, G.P.Ed. Vol.III p.593. The Extract is from Taitt. Bh. III.1 (432) M.Bh. XII.250.4 (433) Severe fasting and other such ascetic practices were regarded as leading to the acquisition of occult powers which could be used to gain one's worldly ends. (434) I.e. the word "constant" occurs only once but must be taken as applying to everything — truthfulness, self-discipline, effort, etc. (435) Praśna I.16. The present Extract is from a Commentary on the Muṇḍaka Upanishad. If the Praśna and Muṇḍaka Upanishads are taken as parts of one text, that text must be the Atharva Veda, to which they both belong. Sac maintains that Śaṃkara is showing that on this point both the verse texts and the prose texts of the Veda agree, the Muṇḍaka being in verse, the Praśna in prose. (436) Muṇḍ. Bh. III.i.5 (437) Chānd. VIII.vii.1 ff. (438) Śvet. VI.23 (439) M.Bh. XII.204.8, G.P. Ed. Vol.III. p.539. The Extract is from Kena Bh.iv.8. (440) The reference is probably to the repetition of Vedic mantras practised as a daily duty by initiated members of the three higher castes with a view to keeping the texts alive in the memory. (441) Ā.D.S. I.xiii.4 (442) Not a transformation into the Absolute but an immediate awareness that one is and always was the Absolute. (444) Bh.G. XIII.2 (445) At Bh.G Bh. XVIII.67 (introduction) Śaṃkara calls devotion to knowledge an "actionless activity". (446) The group of qualities explained at Extract 4 above. (447) Bh.G. VII.17 (448) Bṛhad. III.v.1 (449) Mahānārāyaṇa Upanishad, Āndhra Recension, section 79. (450) *Ibid.* section 78. These same two texts are juxtaposed and quoted in the Adhyātma Paṭala Vivaraṇa (ed. Bhāgavat p.425), which is evidence for the authenticity of the latter work. (451) Bh.G. XVIII.2 (452) Ā.D.S. II.xxi.13 (453) M.Bh. XII.329.40 and 331.44, G.P.Ed. Vol.III p.692 and 694. (454) Cp. Bh.G. V.13 (455) Bh.G.Bh. XVIII .51-55 (456) Bh.G. VII.19 (457) Chānd. VII.xxv.2 (458) Chānd. VI.ii.1 (459) Chānd. VI.xxv.2 (460) External objects are perceived by the Witness mediately through the senses and mind. But the qualities of the mind, such as its pleasure-pain states, are perceived immediately and directly by the light of Consciousness as Witness. (461) The concluding remark shows that Śaṃkara classed the Lord's statement that the attainment of knowledge of the Self was easy as an "artha-vāda", a statement made to encourage the hearer to pursue a certain course. Such statements need not be literally true. So the present statement does not conflict with other statements that enlightenment is rare and hard. (462) The etymological connection of the term asura (demon) with asu = Vital

Energy is supported by modern philology. (463) Śaṃkara's use of the term bhakti is complex. At B.S.Bh. III.ii.24 he associates it with meditation (dhyāna). It was used by the later Commentator Bhāskara to imply dhyāna, as the B.S.Bh. of the latter shows at III.ii.24, saṃrādhanam bhaktir dhyānādinā paricaryyā. At Bh.G.Bh. XI.54, Śaṃkara says "exclusive bhakti" is that through which (in the end) nothing is perceived through any of the instruments of cognition (senses, mind, etc.) but Vāsudeva. At Bh.G.Bh. XIII.10, he identifies the bhakti of the text with jñāna (knowledge). At Bh.G.Bh. XIV.26 he speaks of bhakti-yoga as a preliminary to liberation, making one fit for liberation and as being "of the nature of discriminative knowledge." These texts seem to show that Śaṃkara does not allow bhakti to stand as an *alternative* path, along with knowledge, to liberation. When the passage for comment says bhakti is the means to liberation, he just says that bhakti here means jñāna. Otherwise he makes bhakti a subordinate part of the path to jñāna, interpreting it as meditation (dhyāna) or discrimination (viveka). (464) Bh.G.Bh. IX.1-3 (465) Bh.G.Bh. X.10-11. (466) Bh.G. XII.3, under comment in the present Extract. (467) As described in Bh.G. Chapter XI. (468) upa + āsana = upāsana (469) Bh.G. VII.18 (470) Bh.G.Bh. XII.1-5 (471) Bh.G.Bh. XIII.18 (472) I.e. of how a large and gross effect can proceed from a small and subtle material cause. (473) Bṛhad. I.v.3 The Extract is from Chānd. Bh. VI.vii.1-2.

CHAPTER XIII

THE VEDA AND THE TEACHER

1. THE SELF CAN ONLY BE KNOWN THROUGH THE VEDA

Chapter X contained the main passages in which Śaṃkara refuted faulty theories of liberation based on an incomplete insight into the true nature of Vedic revelation. In Chapter XI came the refutation of rationalistic world-theories by rational means. From there we passed over to the practical side of Śaṃkara's teaching, and in Chapter XII we have just seen the texts indicating the need for a spiritual path and stating the prerequisites for following it. In the present chapter we come yet closer to the culminating point of Śaṃkara's practical teaching, which will be reached in Chapter XV, and study in four sections his views about the main instrument for liberation, namely the Upanishadic texts as communicated by a competent Teacher to a qualified pupil.

In the Extracts of the first section, he establishes that the human mind cannot obtain knowledge of the true nature of the Self through recourse to the empirical means of knowledge, such as perception and inference and argument from analogy, whereas the disciplined and purified mind can be thrown into direct contact with the universal Self, present within it, through the Upanishadic texts. The second section describes the nature of Vedic revelation, and explains the role that reason has to play in its interpretation. The third section describes the nature of the competent Teacher, and the fourth section points out some of the methods the Teacher uses for interpreting the texts.

The Extracts of the present section establish the power of the Upanishadic texts to bring the mind into contact with the Self, and also explain how the empirical means of knowledge are unable to do so. They are divided into four Groups. Group A consists of two texts which bring out the limitations of reason based on sense-experience. Reason never has, never can, and never will discover unassailable truths in the metaphysical sphere, whatever its utility in discovering the laws governing the behaviour of the objects of the world. Group B (Extracts 3-7) sweeps away the pretensions of the Mīmāṃsakas, the Sāṃkhyas, the Vaiśeṣikas and the Naiyāyikas to establish the true nature of the human soul on the basis of perception combined with inference. This negative prelude is important to Śaṃkara, because, if the nature of the Self were accessible to perception and inference, it would mean that the Upanishadic texts were not an authoritative means of knowledge (pramāṇa) on this subject. For if perception and inference yielded genuine knowledge of the Self, then Vedic revelation about the Self would either agree or disagree with that knowledge. If it agreed, it would be a mere recapitulation (anuvāda) of knowledge derived from other sources, and so would not itself be an authoritative means of knowledge (pramāṇa), which, by definition, presupposes a previously unknown object; or else it would disagree, in which case the texts in question would have to be interpreted as being concerned, not with stating a truth, but with incitement to action (arthavāda). This is precisely the doctrine of the Mīmāṃsakas, who wished to eliminate the highest teachings of the

Upanishads, as it threatened the ritualism on which their livelihood depended. But for Śaṃkara perception and inference alone could not yield knowledge of the Self. Hence, for him, the Upanishadic texts proclaiming the Self were authoritative in their own right.

The Extracts of Group C (Extracts 8-17) show that when the knowledge communicated by the Teacher culminates in direct experience (anubhava) it attains a realm where the empirical means of knowledge cannot touch it, as the latter depend on the erroneous identification of the Self with the individual body and mind, which is now broken. None of the empirical means of knowledge can apply to the Self. There is no need to attempt to use them to know the Self. Nor is there any need to defend the Veda's highest teachings logically by dialectical arguments directed against the claims of sense-perception and inference, in the manner of Maṇḍana Miśra and the later Advaita dialecticians who followed him on this path. For sense-perception and inference are valid in the sphere of the experience of external objects, but not in the determination of the true nature of the inmost Self. (1) It may seem that if the Self cannot be known determinately as an object it cannot be known at all. But when the spiritual discipline has been fulfilled, when discrimination has been achieved, and when superimposition has been halted, the Self remains immediately evident in its true nature. Nothing is so close, nothing such a joy, nothing so constant and ineradicable. All possess this knowledge naturally, the only impediment to its clear and full manifestation being ignorance. Once the knot whereby the Self has become falsely identified with the not-self has been cut by the "sword" of discrimination, the not-self no longer has power to blind and delude. Śaṃkara expresses this in his Upadeśa Sāhasrī by saying, "As the ghee, once churned from the milk, cannot be dissolved back into it, so the knowing spirit in man, once it has been separated (through discrimination) from the unreal mind and body can never return to the embodied state." (2)

The Extracts of Group D answer diverse initial objections that had been raised in Śaṃkara's time. One such difficulty has already been dealt with at Volume I p.120 f. above. It is formulated as follows: "If the Absolute were unknown, no one would enquire into it. If it were known, then there would be no point in Vedic teaching on this theme." Śaṃkara replies that it is known in a general way, but that conflicting views prevail about its particular nature. In the first Extract of Group D he disposes of the argument that because the Veda is part of the world-illusion, and thus itself illusory, it cannot awaken one to reality. This objection had been raised by Kumārila even before Śaṃkara's day against those who dismissed the world as illusion (3) After Śaṃkara, Maṇḍana Miśra was to point out that illusions were not without practical efficacy in the world of empirical experience, as the illusory objects of the magician's display could inspire the same terror and joy as "real" waking objects. (4) Śaṃkara himself speaks in a similar vein of the power of illusory dream-visions to affect our waking life.

In the second Extract, a question is raised asking how, if the Absolute is beyond speech, it can be communicated by the Veda at all. This question had been raised before Śaṃkara's day by Bhartṛmitra. (5) Śaṃkara replies that it can be known through negation. It will be seen in Volume VI that he interprets even the supreme text "That thou art" as fundamentally a negation.

(XIII.1) THE VEDA AND THE TEACHER (TEXTS)

TEXTS ON "THE SELF CAN ONLY BE KNOWN THROUGH THE VEDA": GROUP A

1. Moreover, objections based on mere rational considerations should not be raised on topics which can only be known through Vedic revelation. For trains of reasoning on these topics that are not based on Vedic revelation have mere human fancy and speculation for their premises, and lack certitude, since human fancy is unbounded. The arguments of one school of philosophers, though worked out with ingenuity and diligence, are inevitably dismissed as mere pseudo-arguments by a cleverer school that comes later, while the positive arguments of the latter are invariably dismissed as pseudo-arguments by others, so that mere logical argumentation can find no final certitude anywhere, on account of the varied constitution of the human mind.

Well, you will say, why can we not regard the reasoning of Kapila (6) or of some other thinker of universally acknowledged authority as a basis for final certitude? But it is this attitude that leads to that very lack of certitude about which we are complaining. For we find that these great founders of systems, such as Kapila and Kaṇāda (7) and the rest, who are supposed to have universal authority as thinkers, hold mutually opposed views. (8)

At this point you will perhaps claim that it is possible to clear secular reason of the charge of lack of certitude by another line of argument. It is impossible, you will say, to deny that firmly founded reasoning exists in such a way that the denial will be significant. For the assertion that all trains of reasoning are unfounded will itself be grounded on reasoning. And the argument will have to rest on the assumption that, because some trains of reasoning are without foundation, all must be, since they exemplify the same process. (But in that case the argument that all arguments are uncertain must itself be uncertain.) Moreover, it cannot be claimed that all trains of reasoning are unfounded, or all worldly dealing would be at an end. For people are found to act to promote happiness and ward off suffering in the future on the assumption (based on inductive inference) that past, present and future are alike.

Nor is this all. It is by rational processes alone, you will claim, that one can determine the sense of a text when there are divergent interpretations. One has to refute the specious interpretations and establish the true meaning (through reasoning). And Manu has expressed this point in the words, "He who wishes to know the spiritual law (dharma) in its true form should apply himself diligently to perception and inference as well as to the Veda and Smṛti. He alone comes to know the spiritual law, and no one else, who investigates the spiritual teachings of the seers (ṛṣi) in the Veda with the help of reasoning that is not in conflict with the Vedic doctrine." (9)

And you may even go on to claim that the fact that reasoning has no firm foundation is really its great merit. For it means that one can always reject a faulty piece of reasoning in favour of a correct one, on the popular principle, "Just because my ancestors were crazy, it does not follow that I must be crazy too." So we must conclude that absence of total certitude is not a defect militating against the free use of reasoning.

But the Sūtra rejects this view with the words, "Because even so, there will be no escape from the difficulties." Reason, it is true, has certitude when it is used on certain topics. But in the context of the present topic there will be no escape for reason from the charge of having no certitude. For the true nature of Being, utterly transcendent as it is, and the cause of liberation from earthly existence, cannot be so much as conceived except in the light of Vedic revelation as interpreted in a traditional school. The subject-matter here is not within the realm of perception as it has no form or perceptible quality. And we have already explained how it cannot come within the purview of inference, etc., as there can be no inferential sign. (10)

And there is another point. All philosophers who treat of liberation regard it as arising from right knowledge alone. Now, right knowledge can only be one, as it is conditioned (not by subjective human will but) by the nature of its object. And only that which subsists in one (unchanged) form is ultimately real. Knowledge bearing on that is called "right knowledge" in ordinary parlance, as, for example, the knowledge that fire is hot. All this being so, it follows that where there is right knowledge there cannot be conflicting opinion. But it is very well known that conclusions arrived at from secular reason are in conflict, since they stand in contradiction with one another. And it is familiar from worldly experience that what one secular philosopher propounds as right knowledge is demolished by another, and that what he establishes is demolished by another in turn. How, then, can the conclusions of secular philosophy be regarded as right knowledge, when they belong to a domain where uniformity is not attainable?

Again, it is not true that all philosophers agree that the theory of him who maintained that insentient Nature was the material cause of the world (i.e. the theory of Kapila) is the best. So we are not on that account forced to accept his opinions as right knowledge. Nor can all past, present and future philosophers be assembled together at the same place and at the same time so that we could see if their opinions coincided on any subject to establish any universally accepted "right opinion." On the other hand, the Veda is eternal and the one source of right knowledge, and hence that which it teaches can be a fixed reality. And the fact that the knowledge to which it gives rise is right knowledge could not be refuted by all the secular philosophers of past, present and future. Hence it stands proved that the knowledge arising from the Upanishads is right knowledge. And since it is thus impossible that right knowledge should arise from any other quarter, dependence on secular philosophy would involve failure to attain release from transmigratory life. Hence it follows that the Absolute, as a conscious principle, is the efficient and material cause of the world. For this is what we learn from Vedic revelation and from reasoning conducted in conformity with the data of Vedic revelation. (11)

* * * * *

2. As for that view, mentioned earlier, that as the Absolute is already existent and complete it can be the object of the other means of knowledge (apart from Vedic revelation), that was mere wishful thinking. For the Absolute, having no colour or other perceptible quality, is not an object of perception. And because it can have no inferential signs (which are derived from the observation of regular patterns in previous perceptions), it cannot be the object of inference or of other indirect means of cognition (i.e. of any means of cognition apart from Vedic revelation). On the contrary, the Absolute, like the unforeseeable results of our future deeds, is something that can only be known from Vedic revelation. And the Veda itself says: "This insight is not to be gained through dry logic, my dear son, but only as taught by another person so as to be well understood." (12) And again,

"Who knows it well? Who is able to declare it... the source whence this creation arose?" (13) These verses of the Ṛg Veda (14) show that even perfect masters (īśvara) cannot understand the cause of the world. There are texts from the Smṛti on the subject, too, like the following: "These beings are imponderable; one should not approach them through dry logic" and "He is said to be unmanifest, unthinkable, not subject to modification" (15) and "Neither the hosts of gods nor the great ṛṣis (maharṣi) (16) know My origin; for I am Myself in every sense the origin of the gods and great ṛṣis themselves." (17)

True, it has been said that the Veda itself proclaims that reason must be respected, as it enjoins cogitation (manana) over and above hearing (śravaṇa). But this should not be used as a pretext for allowing dry logic to gain entry. For in the present context only those arguments that are sanctioned by the Veda may be resorted to, and that only as an auxiliary to the attainment of direct experience. They should run, for example, on the following lines. Since dream-experience and waking experience are mutually exclusive, they (are unreal and) do not affect the Self; and because in dreamless sleep the world-appearance is lost and one unites with the Self, the real, it follows that only the one Self exists, the real, free from the world-appearance. And because the world-appearance arises from the Absolute (brahman), it follows, from the law that effects are non-different from their material causes, that nothing other than the Absolute exists.

(Reasoning thus conceived is legitimate and even necessary;) it is the deceptive character of *purely* logical reasoning that the author of the Sūtras is going to expose in the Sūtra "Because logical argumentation has no foundation..." (18)

TEXTS ON "THE SELF CAN ONLY BE KNOWN THROUGH THE VEDA": GROUP B

3. This whole Veda is concerned only with enlightening people about the ways of obtaining the desirable and avoiding the undesirable which would not be evident from mere perception and inference. For all men naturally aim to attain the desirable and avoid the undesirable. In the case of perceptible objects, knowledge of how to obtain the desirable and avoid the undesirable comes through perception and inference themselves, so that here no one applies to revelation. But no one will wish to attain the desirable and avoid the undesirable in a future life unless he knows first that his Self (ātman) will exist in such a life, for we have the example of the Materialists (who disbelieve in any future life). Therefore the Veda deals both with the existence of the Self in a future life and also with the particular details about the means to obtain the desirable and avoid the undesirable in such a life....

If you say that a Self such as will exist in a future life is already subject to ordinary perception, that is wrong. For we see that the nature of the Self is differently conceived by philosophers of different schools. And if there were clear knowledge through perception of a Self that would also be connected with a future life, then the Materialists (lokāyatika) and Buddhists would not oppose us and deny that such a Self exists. (19) For, in the case of a pot or other object of perception, no one expresses a contradictory view and starts denying that the pot exists. Nor will it do to propose the example of mistakenly seeing a post as a man as an instance against our view. For there is no perception of a man when the post is properly perceived. There can be no dissensions about a post, etc., when such objects are properly perceived, whereas the Nihilists (Buddhist sceptics) deny the existence of a (permanent) Self existing over against any future body, though they feel themselves to be an "I" (in empirical life, just like anyone else). In fact the existence of the Self cannot be established through perception because it is outside the range of possible objects of perception, and neither can it be established through inference, for the same reason, (since reason, in Indian philosophy, depends on perception to establish a universal law). (20)

It may be objected that the Veda points to signs sufficient for an inference that the Self exists, and that these signs lie within the range of perception. But this objection is wrong, for one cannot perceive the connection of the Self with a body in a future life. The Mīmāṃsakas and Logicians, who on this point simply follow the Veda, first come to know of the Self through the Vedic revelation and through the inferential signs available in worldly experience to which the Veda draws attention. Afterwards they begin to imagine that the metaphysical significance of the ego-consciousness (ahampratyaya), which is in reality learned only through the Veda, has been discovered by themselves in their own private speculations. They then say that the Self is accessible to perception and inference. (21)

* * * * *

4. You will say that it has never been proved that all action is preceded by nescience. But this view is wrong. Though the obligatory ritual can only be known through the Veda, it can only be performed by one who is afflicted with nescience. The same rule applies in the case of the murder of a Brahmin. The fact that the murder of a Brahmin is a special kind of crime can only be known through the prohibitions found in the Veda. Even so, it is a self-injurious act, and can only be performed by one who has defects such as

ignorance and lust, as otherwise its performance is inexplicable. The same rule applies in the case of the daily and occasional rituals. (22)

Perhaps you will say that no one who does not know the Self as distinct from the body and organs can engage in the obligatory ritual. (23) But this is wrong, as people can only engage in any kind of action, which is always of the form of motion and is brought about by the not-self, with the (false) conviction "I am the agent." Nor can you claim that self-identification with the body and its organs is figurative and not false, for, if you did, it would imply that the effects produced by such a figurative entity would themselves be figurative too. (24) To explain:

The (Mīmāṃsaka) opponent's view of action is as follows. He holds that one makes a figurative self-identification with the body and its organs, and also with his possessions (and relatives), like the person in the Veda saying to his son, "My son, you are my very self," (25) or as people in the world say, "This cow is my very life." And this, he thinks, is not a false identification, the latter being what would occur when one could not perceive what distinguishes a man from a post.

All this, however, is unacceptable. A figurative conception is not intended to produce a real result. Its aim, rather, is to praise some agent by a comparison expressed without the word "like." For example, we have "Devadatta is a lion" and "The little fellow is fire." (26) The meaning is that Devadatta is *like* a lion and the little fellow *like* fire in virtue of their ferocity and bright expression respectively. It is just a piece of eulogy. It does not mean that the figurative expression implies that they can do the work of a lion or of fire. Now, a false idea will produce the real result of self-injury which one will have to experience. But in the case of a figurative notion (no self-injury is experienced, because) the one who entertains it is quite clear that his "lion" is not really Devadatta and that his "fire" is not the "little fellow".

Furthermore, action done by the figurative Self consisting in the body and its organs would not be done by the real Self (claimed by the Mīmāṃsaka opponent to be) revealed by the ego-sense. The actions of a figurative lion or figurative fire are not those performed by any real lion or fire. Nor do the "ferocity" and "bright colour" spoken of belong to any real lion or real fire and serve their purposes. They are only mentioned artificially to supply an eulogy. Those who are being eulogized well know that they are not a lion or fire, and that they cannot act like a lion or fire. If, therefore, self-identification with the body were a figurative notion, it would be more reasonable to conclude that the action of the body and its organs was not mine, that I am *not* the agent and perform *no* action. (27)...

Hence it has now been proved that total cessation of transmigratory life (saṃsāra) ensues when there is devotion to knowledge derived from renunciation of all action. And as self-identification with the body is of the nature of nescience, there can no longer be a body when it comes to an end, and hence there can be no more transmigratory experience either.

And self-identification with the body and its organs is of the nature of nescience, without doubt. In ordinary worldly life, no one who realizes that he is different from his possessions, such as cattle, and that they are different from him, proceeds to identify himself with them literally. (28)

Similarly, it is only an ignorant person

who could identify himself with the body and organs through lack of discrimination, thus making an error like a person mistaking a post for a man. One who was not afflicted with nescience and was able to discriminate could not do so.

As for the self-identification with one's son instanced by the text "My son, you are my very Self! " (29) this is figurative usage based on the (close) relation of the son and his father. This figurative self of the father can accomplish no end for him, such as eating, any more than a figurative lion and figurative fire could accomplish the results associated with a real lion or a real fire.

Here you will perhaps object that the body and its organs must be able to accomplish the ends of the real Self, even though they are only a figurative Self, as this is implied by the authority of the Vedic injunctions to perform sacrifices for the unseen gods. But this is wrong, as the body and organs are by nature figments of nescience. They are not figurative Selves (but simply illusions). For it is only through erroneous cognition that the relationless Self appears to enter into relations with anything. Relations exist only when erroneous cognition is in play, and not when it is not. It is only the naīve, undiscriminating souls in their moments of darkness who identify themselves with the body and its organs and think "I am tall" or "I am fair." But when persons of discrimination come under the conviction "I am distinct from the body and its organs," then this crude identification is not made. So the identification of the Self with the body and its organs cannot be figurative, as it is not found in the absence of erroneous cognition. A figurative notion or a figurative verbal expression can only occur when an identical element and a distinct element are separately perceived in two different subjects, as in the case of a lion and Devadatta, or in the case of fire and a young student. (30)

* * * * *

5. Here, (31) an objection is raised claiming that the identification of the Self, that stands beyond the body, with the body, as if the body were its own, is figurative and not erroneous. But this we cannot accept. For figurative, as opposed to literal, use of words is only possible when the difference between the two things denoted by the figurative and literal usage respectively is patent and familiar to all. For instance, regular concomitance shows that it is a certain figure with characteristic features like a large mane which forms the literal meaning of the word and idea "lion." And if we have cognizance of a man in whom leonine qualities such as ferocity and heroism predominate, he is nevertheless well known to be quite different and distinct from a lion.

Now, it will only be a person to whom the two entities are known to be distinct and separate who can apply the word or the idea "lion" to the man in a figurative sense. Such figurative usage cannot be applied by anyone to whom the distinction between the two entities is not clear. If the latter person applies the name or notion of one of the two entities to the other, it will be a case of erroneous judgement and not of deliberate figurative usage. It will be like the application of the name and notion "man" to a post not clearly recognized as a post in the twilight, or like the application of the name and notion of silver to a piece of nacre unwittingly mistaken for such. How, then, can one say that the word and notion "I," when applied quite literally to the bodily organism, are a case of figurative usage, when they rise from failure to distinguish the Self from the not-self? Profound scholars, no less than goatherds and shepherds, apply the name and notion of "I" to the body without discrimination, unless they have achieved practical discrimination between the Self and the not-self. Hence, those philosophers under discussion (the Mīmāṃsakas of Prabhākara's school) who maintain that there exists an eternal Self over and above the body and its organs, apply the notion of "I" to the body and organs not figuratively but erroneously. (32)

* * * * *

6. Some (the Sāṃkhyas) hold that, although the Self does not act in the literal sense, it does in some sense act by its mere presence, and this they regard as real agency on the part of the Self. We speak, for instance, of a king "fighting" on account of his mere presence, when it is his soldiers who do the actual work. Similarly, it is the king who is said to "win" or "lose". (33) And even the general commanding the troops only "acts" in the sense of using his voice, yet the results of the action mainly concern the king and the general. Again, the acts of priests officiating at a sacrifice count as belonging to the sacrificer who pays for them. In this sense, they say, the acts of the body and organs are really performed by the Self, because their results accrue to the Self. The magnet, though itself actionless, causes motion in the iron filings, and is the real agent causing their motion; and similarly, the Self is the real agent in the acts of the body and senses.

But all this argumentation is wrong, for it would make a thing that does not act into a factor of action. You may say that "being a factor of action" can take very different forms (including that of merely being present without acting). But this we cannot accept. For the king and the general are agents in the true sense. The king may (take up arms and) fight literally. He is certainly an agent in causing others to fight by giving them payment, etc. And his agency is confirmed by the fact that it is he who experiences the fruits of (the fighting in the form of) victory or loss. The sacrificer is also an agent in the literal sense, in that he himself personally places the main oblation in the fire, and also pays the priests their fees.

The truth is that to speak of something actionless as an agent is mere figurative usage. If agency in the true sense, involving personal activity, were not found in the case of the king and the sacrificer, one might have attributed it to them figuratively, as one does to the magnet. But in fact they are found to be personal agents. Hence "action" by mere proximity (such as that of the magnet or of the Self (puruṣa) as conceived by the Sāṃkhya) could only be action in a figurative sense. And this being so, the connection of the "fruits" of action with such an "agent" would be figurative also. Action in the true sense is never accomplished by anything which has existence only in figurative thought or speech. Hence the statement (of the Sāṃkhya) that the Self becomes an agent and an enjoyer of the fruits of action through the activity of the body and its organs alone is incorrect. (34)

* * * * *

7. On this point there are some people (the Naiyāyikas or Logicians of the Nyāya school) who imagine themselves to be great sages and who think, on the sole authority of the promptings of their own minds, that all the different means of knowledge are capable of being in mutual contradiction. On this basis, they attack even the Vedic doctrine of the unity of the Absolute as being in contradiction with perception and other valid means of knowledge.(35) Sound and the other sense-objects pertaining to the various different senses

are mutually distinct (our opponents say), so that the doctrine of those (i.e. of us Advaitins) who speak of the unity and sole reality of the Absolute contradicts perception. Furthermore, they infer that the souls undergoing empirical experience, apprehending the various kinds of sense-data through the various senses and doing deeds of merit and demerit, are also different from one another, and exist separately. On this ground they claim that we, who (in following the Veda) hold to the unity and sole reality of the Absolute, contradict inference also. They claim that our doctrine even contradicts the Veda itself. For they say that such passages as "He who desires to possess villages should sacrifice" and "He who desires heaven should sacrifice"show that those who desire villages, cattle and heaven, and apply themselves to the various different means enjoined for these ends, must be different from one another (inasmuch as they have different goals and pursue different means to attain them).

Our reply to this is that these men are the riff-raff of the Brahminical and other castes, whos minds have been deranged by sophistical reasoning, pitiable in condition and quite cut off from the traditional interpretation of the Veda. They say that sound and the other data perceived through the various sense-organs contradict the unity and sole reality of the Absolute. Let us ask them, however, whether the differences amongst the sense-data contradict the unity of the ether. They will say they do not (because the ether is imperceptible to the senses but is known from inference to be partless.) If this is so (on their doctrine), then why should there be any contradiction from perception (to our own doctrine, based on the Veda as revelation,that the Absolute is partless)?

Then there was that point about the souls apprehending the various kinds of sense-data through the various senses and doing righteous and unrighteous deeds, and how they were inferred to be different from each other, one to each body, so that the doctrine of the unity and sole reality of the Absolute contradicted inference also. "Inferred as different by whom?" they should be asked. No doubt we shall hear them reply, "By us, the acknowledged masters in the art of inference." But what are they going to reply if asked, "Who, exactly, are you, the masters of the art of inference?" Very likely they will begin by denying that any of the series formed by the body, senses, mind or soul, if considered separately and in isolation, possesses skill in inference, and go on to claim that they, the experts in inference, are souls *using* the body, senses and mind as instruments, since activity of any kind takes place through a number of separate factors (such as agent, object and instrument, etc.).

Well, if this be so, their skill in inference will reveal that each of them, though one, is many. For their doctrine maintains that an action requires various separate factors. And an inference is a piece of action. And their view is that an action takes place through the instrumentality of body, senses and mind, with the added factor of the soul itself as an agent. If, then, they now go on to say, "It is we who are skilled in inference, it is tantamount to the (self-contradictory) admission "Each one of us, though one, is also many, consisting of a soul associated with the instruments, the body, senses and mind." Oh! The skill in inference of these logicians, oxen lacking only tail and horns! How will he who has not the wit to know his own Self know what is distinct from it or identical with it?

What, indeed, can the Logician infer about his own Self? And on what grounds? One cannot establish the difference of the Self from anything, as there is nothing in its nature to give grounds for such a distinction. Whatever grounds they resort to in trying to prove the distinction of the

Self from anything will have name and form. Whatever pertains to name and form is but an adjunct (upādhi) of the Self (standing only in apparent and not in real relation with it), as the pot or the bowl or the separate apartment within a house or the cleft in the ground are but adjuncts of the ether or space (that do not 'enclose' it or introduce any real distinctions into it). If a person could once come to perceive a ground from which to infer the existence of distinctions in the ether, perhaps then he would be in a position to perceive a ground for inferring distinctions in the Self. (36)

When the Logicians maintain that there are distinctions (and plurality) in the Self, this is based (not on the true characteristics of the Self but) on external adjuncts. But not even a hundred Logicians together could show that there was a ground for such an inference (in any characteristic truly belonging to the Self). It is out of the question that anyone should be able to draw inferences about the Self in its true nature and say that it had distinctions, for in its true nature it is impervious to conditioning from without and is not an object of empirical cognition. Moreover, our opponents themselves maintain that whatever is accepted as an attribute of the Self consists of name and form, and they take name and form as other than the Self. And there are such Vedic passages as "The ether, verily, is that which produces name and form; that within which these two exist is the Absolute (brahman)" and "Let Me bring into manifestation name and form." (37) Name and form are subject to production and dissolution, and the Absolute is different from them by nature. So, since the Self (or Absolute) is not within the range of inference, how can it stand in contradiction with inference? This refutes the notion that there is any contradiction (in our doctrine of the Absolute) with revelation. (38)

TEXTS ON "THE SELF CAN ONLY BE KNOWN THROUGH THE VEDA": GROUP C

8. Therefore, all the Vedic injunctions and all the secular means of knowledge (39) have their scope only before the rise of the conviction "I am the Absolute." For when the non-dual Self that stands above acceptance or rejection has been known, the means of knowledge no longer have any objects to know, or any subject to employ them as his instruments.

In this connection it has been (rightly) said: (40) "When the conviction 'I am the real, the Absolute, the Self' has arisen, when sons and the body and the like have been dismissed as erroneous knowledge and there is no empirical self remaining any longer, how can there be any further action for the sake of knowledge? The 'Self' only applies means of knowledge before there is comprehension of the Self 'that has to be pursued.'

"That Self after which (in Vedanta) we enquire is indeed the same Self that applies the means of knowledge, only free from all defects and evils. Just as the notion of the identity of the Self with the body holds true until the Self has been finally realized, so do all the empirical means of knowledge hold true with it." (41)

9. But how is this state of "no-mind" achieved? The Teacher (Gauḍapāda) explains it by saying that the Self is real. He means that *only* the Self is real, as only clay is real (in the case of clay and pots). For the Veda proclaims this in the text, "A modification is a name, a mere activity of speech: the truth is, there is only clay." (42) To become awake to this through the teaching of the Veda and the Teacher is to become awake to the reality of the Self. When this occurs, there is no more imagining, and nothing to imagine, just as there can be no more burning when there is no more fuel. When this has resulted, a person is in that state of

"no-mind". And because there is nothing to perceive, his mind perceives nothing, and is without that imaginary process called perception.

But you might ask here, "If this world of duality is all unreal, then through what can one become awake to his own true nature as the unborn Self?" To this the Teacher replies as follows. The enlightened ones, he says, proclaim that the pure principle of knowledge, devoid of all false imagination, is identical with the Absolute, the highest reality, that which has to be known. No break is ever found in the knowing of the Knower, any more than there is in the heat of fire, as is proclaimed by such texts as, "The Absolute is Knowledge and Bliss" and "The Absolute is the Real, Knowledge, the Infinite." (43)

It is this knowledge which is further particularized in the text as having the Absolute for its object. That knowledge which has the Absolute for its object is itself the Absolute, non-different from the latter, as heat is non-different from fire. The Self knows itself as unborn through this eternal knowledge, which is its own nature. Like the sun, which is eternally luminous by nature, the Absolute requires no other knowledge to illuminate it, because it is a mass of eternal, homogeneous light. (44)

* * * * *

10. The Lord has said, "Hear how one realizes the Absolute." Now He goes on to describe more explicitly the nature of the realization of the Absolute that He has proposed, and begins by saying that it is the supreme perfection of knowledge. "Perfection" here means the conclusive or culminating point — the culminating point, that is, of knowledge of the Absolute. And this applies to knowledge of the Self, which in turn is the same as the Self. And what is the nature of the Self?

(XIII.1) THE VEDA AND THE TEACHER (TEXTS)

It is taught by the Lord, and by the texts of the Upanishads as interpreted through reasoning.

Now, it might be thought that all knowledge has the form of some object, and that the Self was not an object, and did not possess a form of any kind. True, there are texts which speak of the Self under a certain form, such as, "Of the colour of the sun," "Of the form of brilliance," "Self-luminous." (45) But these texts are only concerned with denying that it has the form of darkness. (46) Since all forms such as substance, attributes, etc., are denied of the Self, it might be supposed that it has the form of blind darkness, and that the texts attributing to it the colour of the sun, etc., are for the purpose of refuting this notion. And in the text "Without form" (47) there is a specific denial that it has any form. And because it is not an object of knowledge, we have such texts as "It has no form which falls within our ken. No one sees it with their eye," and "It is without sound or touch." (48) Hence it is wrong to think that knowledge ever assumes the form of the Self. How, then, can there be knowledge of the Self? All knowledge has the form of its object, as we have already said, and the Self is without form. If knowledge and the Self were both without form, how could there be meditation on the latter or perfect awareness of it?

But this whole objection is wrong. For the Self may be regarded as possessed of perfect purity, transparency and subtlety. And the intellect may be regarded as possessing comparable purity with the Self. Hence the latter may reflect the nature of the former as pure Consciousness. The lower mind receives a reflection of the intellect.(49) And the senses receive a reflection of the lower mind, and the body receives a reflection of the senses. That is why it is that ordinary people think that the body alone is the Self. The Materialists, too, who hold that consciousness resides in the body, maintain that the body, characterized as it is by consciousness, constitutes the whole man. There are others who hold that consciousness resides in the senses, others who hold that it resides in the lower mind (manas), others who hold that it resides in the intellect (buddhi). There are also some who take the Self to be the unmanifest principle interior to the intellect which is called the Unmanifest (avyākṛta) and which belongs to the realm of nescience. In all these cases, from the intellect to the body, the presence of the reflection of the Self as consciousness leads to the erroneous notion that the body, senses and lower mind *are* the Self. (50)

* * * * *

11. In this context, some people who suppose themselves to be very wise (51) say that no one can possibly have such a cognition as "I am the one Self, beyond change, void of the modification into the six states of empirical being beginning with birth (52) and not an agent," on the rise of which it is taught that one should resort to renunciation of all activity.

Such a view, however, is wrong, for it would make a mockery of texts like "It is not born." (53) Moreover, these very people (54) admit that one can come to know of the existence of merit and demerit whereby our past actions affect our future experiences, as well as of the connection of the present agent with other bodies, through the power of revelation inherent in the Veda. They should be asked why the knowledge that that same Self is ultimately beyond modification, and not an agent, should not arise from Vedic revelation in just the same way. If anyone says that the Self is beyond the reach of the mind and senses and other empirical means of cognition, this is not in every sense correct, for the Veda says, "It is to be apprehended by the mind alone." (55) The instrument for the cognition of the Self is the mind purified by resort to inner and outer control, and to the teachings of the Veda and the Teacher. Thus, when both traditional teaching (āgama) and inference (based upon it) yield knowledge of the Self, it is a mere piece of impertinence to say that knowledge of the Self is impossible. (56)

* * * * *

12. "The knower of the Absolute attains the supreme." The Absolute, to be defined later, is called "Brahman" because of its being the "greatest" (bṛhattatamatvāt) thing of all. He who knows it, attains the supreme, which is the Absolute itself. For one does not attain to one thing merely by knowledge of a different thing. And another Vedic text clearly shows that the knower of the Absolute attains to the Absolute, *viz.* "He who knows the Absolute, the supreme, becomes the Absolute." (57)

Here you will perhaps object that the text is going to say that the Absolute is already omnipresent and the Self of all, so that it is not anything that can actually *be* attained. Attainment is always found to be attainment by some finite entity of some other finite entity. But the Absolute is infinite and the Self of all. Hence it is not anything that can be attained, like a finite object which is not one's own Self.

But this objection is unfounded, because attainment or non-attainment of the Absolute depends on whether one does or does not have vision of it. From the standpoint of the highest truth, the individual is already the Absolute. But he identifies himself with the body and other finite external organs composed of the material elements. His mind becomes engrossed in these, and resembles the mind of the villager, who, engrossed in counting the number of his external confederates, failed to take note of his own Self, which would have completed the number, though he was in no way physically separate from it. Like the mind of the villager, he takes his own true Self, the supreme reality, to be non-existent. And on account of this ignorance (avidyā), he identifies himself with various external "selves" such as the physical body, and will not admit that he is anything different from the aggregate of them. In this way the Absolute remains "unattained" through ignorance, even though it is one's own Self.

Such a one, then, fails to attain to his own true nature, to his own Self, to the one thing that would complete his enumerations, through ignorance. But when he is reminded of it by anyone, he "attains" it through knowledge. Hence he may very well be said to "attain" to the Absolute, the Self of all, when he sees it as his own Self, through spiritual awakening, after being instructed by the Veda. (59)

* * * * *

13. It is, however, reasonable to take the reference to "ether" here as a reference to "the ether in the heart", as the passage is concerned with knowledge and meditation. For we know from other texts (in this context) that the term "the ether" may be used to mean "the ether in the heart." Witness, for instance, "That (gross cosmic) ether, verily, which is outside the body ... is the same as the ether which is inside the body (and the locus of dreams)" and "That ether within the heart." (60)

The Absolute rests in the "cave" of the higher aspect of the mind (buddhi), which itself lies in "the ether of the heart." (By "resting" it is not meant that it literally rests there and nowhere else). It means that the Absolute can be apprehended by a modification of the (spiritually educated) mind, as the Witness of the mind, distinct from it. (61) The Absolute cannot have a special relation with any particular space or time. It cannot literally "rest in" (be limited to) the higher aspect of the mind, or the ether in the heart, because it is all-pervading and without internal distinctions. (62)

* * * * *

14. Does it follow that nothing whatever except the Self has to be known? No. But although other things have to be known, they do not require any other knowledge in order to be known apart from knowledge of the Self. For when the Self is known, other things are known through that. (63) We shall be dealing with the objection asking how one can know one thing merely through the knowledge of another in the section relating to the drum. (64)

But why should this realization of the Self be sought? The text goes on, "As in the world by a footprint." One who seeks a lost cow may find it through its footprint: similarly, whoever has found the Self has found all (he could desire).

You will ask why it is that the use of "attaining" has been introduced, when the original proposition was only "When the Self is *known*" all else is known. But this objection does not apply, as in the present context knowledge and attaining mean the same thing. Attainment of the Self is nothing other than knowledge of the Self: attainment is not here, as it is in other contexts, attainment of something one does not already possess, because here there is no difference between the attainer and that which he wishes to attain. If the Self wished to attain the not-self, then the Self would be the attainer, and the not-self,the object of its attainment would be something not already possessed, something which yet required for its attainment some form of action, such as production. It would have to be obtained through resort to some definite act brought about by particular instruments of action. Such an object of attainment, not yet possessed, would necessarily be impermanent. It would proceed from action, which in return proceeds from desire born of wrong knowledge. Its "attainment" would be like the "attainment" of a son in a dream.

But this Self is the opposite. As it is one's own Self, it does not require any action, such as production, for its attainment. Being eternally attained by nature, the only impediment to its possession is ignorance. One may be perceiving a piece of nacre and yet not perceive it, on account of its appearing through error as a piece of silver. Here, the only barrier to possession of the nacre is wrong knowledge, and right knowledge is the only means for its attainment, because right knowledge has the quality of cancelling wrong knowledge, the obstacle to the attainment of the nacre. The same is the case with the Self. In non-attainment of the Self, the only barrier is ignorance. Therefore attainment of the Self can never be anything other than the removal of ignorance regarding it through right knowledge. That is why we shall go on to explain how any other instrument except right knowledge is useless for the attainment of the Self. (65)

* * * * *

15. The Absolute, says the text, "knows itself." It means that it knows itself as the eternal and constant Seer, bereft of the superimposed empirical vision. (66) But is this not a contradiction? For we have that other

text, "Thou canst not know the Knower of knowing." (67) We reply that it is not so, for there is no contradiction when the knowledge is of this kind. In fact the Self is known simply as the Seer (Witness) of seeing, as is also clear from the fact that it depends on no other knowledge for us to be aware of it. And, when once it has been known that the seeing of the Seer is constant and eternal, no other kind of seeing of the Seer is felt to be required. Desire for vision of the Seer as an object breaks off of its own accord, being seen to be impossible. For no desire can arise for a thing known to be impossible. The lower empirical vision, itself an object for the Seer, cannot aspire to see the Seer who sees it. Nor is there any question of the Seer desiring to act reflexively to discover His own nature. (68) Hence, when it is said that the Absolute knew itself, all that is meant is that all superimposition arising through nescience ceased. (69)

* * * * *

16. The pupil has been taught, "Thou art the Self, the Absolute, other than what can be either accepted or rejected." Lest he now think, "I have very well understood that I and I alone am the Absolute" the Teacher (in the Upanishadic text under comment) speaks further with a view to wrest the mind of the pupil away from any such idea.

Perhaps you will say that the conviction "I have very well understood" is exactly what is wanted. It is true that that conviction is wanted, but not the conviction "I have very well understood." If some knowable object were in question, then that could be "very well understood," as an inflammable object can be burnt by fire. But it must be remembered that fire cannot burn up its own nature, and that the settled conclusion of the Upanishadic teaching taken in its entirety is that the Absolute is the Self of every knower. That the Absolute is the Self of every hearer has already been taught in the present Upanishad, in the passage "The hearer of hearing..." through a series of questions and answers. And the passage beginning "That which is not declared by speech" (70) has explained the matter in more detail. The nature of the teaching embodied in the conviction of the enlightened one who has realized the Absolute has been explained in the passage "other than what is known, higher than what is unknown (the Unmanifest Principle)." And the present text is going to sum the matter up later in the words "It is unknown to those who 'know well' and known to those who 'do not know.'" Hence it was right to refute the pupil's notion "I have very well understood." For the Knower of knowing cannot Himself be known, any more than fire can be burnt by fire. (71) Nor is there any other knower separate from the Absolute, that the Absolute could be the object of his knowledge. For the text "There is no other knower but He" (72) precludes the notion that any other knower exists. Hence the idea "I have very well understood that I am the Absolute" is false. And so the Teacher was right to begin a refutation of the idea.

He begins by introducing a doubt and saying, "If by any chance you should have the notion 'I have very well understood that I am the Absolute...'". The "if" refers to the alternative, "Some intelligent people who have overcome their psychological defects can understand even a difficult matter when it is taught to them, while others do not." Now, consider here a text like "'This man (puruṣa) that is seen in the eye, this is the Self,' he said, 'this is the immortal, beyond fear, this is the Absolute.'" (73) Here we see that Prajāpati's words were misunderstood by Virocana, even though the latter was a learned being and the son of Prajāpati and the king of the Asuras (demons). On account of natural psychological defects, he acquired from this teaching the opposite conviction, namely that the Self is the body, even though this was not what had been taught. On the other hand, Indra, the king of the gods, when taught once, twice and thrice did not understand, but on overcoming his natural defects finally understood, on the fourth occasion of teaching, that same Absolute that had already been taught to him on the first occasion. And, moreover, we see, even in the case of secular teaching, that of a group of pupils listening to a teacher, some will understand what he has to say correctly and others incorrectly, while some will understand the exact opposite of what has been taught, and others will understand nothing at all. How much more will this be the case when the subject of the teaching is the Self which transcends the senses! And it is noteworthy that all rationalist philosophers contradict one another on the topic of the Self, some affirming it, while others deny its very existence. Thus, even where the statement "I have understood the Absolute" was made confidently, the Teacher (in the Upanishadic text) was only right to introduce a doubt and say "If you think..."

If you think "I have understood the Absolute very well" you only know a small aspect of the Absolute. Do we maintain that the Absolute has many aspects, some smaller, some greater, that we say "a small aspect"? Yes, we do. The Absolute has many aspects, engendered through the adjuncts of name and form, though it has none in itself. In regard to its intrinsic nature, the text "That which is without sound, without touch, without colour, indestructible, without taste, eternal, without odour" (74) denies all visible form of it, along with sound and other sensed qualities.

Now, you might raise an objection here and

say that whatever quality (dharma) characterizes a thing constitues its essential nature, so that we must conclude that whatever particular quality was used to define the Absolute constitutes its essence. Consciousness, you might further argue, is neither a quality of earth nor of any of the other elements or of the forms into which they evolve. Nor is it a quality of the sense of hearing, or of any of the powers of perception, or of the mind (antaḥ-karaṇa). Hence, consciousness is the form of the Absolute, and the Absolute is constituted of consciousness. And the nature of the Absolute is in fact described in this way by the Vedic texts, for instance in "The Absolute is Consciousness and Bliss", "A mass of Consciousness only", "The Absolute is the Real, Knowledge, the Infinite" and "The Absolute is Consciousness". (75)

All this is very true. But the Absolute is referred to by such words as "Consciousness" (vijñāna) only in virtue of its external adjuncts, such as the mind, the body and the sense-organs, that is to say, because it seems to conform to the various vicissitudes of the body, sense-organs and mind, such as growth, contraction, being cut off and undergoing destruction. But it is not referred to as "consciousness" in its own right. It will be shown below that the formula that applies to the Absolute in its true nature is "Unknown to those who know, known to those who do not know."

Where the text goes on to speak of "the aspect of this Absolute (amongst the gods,)" this has to be completed by what has gone before, namely, ("is little.") It is not only that you know little when you know the form of this Absolute as limited by the adjunct of the individual soul. One must go further. My view is (says the Teacher in the Upanishadic text) that the aspect of the Absolute which you recognize in the gods is something small too.

It is the form apparently assumed by the Absolute when the latter is viewed as limited by the adjuncts of the divine cosmic powers. This form, too, because limited by external adjuncts in the form of the divine cosmic powers (deva), does not escape the epithet "small". The implication here is that the Absolute (in its true nature) is void of any kind of adjunct, for it is of the nature of peace, it is infinite and non-dual, it is called "abundance" (bhūman), it is not open to being known as an object. "This being so," the Teacher observes, "I think your present ideas require further investigation."

Thus addressed by the Teacher, the pupil went away and sat down in a lonely spot, collected his mind in inner contemplation and began to reflect deeply on the content of his preceptor's teaching, brought reasoning into play, and was eventually visited with some direct experience. Then he went back into the presence of his Teacher and said, "I think I have now understood the Absolute."

The Upanishad next goes on to explain in what sense the pupil thought he had understood. "I do not think I know it completely," he said. But when the Teacher said, "Then you do not know it at all," he replied, "It is not that I do not know it: I do know it, and yet (I do not know it)." Here the words in the text "and yet" imply "and yet I do not know it."

The Teacher then proceeds as follows: Is it not a contradiction (he asks) to say, "I do not think I know it completely; it is not that I do not know it; I do know it, and yet I do not know it"? If you do not think you have known it completely, how can you also say that you know it? If, on the other hand, you think you know it, how can you also think you do not know it? It is a contradiction for a person who knows something to say that he does not know it properly, unless by "knowing" it he only means doubt or wrong knowledge. But it is not possible to speak of knowing the Absolute if doubt or wrong knowledge are in play. Doubt and wrong knowledge are everywhere acknowledged as sources of evil.

But even under this cross-examination on the part of the Teacher the pupil did not waver. For he was now in possession of the traditional instruction of the Teacher to the effect that the Absolute is other than what is known and higher than what is unknown (i.e. higher than the Unmanifest Principle), (76) which he had moreover confirmed both by abstract reasoning and by direct personal experience. On the contrary, he roared out in a loud voice to show how complete was his conviction that he had gained knowledge of the Absolute (brahma-vidyā). And what he roared out was, "Whoever else amongst us Brahmacārī pupils clearly understands what I say knows the Absolute." "Well then," says the Teacher, "what is it you say?" "What I say is, 'It is not that I do not know. I know and yet (I do not know)'." The Teacher had said, "It is other than what is known and higher than what is not known (the Unmanifest Principle)." The pupil, in saying "It is not that I do not know. I know and yet (I do not know)," was in substance repeating this, only in different language, and backed by the combined reinforcement of abstract reasoning and concrete personal experience. His purpose was to show the affinity he had attained with the Teacher's own standpoint, and to show how he rejected the constructions that the less gifted pupils might have put on the Teacher's words. Hence he was quite justified in exclaiming emphatically "Whoever amongst us know this, knows truly."

At this point the text discontinues the framework of an imaginary conversation between a Teacher and a pupil, and presents the conclusion of the whole conversation in its own words. He who, while knowing the Absolute, cherishes the conviction that he does not know it (as an object), he has right knowledge of the Absolute. But he, on the other hand, who cherishes the conviction that he knows the Absolute (as an object) does not in fact know it.

The text then goes on to specify more clearly the views of those who do and those who do not know the Absolute. Those who in fact know the Absolute feel that they do not know it determinately. Those who feel that they have determinate knowledge of the Absolute do not in fact have right knowledge of it. In practice, the latter take the senses, mind and intellect for the Self. The Upanishad refers to them as "knowers" because those whose minds are completely undeveloped do not (even) acquire the (faulty) conviction "We have known the Absolute." But the case of those who take the senses, mind and intellect for the Self is different. They are aware of such adjuncts as the intellect, etc. But they fail to distinguish these adjuncts from the Absolute. Hence, they acquire the erroneous conviction, "We have known the Absolute." Their view is therefore expounded as a preliminary hypothesis, which is later to be rejected through the words "Those who feel that they have determinate knowledge of the Absolute do not in fact have right knowledge of it." Or it may be that the phrase "those who feel that they have determinate knowledge of the Absolute do not in fact have right knowledge of it" is primarily a statement of the reason why the following phrase ("Those who in fact know the Absolute feel that they do not know it determinately") is true.

It has been shown how the Absolute is not determinately known by those who know it. Now, if the Absolute were *entirely* unknown there would be no difference between knowers of the Absolute and materialists of the world. And again, the statement, "Not known to those who know it" seems to be a self-contradiction. To answer the question "In what sense is the Absolute truly known?" the text says, "Known through every cognition." Cognition" here means the mental presentations. The Self which takes all mental ideas for its object illumines all cognitions. It is pure Consciousness in its true form. It is revealed by the cognitions as that which is non-different in each. There is no other way to have knowledge of the inmost Self but this.

When, therefore, the Absolute has been "known" as the inmost Self witnessing the stream of mental ideas, then, says the Upanishad, it is apprehended, that is to say, rightly known. Since it is the principle that beholds all mental presentations, it follows that it is the essence of pure Consciousness, which neither rises nor falls, which is eternal, pure, the Self as a metaphysical principle (tattva), undifferentiated, and one and the same in all beings. For it has no characteristics which introduce distinctions into it anywhere, being in this respect like the one ether of space spread out equally in (small cavities like) pots and (large ones like) mountain caves (and not differentiated by any of them). Hence the present text elucidates and sums up the statement of the earlier text which said that the Absolute was other than what was known and higher than the unknown. And it is confirmed by that other text, "The seer of seeing, the thinker of thinking, the knower of knowing." (77)

But what if the word "knowledge" were here interpreted in a different way to mean the act of knowing? It would then be that, given the fact of the act of knowing, one reasoned from that to affirming the existence of an agent for each act of knowing, in the same sort of way that one says "That which sets the branches of the trees in motion is the wind." (78) The Self would then be a substance, possessed of the active power of knowing: it would not be the very essence of Consciousness. Empirical cognitions, however, rise and pass away. Whenever, therefore, an empirical cognition arose, the Self, as agent in the act of knowing, would undergo a modification through performance of that act. And whenever an empirical cognition passed away, then the Self, now bereft of that empirical cognition, would stand undifferentiated as a mere (non-conscious) substance. In these circumstances it would be impossible to avoid imputing to the Self a nature subject to modification, resolution into parts, non-eternity, impurity and other defects.

The Vaiśeṣikas regard empirical cognition as arising with "intimate inherence" (samavāya) in the Self, but only through the contact of the mind with the Self. For them, therefore, the Self is the knower, and yet it does not undergo modification. They regard the Self as a mere substance, in which empirical cognition "inheres" in the same sense that dye (rāga) "inheres" in a pot (though distinct from the pot). Even on this view, Upanishadic texts such as "The Absolute is Consciousness and Bliss" and "The Absolute is Consciousness" (79) would stand contradicted, as the Absolute would be a mere non-conscious substance (in which consciousness "inhered", but as something distinct). Moreover, in the theory of the Vaiśeṣikas the Self is (all-pervading and) without parts. Since it therefore contains no particular places, the mind must be in constant connection with it. This being so, it is impossible to explain memory. (80) Again, the hypothesis that the Self is a substance that enters into external relation with any other principle (in this case the mind) stands in contradiction with the teaching of the Veda and Smṛti, also with reason. As regards the Veda and Smṛti, we have texts such as "It is relationless, for it does not enter into relations" and

"Unrelated, the support of all." (81) As for reason, it establishes the principle that only that which has empirical attributes can enter into relation with another thing that has empirical attributes. To say, therefore, that that which is without empirical attributes, undifferentiated, and distinct in all respects from everything else, enters into relation with something else which (does have empirical attributes and) is (therefore) incommensurable with it, is to contradict reason. Hence we must conclude that, if the Self is to be taken as that which illumines all cognitions, this can only be done if it is taken as the Self which is the light of eternal and unbroken Consciousness by very nature. The text, therefore, which says that the Self is rightly understood when it is known as that which illumines all empirical cognitions must be understood as we ourselves have explained it.

Another attempt has been made to explain the words "known in every empirical cognition" as meaning that the Self is known to itself. Here the Self is taken in association with its external adjuncts. The Self imagines the distinctions through assuming the form of the intellect and other adjuncts, and has the experience of "knowing Himself through Himself," as in such texts as "The Self sees Himself in Himself" and "Thou, the supreme Spirit, knowest Thyself through Thyself." (82) But the Self as void of all adjuncts can be known neither by itself nor by another, because it is one and is the sole reality. As it is of the very nature of knowledge, it cannot depend on any knowledge, any more than a light can depend on another light.

If, on the other hand, an attempt were made to establish that the Self knew itself in the sense (implied by the doctrine of the self-luminosity of momentary cognitions) held by the

Buddhists, then Consciousness would turn out to be subject to destruction every moment and to have no Self at all. But this would contradict such Vedic texts as "No break is found in the knowledge of the knower, as it is indestructible," "Eternal, omnipresent, all-pervading," "Verily this great unborn Self is ageless, deathless, imperishable and beyond fear." (83)

* * * * *

17. Only a knower which, like the mind, depends on instruments (84) for its cognition of objects (and is consequently an agent), and which knows but a limited portion of the knowable field, can be subject to change (pariṇāmin). (But the Self as Witness is knowledge absolute, not an agent and not subject to any change.)

The conviction "I am the Witness" can belong only to the intellect; it cannot belong to the Witness because the latter has no (internal) distinctions and nothing beyond it. (85) It is not, however, to the ego as agent that the experience of liberation falls, for freedom from pleasure and pain is impossible in the case of the ego as agent. In this situation (i.e. at the time of liberation) the non-discriminatory notion "I am the sufferer," arising from self-identification with the body, etc., is permanently cancelled by the discriminatory notion revealing one's identity with the inmost Self, just as the notion "I am the one with the ear-rings" is permanently cancelled (when one takes them off). (86) This discriminatory notion must be admitted to cancel the non-discriminatory one, (87) for if the reverse were to occur, we should have a means of knowledge that led to the unreal and so was no means of knowledge. (88)

TEXTS ON "THE SELF CAN ONLY BE KNOWN THROUGH THE VEDA": GROUP D

18. But how (an objector might ask) can the texts of the Upanishads, being unreal, (89) communicate the knowledge that the Self is the Absolute, which is a truth? No one bitten by a rope-snake (90) dies. Nor does the water of a mirage serve for drinking or for bathing.

But the Advaitin replies that there is nothing wrong in his position. For we see that results, such as death, do in fact flow from merely mental causes, such as grief and despair. And we also see that the bite of a snake and bathing in water produce results (dream-results) in the case of one who is in the state of dream. You might say that these results, too, were illusory. Well, we admit that the effects produced by the bite of a snake and bathing in water and the like in the case of someone dreaming are illusory. But the consciousness (avagati) whereby they were known was real, because it is not contradicted on awakening. (91) One who awakes from a dream will no doubt come to think that the effects of the snake-bite, and of bathing in water and the like, that he beheld in dream, were illusory. But he will never think that the consciousness whereby he beheld them was illusory. And one might add that the fact that the consciousness which enabled the dreamer to see his dream is not cancelled or contradicted *as consciousness* (in the waking state) refutes the view that the Self is none other than the body. (92)

The Veda also teaches that one may come to know of real (future) success through dream-visions that are in themselves illusory, as in the text, "If a person sees a woman in his dream while he is in the course of performing optional rituals for an individual end, he should see the success of his ritual prefigured in the dream-vision." (93) And another text, after mentioning certain objects of ill-omen in waking perception as signs that one will not live long, goes on to show that death, as a reality, can be indicated by unreal dream-visions, in the subsequent passage beginning "But when in dream one sees a dark man with black teeth who kills him (the dreamer)...". (94) And it is a well-known fact in the world that the experts in enquiry by the method of agreement and difference are prepared to say that such and such a dream-vision is auspicious and such and such another inauspicious. And, in the same order of ideas, we see that there can be knowledge of sounds, which are (eternal) realities, through the vision of lines (i.e. written letters), which cannot truthfully be identified with sounds. (95)

Further, the means of knowledge (*viz.* the Upanishadic text) which reveals the sole existence of the Self is an "ultimate" means of knowledge. Nothing further is required after it. For example, when the phrase "One should perform ritual" arises in the ordinary course, further questions arise, such as "Who should perform it?" and "What ritual should he perform?" But when "That thou art" or "I am the Absolute" (96) are uttered, nothing further is required to be known, as this knowledge bears on the identity of all with the Self. Nor can it be denied outright that any such knowledge can arise, as we have such Vedic texts as "Then he understood it from him." (97)

That this knowledge can be attained also follows from the fact that the means to it, such as hearing of,(cogitation over and sustained meditation on) the Upanishadic texts, are enjoined. Nor can it be claimed that this knowledge is either useless or erroneous. For it is seen to have the fruit of putting nescience to an end, and we find that no further knowledge comes to contradict it afterwards. And we have already explained how all practical experience and Vedic teaching either holds true or turns out to be false in its ordinary nature as empirical experience before the rise of the knowledge of the sole reality of the Self. But when one has learned from the ultimate means of knowledge that only the Self exists, then all previous experience of distinctions is contradicted and cancelled. And from then on there is no longer any room for the vain supposition that the Absolute has any plurality in its nature. (98)

* * * * *

17. And because the Absolute has no particular characteristics, the Veda indicates its nature by denying of it the forms of all other things, as is shown, for instance, in the following passages: "And so, therefore, the teaching is 'Not this, not this'", "It is other than what is known, and higher than what is unknown", "That from which speech turns back, without reaching it, together with the mind." (99) And the Vedic texts (100) also relate how when Bādhva was questioned by Bāṣkalin he gave his answer merely by not speaking. "Sir, teach me in words," Bāṣkalin said. But the Teacher remained silent. Finally at the second or third time of asking, Bādhva replied, "I am telling you, but you do not understand. This Self is silence."

And in the same way, in the Smṛti, the Absolute is taught by mere negation, as for example in such passages as, "I will tell thee what thou hast to know, knowing which thou wilt attain immortality. The beginningless Absolute (brahman) in its highest form is not said to be real or unreal." (101) And in the same way we have the further text (from the Smṛti) (102) in which Nārāyaṇa, putting on the form of the entire universe, spoke to Nārada and said, "O Nārada, this is a mere illusion (māyā) projected by Myself, whereby you see Me associated with the attributes of all creatures. Do not suppose that this is my true nature." (103)

2. THE VEDA, SMṚTI AND REASON

The Extracts of this section are divided into five groups. Group A deals with the manner in which the Veda is manifested. In Śaṃkara's doctrine, it is projected anew by the Lord at the beginning of each new world-period, and then "seen" or "discovered" by great sages (maharṣi) projected by the Creator at the beginning of the world-period, who mediate and preserve it for mankind. (104) Historians today tell us that the earlier poets of the Ṛg Veda regarded the hymns as their own handiwork, their own creation and personal offering to the deity they were addressing. (105) But Śaṃkara quotes a "late" Ṛg Veda text revealing a different conception. "They sought the traces of (the eternal deity) speech through sacrifice, and found her already resting with the Seers." (106) This view that the Ṛṣis "saw" or "mediated" the texts of the Veda in moments of high inspiration, and did not compose them, is associated with the doctrine that the Veda and all its texts are eternal. It goes back to Jaimini's Pūrva Mīmāṃsā Sūtra, and had been elaborated by the Mīmāṃsaka Śabara before Śaṃkara's day. (107) It was accepted by Śaṃkara, but modified in accordance with the doctrine that the Veda and the world emanate from the Lord anew at the beginning of each world-period, a doctrine to which the Mīmāṃsakas, as we have seen, did not subscribe. Extract 3 in the present group shows how Śaṃkara accepted the teaching of the Chāndogya Upanishad that the Vedic texts were communicated by Brahmā to Manu, who, in turn, passed them on to men. As he also maintained that they were eternal, it must have been his view that the communication of the eternal texts to Manu took place at the beginning of each world-period (kalpa), though this is not implied by the Chāndogya text quoted. The final Extract in this group shows that, in Śaṃkara's view, the world is projected *in accordance with* the thoughts expressed in the words of the Veda, but that it is not a mere materialization of those words in time.

Group B explains how the Veda is an authoritative source of knowledge of the Self, and how this teaching, though it ultimately cancels the notion that the Self is an agent, does not undermine the authority of the injunctions and prohibitions of the Veda in the practical sphere. Group C shows how the texts of the Smṛti and the assertions of reason are authoritative only if they do not contradict the Veda as interpreted by a traditional school. Group D explains how, and to what extent, reasoning by analogy with experience can be used to confirm and interpret the Veda. Extract 4, the last, is important as modifying somewhat the stance taken at Extract 11 in Group C, according to which, the Smṛti, as opposed to the Veda, was composed by fallible humans, and must be rejected or re-interpreted when it contradicts Vedic teaching. In this later Extract it is claimed that the authors of the Smṛti, and yogīs generally, may have or have had extraordinary experiences inaccessible to lesser mortals. We are not entitled to reject their statements out of hand.

The texts of Group E declare that the Veda is the "final" authoritative means of knowledge (pramāṇa), in the sense that when its final message is not merely understood but known in immediate intuition (anubhava) all other means of knowledge (such as perception, inference and so forth) stand negated. As the notion of a real connection between the Self and an individual body and organs of knowledge is then negated, the active personality, the "agent and enjoyer," is himself dissolved. There is no longer a knower, and even the Veda is itself no longer a means of knowledge. In his Brahma Sūtra Commentary, (108) Śaṃkara abstracts the Upanishadic text "There the

Veda becomes no Veda" (109) from the context of dreamless sleep and applies it to the state of enlightenment generally.

What makes the Veda authoritative is not, as the Mīmāṃsakas would have it, the fact that it gives commands, but rather the fact that it gives fruitful knowledge not available from any other source. Śaṃkara's views on the relation between the Veda and the Smṛti are worth noting. For him, the "Veda" includes all the "Brāhmaṇas" or prose passages traditionally handed down by the various Vedic schools, along with the hymns (mantra, verse, sūkta, hymn). In other words, for him "Śruti" consists collectively of the Vedas, Brāhmaṇas, Āraṇyakas and Upanishads. The Smṛti includes mainly the Sūtras or aphorisms composed to summarize the rules of ritual, the classical treatises on the auxiliary sciences needed for practising the Vedic ritual, like Grammar, Prosody and Astronomy, and also the Law Books (dharma-sūtra), the Epics (itihāsa) and the Purāṇas. Śaṃkara quotes from Jaimini's Pūrva Mīmāṃsā Sūtra I.iii.3 the rule that a text from the Smṛti may be assumed to be a human tradition preserving a lost piece of Vedic teaching when (but only when) it does not conflict with known Vedic doctrine. (110) But, whereas the Veda is the outbreath of the Lord and infallible (it is only *mediated* by the ṛṣis), the Smṛti stems from fallible humans. Where two Vedic texts conflict, one must be treated as metaphorical. Where two Smṛti texts conflict, the case is different. If neither conflict with the Veda, one may apply the maxim that the *unintelligible* one is to be accepted, (111) as this saves the authority of both texts, since the intelligible one may be applicable in some other context. But, for Śaṃkara, nothing can save a doctrine, such as the dogmatic dualism attributed to the sage Kapila, which conflicts with the Upanishadic texts teaching that the Self is non-dual. The parts of it that conflict with Upanishadic Advaita have to be rejected. Nor can one accept that the Upanishadic texts have to be interpreted in accordance with the tenets of the dualistic form of the Sāṃkhya system merely because the latter are attributed to a Vedic sage of the name Kapila. (112)

Śaṃkara adhered to the principle that before enlightenment all means of knowledge were authoritative within their respective spheres (sva-viṣaya). (113) Thus the Vedic hymns, the eulogistic passages of the Veda and the texts of the Epics and Purāṇas are all to be regarded as having authority and value, though they have to be interpreted metaphorically if their literal meaning would conflict with common experience in an area (such as that of perception) where the latter was valid, or else if they conflicted with other Vedic teaching properly interpreted and understood. True, as emanating from mere *men*, the texts of the Smṛti require to be confirmed by the Veda, and cannot be accepted if they contradict it. But extraordinary statements made in such texts may rest on the direct perception of the men who made them. Take the traditions that the gods have real bodies, contested by the Mīmāṃsakas. (114) We are told that Vyāsa and other authors of the Smṛti were able to converse with the gods and actually see them, and we ought not to disbelieve this merely because humans are no longer able to achieve this feat. (115) Even the common beliefs of mankind (loka) on supersensual matters have *some* weight, and should not be rejected unless there is some reason for doing so. (116)

It remains to say a word on the relation of revelation to reason and other means of knowledge. We have seen that before enlightenment each means of knowledge is authoritative in its own sphere (sva-viṣaya). A means of knowledge is only authoritative in that area into which it alone can penetrate, not where it can only confirm knowledge obtainable by more direct means, the most direct always being immediate perception. This means that the Veda is not an authoritative means of knowledge in matters covered by sense-perception. (117) Śaṃkara here follows the established Pūrva Mīmāṃsā view. As Śabara had said that one could not accept the Veda as an authority if it said "Gourds sink while stones float,"(118) so Śaṃkara remarks that not even a hundred Vedic texts could make fire cold. Sense-perception, however, can bear only on the elements which compose matter, which are of the same composition as the sense-organs. (119) And inference, except when applied to the data of revelation, depends entirely on perception and can never contradict it.

Inference, for Śaṃkara, depends on an inferential sign (liṅga). A sign in this sense is a perceived object known according to laws derived inductively from previous sense-experience to be invariably concomitant with (literally, to "pervade") another object, as smoke is a sign of fire. But the Absolute in its true form is not an object of sense-experience, because it has no colour or other sensible quality. (120) And hence it is not subject to inference conducted independently of the revealed texts. For the fact that it is beyond sense-experience means that it cannot have an inferential sign. (121) G.V. Devasthali is therefore correct to point out that the opponent at Brahma Sūtra Bhāṣya II.i.4 (122) is wrong in principle to raise the question of the relative strengths (balābala) of perception and inference against Vedic revelation in the matter of knowledge of the Absolute, as in this area perception and inference, considered as independent sources of knowledge, have no scope *at all*. We cannot here even argue by analogy with experience (sāmānyato-dṛṣṭa). (123) And again, it is wrong to suppose you can use inference to *prove* the truth of the Vedic dicta about the Absolute, as if the Veda depended on any external support for its authority, in the manner of a human speaker, or as if its authority as an independent means of knowledge would not be undermined if it did. On these points Śaṃkara differs slightly from his contemporary, Maṇḍana Miśra. Maṇḍana envisages the possibility of a conflict between the metaphysical teachings of the Upanishads and the deliverances of sense-perception, and claims that the Veda constitutes a "higher" or "more powerful" (balavān) authority. Hence we find attempts in the works of Maṇḍana, and of many post-Śaṃkara Advaitins, who followed Maṇḍana on this point, to prove *a priori* that perception cannot supply genuine knowledge of difference. No such attempt is found in the works of Śaṃkara, and it would not be required from his standpoint. But Śaṃkara and Maṇḍana are at one in holding that there can be no knowledge of the Absolute except through the Upanishadic texts. (124)

Śaṃkara, however, evidently makes a copious use of inference in his own interpretations of the Vedic texts. What, according to him, is its scope? It protects the student from wrong ideas, by subjecting them to criticism. (125) It is used, in an extension and modification of the methods of the Pūrva Mīmāṃsakas, to harmonize the texts, in a way which has continually been exemplified throughout the course of the present book, but of which some particularly explicit examples will be given in the final section of the present chapter. But beyond these methods of harmonizing the texts, that derive from the Pūrva Mīmāṃsā, Śaṃkara also made use of what Saccidānandendra Svāmin has called "a unique principle of interpretation which deserves specially to be kept in view." (126) The reference is to the principle that Vedic revelation on the subject of the Self is incomplete as long as it remains a matter of mere faith — it must culminate in direct experience. (127) Since the part of the Vedic revelation that teaches the true nature of the Self can only be said to have been truly understood when it culminates in immediate experience (anubhava), a special kind of critical reflection and counter-suggestion is required to negate the firmly entrenched prejudices arising from the natural experience of duality. One has to use reason to reflect critically on the implications of one's ordinary secular experience in the light of the Upanishadic texts communicated by the Teacher. More light on the nature of this process will be thrown by the Extracts in Volume VI Chapter XV, sections 3 and 4.

TEXTS ON THE VEDA, SMṚTI AND REASON: GROUP A

1. Now begins the explanation of speech (vāk). Speech (in the broad sense) includes any phoneme, such as a vowel or consonant, pronounced by living creatures with the help of the palate or other resonant organ, and also other sounds, such as those issuing from a musical instrument or a cloud.

So much for the nature of speech (which includes all sound as such). But what is its use? It serves to communicate a meaning. Because it illumines a meaning, it cannot itself be illumined, as it is itself of luminous nature, like a lamp or other instrument of illumination. No light or other instrument of illumination can be illumined by any other light; and, in the same way, speech illumines and therefore cannot itself be illumined. By accepting this view, the Veda avoids an infinite regress. Illumination is the only function of speech. (128)

* * * * *

2. And the authoritative treatises of Śaunaka and other (authors of Prātiśākhyas) (129) teach that the various groups of ten hymns in the Ṛg Veda (after first being entrusted to Hiraṇyagarbha) were seen by the seers (ṛṣi) such as Madhuchhandas (130) and the rest. And the Ṛṣi presiding over each section (kāṇḍa) of each Veda is mentioned in

the supporting literature. The Vedic teachers themselves proclaim that one should only recite the hymns if one knows the name of the seer, in the passage which begins, "Whoso, verily, employs a Vedic verse in a sacrifice or teaches anyone to recite it without knowing who its seer was, its metre, its presiding deity and its proper ritual application, will either bump into a tree-stump or fall into a ditch," and which concludes, "Therefore one should know these in the case of each verse." (131)

* * * * *

3. The words "This, verily," occurring in the text refer to this teaching of Self-knowledge with its accessory parts, beginning with the words "This syllable OM," (132) that has been given with all its subsidiary meditations and its eight chapters, by Brahmā or Hiraṇyagarbha, which term may here stand for the supreme Lord, to Prajāpati, that is to say to Kaśyapa. He gave it to his son Manu, and Manu gave it to men. The Vedic teaching has been handed down traditionally in this way, and is still so understood to this day by those who possess the true wisdom. (133)

* * * * *

4. The author of the Sūtra now strengthens his claim that the Veda is eternal in the words, "And this shows that it is eternal." "This" means the fact that the fixed, eternal specific forms (ākṛti) of the gods and the world arise from the words of the Veda. From this fact, we conclude that the words of the Veda, too, must be eternal. And in support of this there is a Ṛg Vedic verse, "They sought the traces of (the eternal deity) Speech through sacrifice, and found her already resting within the Seers (ṛṣi)," (134) which shows that the deity Speech (vāc) was *already*

existent (and hence fixed and eternal). And Veda Vyāsa (the author of the Vedas and Purāṇas) records the same thing in the Smṛti in the words, "After performing austerity and acquiring the permission of Brahmā, the great (ṛṣi) received the Vedas, along with the Epics, which had disappeared at the end of the previous world-period." (135)

* * * * *

5. Further, the doctrine that the world arose from the words of the Veda does not mean that the latter were its material cause, in the sense that it is held that the world arose from the Absolute as its material cause. All that the phrase "arising from the words" means is that an individual, subject to designation by words, can only come into being if words are already established in eternal relation with their meanings.

But how do we know that the world "arises" from the words at all? Through "perception" and "inference," says the author of the Sūtras. "Perception" (pratyakṣa) here means the Veda, because it is dependent on nothing external for its authoritativeness. "Inference" (anumāna) means the Smṛti, because the latter is dependent on an external authority (*viz.* the Veda) for its own authoritativeness. Both these authorities (the Veda and the Smṛti) exhibit creation as based on words.

There are several texts in the Veda which teach that creation is associated with words, as, for instance, "Prajāpati projected the gods remembering the word "these" in the Vedic text, he projected men remembering the words "are pressed", he projected the ancestors (pitṛ) remembering the word "drops (of Soma)", he created the demons remembering the words "through the sieve", the hymns of praise remembering the word "swift", the spoken prayers remembering the word "all", and he projected all other creatures remembering the word "joys"; (136) or again, (we have the text) "He brought about the union of Speech (vāc) with mind."(137) The Smṛti, too, says the same thing, as in such a text as "Beginningless, endless and eternal is the Speech uttered forth by the self-existent one (brahmā) of old— that divine Speech consisting of the Vedas, from which all actions proceed." (138) This "uttering forth" is to be understood as no more than the revivification of an already existent tradition (sampradāya), (139) as the "uttering" of Speech cannot be conceived otherwise if that Speech is beginningless and endless. Hence (the next verse follows), "That great Lord created in the beginning the name and form of beings and (the injunctions containing) prompting to act." (140) Manu Smṛti also says, "In the beginning He (Hiraṇyagarbha) created all the separate names and forms and deeds (karma) of all creatures in accordance with the words of the Veda, as well as their different forms." (141)

(Perception and inference may also be taken to prove the same point in another way, that is, if we take the direct and normal meaning of these terms). It is a matter of common perception that someone who wishes to produce some desired effect invariably calls the name for it to mind before setting about the necessary work. From this we conclude (by inference through analogy) that in the case of Prajāpati, the Creator, too, the words of the Veda appeared first in His mind, and that He projected the universe in accordance with them afterwards. Thus, the Veda says, "He cried 'Bhūḥ' (this lower earth) and projected the earth (bhūmi). (142) Passages like this show that planes of being such as "the earth" were created as a result of the words "bhūḥ," etc., that arose in the mind of the Creator. (143)

TEXTS ON THE VEDA, SMṚTI AND REASON: GROUP B

6. You might object that if texts like "The Absolute is one only, without a second" (144) were mere statements of fact, not associated with any injunction, they would lose all authority, (145) on the analogy of the mythological passages of the Veda like, "So he wept, and because he wept (arodīt) he became known as Rudra." (146) Here (the opponent might claim) we are not obliged to take the statements literally because they are merely concerned with reporting matters of fact (and do not enunciate commands). And the same, he would say, is true of the texts proclaiming the existence of the Self.

But this view is wrong, as it neglects an important distinction. It is not the question of whether a text proclaims a matter of fact or enjoins an action that settles whether or not it is authoritative. The real test that has to be applied is, "Does it produce knowledge that is of undeniable practical benefit to man?" Texts that do so are authoritative, texts that do not do so are not.

We ask you, therefore, "Do the texts which proclaim the true nature of the Self produce indubitable and fruitful knowledge or do they not?" If they do, how can they help being authoritative? Have you not seen examples of the fact that knowledge of the Self results in the benefits of cessation of nescience, grief, delusion and fear, and all the other defects which cause continuation of transmigratory life? Even if you have not, are you not acquainted with hundreds of Upanishadic texts proclaiming that this is the case, such as, "Where, then, is delusion, where is grief for the one who sees the unity of all?" (147) and "I am only a knower of the texts, my lord, not a knower of the Self. Hence I grieve. Take me beyond grief, my lord." (148) Now, we ask of you, do we find the same indubitable and beneficial knowledge in the texts like "He wept"? If we do not, let us by all means dismiss the latter as inauthoritative. But why should it follow that just because *they* are not authoritative, texts which produce indubitable and beneficial knowledge should be inauthoritative? And if the passages which produce indubitable and beneficial knowledge are not to be regarded as authoritative, what faith can there be in the texts enjoining the performance of the New and Full Moon Sacrifices and the like? (149)

Perhaps you will reply that the texts enjoining the performance of the New and Full Moon Sacrifices are authoritative because they promote knowledge of a course of action (for a stated goal) open to man. And you will add that this feature is lacking in the texts proclaiming the existence and nature of the Self. You are quite right, it is lacking. But this is no defect in our position, as it in no way undermines the authority of such texts. For the test of authoritativeness is just what we have declared it to be, and no other. And indeed, so far from being a reason for denying them authority, it is a great point in favour of the authority of the texts proclaiming the Self that they should occasion knowledge which results in the destruction of the very seeds of action. (150)

* * * * *

7. As for the claim (that the Mīmāṃsaka's "figurative Self" in the form of the body and its organs (151) must be able to accomplish the ends of the real Self) "as this is implied by the authority (of the Vedic injunctions to perform sacrifices for the sake of unseen goals)," it is not relevant to the matter in hand. For that authority covers only the realm of the unseen. The Veda is authoritative only in matters

that cannot be known through perception and the other empirical means of knowledge, as, for example, the hidden connection of means and ends in the case of the Agnihotra and other Vedic rituals. But it is not an authority in matters which come within the sphere of perception and the other empirical means of knowledge, on account of the principle that authoritative means of knowledge exist to reveal (152) what has not been revealed (in any other way). So one cannot conceive how self-identification with the body and its organs could be a figurative notion, when it is an error of perception. (153) Not even a hundred Vedic texts saying that fire is cold or non-luminous could be accepted as authoritative. If the Veda were to say that fire were cold or non-luminous, one would have to resort to some form of metaphorical interpretation, if its authority was to be safeguarded. It cannot contradict either its own texts or the other means of knowledge.

Perhaps you will say that if the agent of any act must be in the grip of error, then there cannot really be any agent; and in that case the Veda, which enjoins action, cannot command authority. But this would be wrong, for the utility of the Veda lies (ultimately not in the realm of action but) in the sphere of the knowledge of the Absolute.

But would it not follow that if the Veda lacked authority in the sphere of the injunctions to action it would equally lack authority in its injunctions towards knowledge? Not so, for no notion can arise to contradict its deliverances in this sphere. When awareness of the Self has come through the deliverances of the Veda in the realm of knowledge of the Absolute, the notion of identity with the body and its organs is contradicted. But that awareness of the Self which takes place in the Self can never be contradicted in any way by anything. For awareness is inseparable from its own "result" (phala), as fire is invariably hot and luminous.

Nor do we admit that the Vedic texts concerned with ritual lack authority. For their purpose is to turn men's attention more and more towards the inmost Self by continually generating new and higher modes of activity and suppressing old, natural modes of activity. Even if the means are not real in themselves, they become real (and true) if the goal towards which they lead is real, as is the case of the eulogistic passages at the end of the ritualistic injunctions. (154) In ordinary worldly dealings, too, people say to children and lunatics "This will make your hair grow" when trying to coax them to drink milk and the like.

Moreover, the texts in those parts of the Veda which do not deal with knowledge of the Absolute are directly authoritative before knowledge of the Self arises, in just the same way that perception and the other empirical means of knowledge are, even though the latter depend on false self-identification with the body and its organs. (155)

* * * * *

8. (An objector against Advaita might develop the following position). If all the Upanishads (he might say) are concerned merely with teaching the unity and sole reality of the supreme Self, then why does the contradictory hypothesis occur that something different from the supreme Self exists, namely the individual soul? Some say that this hypothesis is necessary in order to safeguard the authoritativeness of the ritualistic portions of the Veda. For the texts dealing with the ritual presuppose a plurality consisting of

actions, factors of action, results of action, agents and experiencers. If there were no separate individual soul, and only the supreme Self existed in perfect unity and transcendence, then how could these texts cause anyone to engage in ritual for desirable ends (which is manifestly their function?) Or how could they cause anyone to desist from acts whose consequences would be evil? And what soul could exist in bondage, for whose sake an Upanishad could begin its teaching?

Furthermore, on the view that the supreme Self is one and the supreme reality, how could the sole reality of the supreme Self be *taught* ? Or how could such teaching bear fruit? Such teaching is for the sake of destroying the bonds of those in bondage, and if there were no bondage, the Upanishadic teaching would have no scope. So that in this matter the exponents of the Upanishads stand or fall by the same arguments as the exponents of the ritualistic portion of the Veda. If no differentiation really exists, then neither the ritualistic portion of the Veda nor the Upanishads can claim any absolute authority. But we ought to dismiss the Upanishadic teaching of the unreality of existence, and accept the authority of the ritualistic portion of the Veda, because at least the teachings of the latter are such that, if authoritative, they would not be the negation of the Veda's own meaning and purpose. One should reject the authoritativeness of the Upanishads because, if accepted, it would negate (a part of) their own meaning. (156) But the authority of the ritualistic portion of the Veda, once accepted, cannot be rejected. A lamp cannot both illumine and not illumine the objects within its range.

The authority of the Upanishads (the objector goes on) is also to be rejected because of the conflict with the empirical means of knowledge such as perception and inference. In teaching the sole existence and reality of the Absolute (and the absence of all difference), the Upanishads not only negate their own meaning and undermine the authority of the ritualistic portion of the Veda, they also conflict with perception and other empirical means of knowledge, which yield a definite conviction of the existence of differentiation. So the Upanishads cannot be an authoritative means of knowledge. Or, if authoritative, their real teaching cannot be the seamless unity and sole reality of the Absolute, but must be something else.

But we (Advaitins) say to the objector that all this is wrong, for the answer to it has already been given. What makes a means of knowledge authoritative or inauthoritative is the circumstance of whether it does or does not convey right knowledge. Otherwise (the sight of) a pillar could be an authoritative means of knowledge for hearing sounds. If the Upanishads convey right knowledge of the sole existence and reality of the Absolute, how can they fail to be authoritative?

Perhaps you will say that they do not produce right knowledge any more than the statement "Fire produces cold" would. If so, we must ask whether your statement denying the authority of the Upanishads does in fact negate their authority and whether fire illumines colour. If they do, then your statement expressing a negation is an authoritative means of knowledge, just like fire (in the form of light) when it illumines colour. If negations are an authoritative means of knowledge, the Upanishads are an authoritative means of knowledge. (157) So please tell us how you reply to that.

Perhaps you will reply that the knowledge conveyed by your negation of the authority of the Upanishads and the knowledge of colour are evidently cases of right knowledge. But, if so, we (Advaitins) ask why you have such a bias against the (equally) evident right knowledge expressed by the idea that the Absolute is the sole existent reality, which arises when the Upanishads are known? For your refutation does not hold at all. We have already declared (158) how grief and delusion and so on come to an end as an immediately evident result flowing from an intuitive knowledge of the identy of one's true Self with the Absolute. Hence the objections have been answered, and there is no room to doubt the authoritativeness of the Upanishads.

Nor can we accept your criticism that the Upanishads are not an authoritative means of knowledge because their doctrine negates (part of) their own meaning. For there is nothing contradictory in their teaching. From the proposition "Fire is both hot and cold" we would collect a pair of contradictory ideas. But we do not collect from the Upanishads the contradictory ideas that the Absolute both is and is not one without a second. And we only mention this at all on the basis of a hypothetical concession to your position. For if the texts are to be treated as authoritative, the tradition is that they cannot have more than one meaning. If a text could have more than one meaning, there would be a certain meaning, plus another contradictory one that nullified it. But the traditional Vedic exegesis does not admit that one and the same passage can have different meanings, one appropriate and the other contradictory to it. For it maintains that the words can only be construed as a single significant passage if their collective meaning is itself a unity, (159) and we do not find any Upanishadic texts that contradict the unity of the Absolute.

As for the proposition pertaining to secular life "Fire is both hot and cold," this cannot be accepted as forming a single significant passage, for part of it is (not an idea freshly communicated by the sentence in question but) a mere restatement of matters already known from other sources. Thus we have to analyse such a proposition into two separate parts. On the one hand we have the "informative" statement "Fire is cold." (160) And on the other hand we have the passage "Fire is hot," which merely reminds one of what has already been a matter of experience through other sources of knowledge (*viz.* perception) and which has no special information of its own to convey. The phrase "Fire is hot" can therefore not form a single passage with the informative statement "Fire is cold," because it (conveys no new information but) is limited to reminding us about what has already been a matter of experience through other means of knowledge. As for the notion that the words "Fire is hot and cold" form a single self-contradictory proposition, this is simply an error, induced by the fact that the words "hot" and "cold" are both in the same grammatical case as "fire," (whereas "cold" is in fact included in an informative statement and "hot" is not, being part of a mere reminder). The truth is that no single proposition, whether secular or Vedic, can have more than one meaning.

The opponent's statement that the metaphysical texts of the Upanishads would invalidate the ritualistic section of the Veda if they were accepted as authoritative was also wrong, for they deal with a different subject-matter. The function of the metaphysical texts of the Upanishads is to proclaim that the Absolute is one, and the sole existent. They do not either teach the means to obtain desirable ends in the empirical world or negate injunctions to do so (found in other texts). For they cannot (according to the rules of Vedic exegesis) have more than one meaning and purpose. Nor is there anything to prevent the texts of the ritualistic part of the Veda from conveying valid knowledge in their own particular field. If a text promotes valid knowledge in its own particular field, how could it fall into contradiction with another text belonging to a different field?

It is true that the opponent has said that, if the Absolute were one and the sole existent, then the texts of the ritualistic part of the Veda could not convey valid knowledge within their own field, for lack of any field to apply to. But this we deny, for we actually perceive them to convey valid knowledge. We actually perceive valid knowledge arising from such texts (in the ritualistic portion of the Veda) as "Let him who desires heaven offer the New and Full Moon Sacrifices" and "A Brahmin should never be slain." That this would be impossible if the Upanishads conveyed the knowledge that the Absolute was one and the sole existent is a mere inference, and inference cannot be accepted as a valid means of knowledge where it contradicts perception. So your statement that (if the Upanishads were a valid source of knowledge) right knowledge could not arise from the ritualistic portion of the Veda was simply wrong.

The Veda neither affirms nor denies the truth or untruth of the distinction between actions, their factors and results — a distinction which is a matter of universal experience in the world. People rely on this distinction as set up by nescience and engage in action in a general way to obtain the desirable and avoid the undesirable on the basis of it. What the Veda does is to give them some information about particular means to particular ends that they were not previously aware of. For in its ritualistic section, the Veda is only concerned with explaining the means to attain the (empirically) desirable and avoid the undesirable.

Though desire proceeds from false knowledge, the part of the Veda which is concerned with the satisfaction of desires accepts them as they come, and explains the means for satisfying them. It does not abstain from doing so merely on the ground that desires are harmful because they rest on false knowledge. The same is true of that part of the Veda which deals with the obligatory rituals like the Agnihotra and others. (161) It accepts the distinctions, proceeding from nescience, between actions, their factors and results, just as they arise. And on this basis it prescribes the Agnihotra and the other obligatory rituals, with the idea that even they serve some unseen purpose or other, whether it be the attainment of a positive end or the avoidance of some calamity. It does not abstain from prescribing them on the ground that they concern the unreal in the realm of nescience. It treats them in the same way that it treats the optional rituals. Nor would men cease to act from desire if the Veda abstained from prescribing action for particular ends. For we see that men under the influence of nescience invariably act, as, for instance, those who fall under the influence of desire.

But, you will say, is it not the rule that only those who have knowledge are competent to perform ritual (and not those in the grip of nescience)? (162) But we reply that this is not so, for we have already explained how knowledge that the Absolute is one and the sole existent contradicts all capacity for action. And this should be taken also to answer the objection that, if the Absolute is one and the sole existent, there is no advantage to be gained from receiving the ritualistic instruction, because there could not be any scope for it.

Another reason for the significance of the ritualistic part of the Veda is the diversity of men's longings and desires. Various indeed are the longings and desires of men, each to be accounted a defect. The Veda has no power to restrain men when their minds are captivated by desires for external objects. Nor can it prompt those whose minds are naturally indifferent to external objects to action in that realm. All that the Veda does is to give information saying, "This leads to the desirable, that to the undesirable." It states certain details about the relations of means to ends, as a lamp gives knowledge of colours in the dark. But it never forcibly restrains anyone or forcibly makes anyone act, as a master might do to his servants. For it is seen that the force of passions is so strong that men transgress even the Veda. Hence the Veda teaches many particulars about the relation of means and ends, in order to conform to the widely different ideas of different men. Men adopt this means or that from Vedic teaching, according to their private wishes, while the Veda illumines all without taking sides, like the sun or a lamp. To one man, what is really the highest good will not seem like a human good at all. Each one interprets the end of human life according to his lights, and seeks means to fulfil that end....

Hence we conclude that the Upanishads do not contradict that part of the Veda that deals with ritual, nor do they deprive the ritualistic texts of their legitimate scope. Neither do the ritualistic texts, which imply a distinction between action, its factors and results in the manner described, undermine the authority of the Upanishads when the latter proclaim that the Absolute is one, and the sole existent. For all the different means of knowledge, like the power of hearing and the rest, are incontrovertible in their own sphere. (164)

* * * * *

9. Nor can you argue that, as the Veda is eternal, it must hold sovereign sway and be able to bind everyone by its commands. For the same

fallacy will arise as before. The absurd conclusion will inevitably follow that everyone will have the duty of performing all the enjoined ritual at the same time.

Perhaps you will say that, all my theoretical argumentation to the contrary notwithstanding, the fact remains that the Veda does actually enjoin both performance of action and knowledge of the Self on the active ritualist. But this is wrong, because no one can communicate anything that is inherently self-contradictory. One cannot inform anyone that he is connected with past or future action and also assert the exact opposite at the same time. It would be like trying to say that fire was hot and also cold.

Nor is the desire to act for one's advantage or to stave off evil prompted by the Veda, as it is characteristic of all living beings. If these two characteristics only arose from the Veda they would not be observed (as they are in fact) in cowherds, as the latter have no knowledge of the Veda.

The function of the Veda is to acquaint one with things that cannot otherwise be known. If its function were to convey knowledge of the Self, which notion is contradictory to all notions of activity and duty, how could it afterwards revive the contradictory notion of duty? It would be like trying to say that fire was cold or the sun dark.

If you try to deny that the function of the Veda is to convey knowledge of the Self, we say you are wrong, as is shown by many texts including the following, "One should know 'He is my Self'," (165) as also the recapitulating-formula of the present Upanishad, "(Consciousness is the support of the world): Consciousness is the Absolute (brahman)."(166)And as the direct intuition that one's Self is the Absolute is uncontradictable once it has arisen, it can never be asserted that it never arose or that it was erroneous. (167)

* * * * *

10. The Veda does not proclaim distinctions such as that between goal and means, for such distinctions spell continued transmigratory life, the very thing that has to be avoided. The ordinary man is ignorant and fancies himself to be affected by the desirable and undesirable states of his body, and does not know what means to apply to obtain the desirable and to prevent the undesirable. What the Veda first does is gradually to remove his ignorance about how to obtain what he desires and prevent what he does not desire. Then afterwards it eradicates nescience proper, which is vision of difference, and which is the source of transmigratory life. It does this by showing that it is correct to regard what appears as many through the creation, maintenance and withdrawal of the universe, as in reality only one. (168)

* * * * *

11. In the world, only he who knows the truth about some matter attains what he wants or avoids what he does not want, while through ignorance of the truth one fails. In the same way, in the present context, one can obtain beneficial results only through correct knowledge of what the words of the Vedic text actually say.

Now, there is nothing whatever to show that what is taught in Vedic texts as a theme for meditation is necessarily untrue. Nor are there any passages in the Veda which contradict the truth of the theme here taught. (169) We accept it is true because beneficial results flow from it, whereas evil invariably comes from what is not true. Whoever in the world fails to see things in their true light invariably suffers, as for instance, when a person takes a man for a post, or an enemy for a friend. If what one heard from the Vedic texts about the Self or about the Lord or about the various deities proved false, one would certainly conclude that the Veda led one into harm, on the analogy of what arises from false knowledge in the world. And such a conclusion is not acceptable. (170) Hence it follows that what the Vedic passages concerned with themes for meditation teach about the Self, and also about the Lord and the various deities, is true.

Perhaps you will say that this is wrong because there are Vedic passages which speak of meditating on "name," etc., as the Absolute, (171) when it is clear that "name" and the rest are not the Absolute. For the Veda to recommend meditating on "name" as the Absolute is equivalent to inculcating a wrong notion about a post to the effect that it was a man. From this you might conclude that we were wrong to claim that spiritual welfare only arises from the Veda when the latter conveys knowledge of things as they really are.

Such a view, however, is wrong. For the one practising this meditation remains quite clear that what he is meditating on (name) is different from what his meditation is representing it to be (the Absolute), as one worshipping a statue as if it were Viṣṇu is perfectly clear that it is only a statue.... One's idea of "name," etc., are mere frameworks for the meditation on the Absolute. The text does not affirm that "name" and the rest *are* the Absolute....

The Pūrva Mīmāṃsaka may perhaps intervene here and claim that in the case of Vedic injunction to meditate on this or that as the Absolute, there is only the *idea* of the Absolute in play, but that no real Absolute exists. Similarly, when a statue is worshipped as Viṣṇu, Viṣṇu is not really present in the statue, and when one's ancestors are worshipped through offering hospitality to Brahmins, one's ancestors are not really present in the Brahmins. So here, there is but an injunction to meditate on "name" (spoken of eulogistically as the Absolute to encourage the meditator). (172)

But this view is wrong, as we find cases of injunctions to meditate on well-known things like the Ṛg Veda, identifying them with equally well-known things such as the earth, (173) which imply the projection (in thought) of already existing entities like the earth onto objects like the Ṛg Veda. Hence, because of parity of form, (174) we must assume that when there is an injunction to project (in thought) the Absolute over "name," this is already a proof that the Absolute actually exists. It also shows that when there is worship of a statue as Viṣṇu or some other god, or of Brahmins (in hospitality) as one's ancestors, the idea of Viṣṇu, etc., or of one's ancestors, corresponds to some existent reality.

There is also another argument which shows that the notion of the Absolute implied in such a text as "Meditate on name as the Absolute" must refer to a reality. A figurative meaning of a word implies a true meaning. (175) There can only be meditation on Five Fires conceived figuratively (176) if fire in the true sense exists. Similarly, if the Absolute is to be regarded as only figuratively present in "name" for purposes of meditation, this already proves that the Absolute in the true sense of the word must be an existent entity.

Furthermore, the same rules apply in the case of meditations as apply in the case of rituals. It is only from the Veda that we can learn of such supersensuous matters beyond perception and inference as the due order of performance and future results of the New Moon and Full Moon Sacrifices. (177) And it is likewise only from the Veda that we can learn about such supersensuous realities as the supreme Self, the Lord or the deities, as for instance, that they are impalpable to our senses and above hunger and so forth. In both cases the information must be correct, since it transcends the range of empirical knowledge. (178) There is no difference between the texts conveying knowledge and the texts enjoining rituals in point of communicating ideas, nor is there anything to show that the ideas they produce in regard to the highest Self and other beings of the supersensuous realm are either unfounded or erroneous. (179)

The Mīmāṃsakas will perhaps intervene here and claim that there *is* a fundamental difference between Vedic texts purporting to convey knowledge and those enjoining rituals. In the former there is nothing to be done. In the latter, knowledge about some matter that transcends natural cognition is admittedly conveyed. But what is conveyed is information about a creative ritualistic act (bhāvanā) that has to be performed, such information including the three aspects (of goal, means and method). (180) Since the texts concerned with conveying information about the highest Self and the Lord, etc., do not include any information about any act that has to be performed, it is not right to say that there is no fundamental difference between them and the texts enjoining rituals.

This, however, we cannot accept. For all knowledge alike has, as such, true correspondence with its object. It is not the fact that it has to be done that guarantess the effectiveness of the creative ritualistic act with its three aspects, but the fact that it is known through an authoritative means of knowledge. (181) Nor is it the fact that one's conception of this creative act is associated with something to be done that makes it true (as the followers of

Prabhākara would maintain), but the fact that it arises from a Vedic text. When a matter is known from a Vedic text it is true as such, and a person will proceed to do it if it is some duty to be done, or will abstain from doing it if it is something that should not be done.

To this the Mīmāṃsaka will doubtless reply that no sentence can be an intelligible piece of knowledge unless it contains a reference to something to be done. For words (he will say) cannot be connected (to make an intelligible sentence) except as related to something to be done; only when this element is present can they be brought together to form a definite meaning. Only that sentence can be an authoritative means of knowledge which is concerned with something to be done and has the form "this must be done with such and such an instrument in such and such a way." But you can go on piling up hundreds of words for the "this" which has to be done, and also for the ways in which it has to be done, without ever being able to construct a sentence out of them unless you have a verb issuing some form of a command. Hence "the highest Self" and "the Lord" cannot be established as existent on the mere authority of the Vedic texts affirming it. (182) If you say that they (the "highest Self" and "the Lord") constitute the meanings of certain words found in the Veda, then (if those words are to be intelligible) the real existence of what they refer to will have had to have been established by some other means of knowledge (since words by nature refer to things whose existence has been established by other means of knowledge.) So the view that the existence of the Absolute is established by the Vedic texts is wrong.

But this argument (of the Pūrva Mīmāṃsaka of Prabhākara's school) is unacceptable. For we find texts like "There is a mountain called Meru which is of four colours." Such texts do not speak of anything that has to be done, and no one on hearing phrases like "Meru which is of four colours" thinks that Meru and the like are something that has to be done. So what is there to prevent the words in sentences propounding the existence of the highest Self and the Lord from forming connected sentences of subject-predicate form based on the word "is"?

Nor should it be said that our argument is wrong on the ground that knowledge of the supreme Self cannot really be what the Veda means to teach, as such knowledge no more serves the real purposes of man than a knowledge of Mount Meru would. (183) For there are other texts, such as "The knower of the Absolute reaches the supreme" and "The knot of the heart is loosed" (184) which teach that such knowledge has a favourable result. And we also see in practice that it leads to the cessation of nescience and other evils. (185) Again, we cannot say, in the case of knowledge of the Self, that mention of a favourable result arising from it is a mere fanciful eulogy, as we can in the case of the eulogy of the sacrificial ladle, (186) because it cannot be shown to form a subsidiary part of anything else (e.g. a ritual).

Moreover, the fact that deeds forbidden in the Veda have unpleasant results for the performer is learned from the Veda alone. And you cannot say that a forbidden deed is something "that has to be done." One who is about to engage in a prohibited deed has nothing to do except to desist from doing it. The function of prohibitions is to promote knowledge of what one should *not* do. When a hungry person who knows the prohibitions comes upon food that is prohibited, either because it comes from an animal that has been killed by a poisoned arrow, or else because it is offered by a person under a curse, his first idea is that it should be eaten, but this idea is cancelled by the recollection of the prohibitions. It is like the notion that a mirage is something from which you can get water to drink being cancelled by the realization that it is only a mirage; when the natural but erroneous idea has been cancelled, the harmful process of eating does not ensue. All that is involved is the cessation of the determination to act that arose from erroneous knowledge. There is no effort involved, as the determination just ceases of its own accord. Hence it follows that the Vedic prohibitions are concerned with proclaiming true knowledge only, without even a suspicion of a concern with human action. (187) There is therefore no reason why the affirmations giving true knowledge about the Self, etc., should not be limited to that function (of conveying knowledge) alone. In their case, too, one who knows their content will realize that action proceeding from opinions opposed to it will bring harm. When he remembers his right knowledge about the supreme Self, etc., the natural erroneous opinion that leads to such action will just cease of its own accord.

Here you will concede, perhaps, that in such cases as that of eating food that comes from the body of an animal that has been poisoned, remembrance of the harmfulness of the act from the standpoint of true knowledge may very well result in the cessation of the erroneous idea that it should be eaten, and consequently of the harmful determination to eat it. But it would be wrong, you might contend, to think that desistance from action enjoined in the Veda could arise in this way, because such action is not the subject of any prohibition. Such reasoning, however, is not sound. For in this case, as well as in the former, there is the common factor that the action originally contemplated is based on erroneous ideas and is harmful. Actions like eating food derived from animals killed with poisoned arrows arise from false knowledge and are harmful; but so, equally, are actions based on the Vedic injunctions! In the case of one who knows the truth about the supreme Self, therefore, it is but right that even actions enjoined by the Veda should cease. For they are caused by erroneous opinion and are harmful, just like the action of eating food derived from killing by poisoned arrows, and this wrong opinion will have to be put to an end by right knowledge of the supreme Self.

Very well, you will say, suppose we grant your position here. But it will not be right to say that the obligatory daily rituals cease in the case of one who has known the true nature of the supreme Self. For here the impulse to activity is (not erroneous opinion but) only the Vedic injunctions, while no harm results from their performance. But this argument is no better, as the obligatory daily rituals are enjoined only for those who are afflicted by such defects as nescience, attachment, aversion and the rest. It is quite evident that the optional rituals such as the New and Full Moon Sacrifices are laid down for the benefit of those afflicted with such defects as the desire for heaven and the like. And, in the same way, the obligatory rituals are enjoined for the benefit of those who are afflicted with nescience and the other (psychological) defects which are the cause of all evil, and who are likewise afflicted with a consequent attachment and aversion, expressed in seeking the desirable and avoiding the undesirable, and who habitually act under both these impulses in the aim of attaining the desirable and avoiding the undesirable. It is not right to say that such rituals are performed at the behest of the Veda alone.

Furthermore, the question of whether the Agnihotra or the New and Full Moon Sacrifices or the Four Month Sacrifice or the Animal Sacrifice or the Great Soma Sacrifice are optional or obligatory rituals does not depend on their intrinsic nature (but on the attitude of mind of the sacrificer while he is performing them). They become "optional" if the sacrificer has the defect of desire for heaven. And it is but right to say that, in the case of those who are afflicted with nescience and other (psychological) defects, and who are prompted by their very nature to seek the desirable and to avoid the undesirable, the obligatory rituals serve these very ends. For they are enjoined on just such persons. No action is enjoined on those who have a right knowledge of the Self, except such action as leads to the cessation of all activity whatever. (188) For what is enjoined is knowledge of the Self through obliterating the consciousness of all the means to ritualistic action, such as consciousness of presiding deities and of the other necessary component factors of the sacrifice. Indeed, one who has lost all consciousness of actions and of the factors of action cannot act. For one can only act if one has a clear idea of the action one is proposing to carry out, and of the means to do it. There is no question of ritualistic action on the part of one who sustains only the vision of the Absolute as non-dual, as void of all empirical attributes beginning with perceptibility, and as beyond all determinations such as those of time and space.

Here you might object that there could be ritualistic action on the part of such a one in just the same way that he eats and performs other such physiological functions. But this is not so. Eating and the like arise simply from defects like nescience. There cannot be any fixed laws about their occurrence. The obligatory ritual cannot be haphazard in this way, sometimes done, sometimes not done; but a haphazard attitude can well be adopted towards such actions as eating, as they arise only from defects. Defects rise and fall spontaneously, and not at regular intervals. In this they are like the desires prompting people to perform optional rituals. But the obligatory rituals, (even though the prompting cause of their performance be the above-mentioned psychological defects,) cannot be performed in an irregular way, because they depend on special times and occasions prescribed by the Veda, and even the optional form of the Agnihotra (i.e. the performance with desire for heaven) must be performed morning and evening, and with due observation of other rules, too, on account of the Vedic injunctions.

Perhaps you will say that the man who rightly knew the Self could be subject to restrictions (in performance of the Agnihotra) because there are restrictions (for monks) about eating and other such acts. (189) But the inference you have drawn is not right. For restrictions are neither actions nor motives for action. They do not imply any contradiction with knowledge. Hence we must conclude that the Vedic affirmations conveying right knowledge about the supreme Self amount also to prohibitions of all action, because they put an end to all erroneous ideas of the Absolute, such as that it is gross and palpable and characterized by duality. Their net result, therefore, is the same as that of a prohibition, namely, absence of all further action. Hence it is proved that enunciation of the nature of the real stands alongside prohibition and affirmation as one of the concerns of the Veda. (190)

TEXTS ON THE VEDA, THE SMṚTI AND REASON: GROUP C

12. Our opponents argue as follows. The view, they say, that it is the Absolute, the Omniscient, and nothing else, that stands as the cause of the world, is wrong. Why? Because such a view commits the error of denying scope to the Smṛti. The texts of the Smṛti go back to the Tantra (191) composed by the great seer (ṛṣi, i.e. Kapila), which is accepted by all persons of culture and education, along with other texts that are based on it. If the principle that the Absolute alone was the cause of the world were accepted, these texts would be ruled out. For their doctrine is that non-conscious Nature is the sole independent cause of the world.

(XIII.2) THE VEDA AND THE TEACHER (TEXTS)

It is true (continues the opponent) that there would still be scope for other texts of the Smṛti, such as the Law Books of Manu and others, which deal with the whole subject of the spiritual law (dharma) and give injunctions about the performance of the Agnihotra and other rituals. They give the rules about when and by what form of ceremony a boy of a particular caste should be initiated as a student. They prescribe his daily mode of living, the way in which he should repeat the Veda, the way in which he should break off his student life and how he should be joined with his future partner (i.e. wife) in the pursuit of the spiritual law. And they lay down the various duties of the different castes and stages of life (āśrama), performance of which serves human ends and interests. But the Smṛti works like those of Kapila and others of his school do not have their scope in prescribing things that have to be done. Their chosen subject-matter is true metaphysical knowledge, taken as the means (not to ends and interests within the world but) to final liberation. If these texts are ruled out as a means to true metaphysical knowledge, then they will be completely useless. So (to avoid this) the Upanishads have to be interpreted in such a way as not to conflict with them.

In face of this, we (Advaitins) might well ask how anyone could again raise difficulties about the absence of scope for the Smṛti when we have already established that the omniscient principle, the Absolute, is the sole cause of the universe, on account of texts like, "He took thought" (192) and on other grounds as well. To this the Sāṃkhya might reply that our objection to his claims could only be made by people of independent judgement. But most people have to rely on some one else's system of interpretation of the Upanishads, being unable to construct one for themselves. And such people rely perforce on the texts of famous Teachers of the Smṛti, and understand the texts of the Veda in their light.

Such people will never place confidence in the explanations of the Advaitin on account of their great reverence for the classical Teachers (of other schools) whose work survives in the Smṛti. To add to this, we have the Smṛti texts saying that the knowledge of a Seer (ṛṣi) never proves wrong, while the Veda (shows that Kapila was a ṛṣi in this sense when it) says, "One should know that Lord who acquaints His son ṛṣi Kapila, born at the beginning of the creation, with knowledge of past, present and future."(193) No one, therefore, can show that the Sāṃkhya system is untrue. And it is also supported by logical argumentation.

To this the author of the Sūtras replies: "No: because your own view would deny any scope to *other* texts of the Smṛti." That is to say, if the doctrine that the Lord (īśvara) is the cause of the world is objected to on the ground that it would deny scope to certain texts of the Smṛti (viz. those of the Sāṃkhya Śāstra), this would itself imply denial of scope to certain other texts of the Smṛti which *do* teach that the Lord is the cause of the world .... And there is the text in the Bhagavad Gītā, "I am the origin and end of the whole universe."(194) ... In these and similar ways the Smṛti sets forth the doctrine that the Lord is both the efficient and the material cause of the universe. The author of the Sūtras only speaks of the denial of scope to other texts of the Smṛti because he wishes to refute those who would like to argue with him about the nature of the authority of the Smṛti, and refute them on their own ground.

As for the Veda itself, we have already shown that the doctrine towards which all of its texts point is that of the Lord as the cause of the universe. If the texts of the Smṛti, on the other hand, contradict one another on the point, then a choice of one group of texts and a rejection of another is inevitable. In these circumstances, one has to take those texts of the

Smṛti which follow the Veda as authoritative, and ignore the others. For the principle has been laid down (by Jaimini), in defining textual authority, "Where a text of the Smṛti conflicts with the Veda, it must be ignored. For one may only assume (the existence of a lost Vedic text as the source of a text from the Smṛti) where there is no contradiction (with existing Vedic texts)." (195) And one cannot prove that supersensuous matters can be known in any way except through the Vedic texts.

"But," you will say, "such proof *can* be produced. For Kapila and other seers were 'perfect men' (siddha) and their knowledge never proved wrong." But this we cannot allow. For their "perfection" was conditional. "Perfection" (siddhi) depends on following the spiritual law (dharma). This spiritual law is expressed (in the Veda) in the form of injunctions. These injunctions must exist prior to him who acquires "perfection" by carrying them out, and their meaning cannot be called in question by anything said by him. Even on the supposition that one can appeal to the sayings of "perfected" men, the fact remains that the "perfected" men are many, and this circumstance has introduced contradictions into the Smṛti in the manner already explained. This being so, there is no other source for determining the truth apart from the Veda. Nor should those who have to rely on the systems of others plump blindly for one particular system without any special reason. For if one picked out one man's view here and another man's view there, truth could not form a stable consistent system. For there is a world of difference between the opinions of different men. Hence the mind even of one who relies on the systems of others has to be brought back to the right source by exhibiting the contradictions latent in the texts of the Smṛti, and analysing them to see whether or not they are in conformity with the Vedic teaching.

Now, it is true that the opponent quoted a

Vedic text referring to the extraordinary knowledge possessed by a certain "Kapila." But this text would not justify us in placing faith in any doctrine of any Kapila that contradicted the Veda. The only connection between the Veda and the Sāṃkhya system is the accident that the Veda happens to refer to the name "Kapila." For the Smṛti itself shows that there was another Kapila, the one also called Vāsudeva, who burned the sons of Sagara. (196) And when a Vedic passage is primarily concerned with one thing, it cannot serve as a proof of the truth of anything else that it happens to mention incidentally, if the latter is not also known by some other means. (197)

Moreover, there is another Vedic text which sings the glories of Manu, namely, "Whatever Manu says is medicine."(198) And Manu implicitly attacks the doctrine of Kapila when he eulogizes the vision of all in the Self in the passage, "The one who sacrifices to the Self, and sees the Self in all beings and all beings in the Self, acquires spiritual sovereignty." (199) For Kapila takes selves as different from one another, (200) and hence does not admit that there can be vision of all as the Self.

Consider also the following passage in the Mahābhārata. First the question is raised, "Are souls (puruṣa) many, O Brahmin? Or is there only one?" The opponent's view is stated in the words, "According to those who follow the Sāṃkhya and Yoga systems, O King, souls are many." Finally, this is refuted in a passage which begins, "I will explain to you how it is that the one Spirit associated with His qualities (of Omniscience and Omnipotence) is said to be the ground of all in the same way that the one earth is said to be the one womb of the many souls that assume bodily form." (201) Later in the passage, the doctrine that all is the one Self is expressed quite clearly in the words: "He is my inner Self and also your own. He is the Witness present also in all other embodied beings. He is never apprehended (as an object) by anyone anywhere. All heads are His head, all arms are His arm, all feet are His foot, all eyes His eye, all noses His nose; He is one, but He moves about among the creatures at will and wherever He likes." (202)

The Veda also teaches the doctrine that all is the one Self in such passages as, "When, for the enlightened sage, all creatures have become his own Self, then what delusion or what grief could there be for the one who feels the unity of all?"(203)

Hence it stands proved that the system of Kapila contradicts both the Veda and those texts (of the Smṛti) which follow the Veda, because it supposes that selves are different and many, and this in addition to the fact that it wrongly imagines Nature (prakṛti) to be an independent self-existent power. The Veda is an independent authority in regard to its own specific subject-matter, just as the sun has the special power to illumine colour and form. Different, however, is the case with the words of mere humans. They depend on knowledge gained from some other source and mediated by the (fallible) memory of the speaker. Hence there is nothing wrong in our view if it denies scope to the texts of the Smṛti on points that are contradictory to Vedic teaching.

And there is another context where the same rule holds good. The principles (tattva) other than Nature, beginning with the Cosmic Intellect (mahat), which are taught in the Smṛti as so many modifications of Nature, are not found in the Veda, and are never found in worldly experience either. We accept the doctrine of the material elements and the sense-powers found in the Smṛti, because it is in line with what is experienced in the world and taught in the Veda. But the Cosmic Intellect and the rest should not, properly speaking, be taught in the Smṛti at all, as they are unknown either to worldly experience or to the Veda, and are quite beyond the purview of human knowledge, like the objects of some (imaginary) sixth sense. We have already explained in commenting on the aphorism "If you maintain that the texts of some Vedic schools mention entities which have been established through inference (by us, the Sāṃkhyas) ..." (204) how some Vedic texts which appear to deal with the Cosmic Intellect do not in fact do so. The present aphorism means to imply that if the Smṛti is not authoritative when it speaks of certain effects (such as the Cosmic Intellect and so forth), it is not authoritative when it speaks of their cause (Nature conceived as an independent principle) either. So here is another case where it is no fault on the part of our doctrine if it denies scope to certain texts of the Smṛti. As for the dialectical argumentation offered (by the Sāṃkhyas) in support, this will be dealt with in commenting on the series of Sūtras beginning at Brahma Sūtra II.i.4.

And now the author of the Sūtras extends the refutation to the Smṛti associated with the Yoga system (of Patañjali), on the ground that this refutation of the Sāṃkhya system will serve to refute the Yoga system as well. In this system too, Nature is set up in contradiction with Vedic teaching as the independent cause of the world, and it is imagined to have effects like the Cosmic Intellect which are unknown either to worldly experience or to the Veda.

Now, one might wonder, if all this proceeds from what has gone before by simple analogy, why should there be the formality of extending the argument to cover the new topic. But the fact is that it is necessary to show that the Yoga system is contradicted by the Veda on certain points. (Otherwise it will be assumed that the teachings of the Yoga system agree with the Veda in every detail, for) Yoga is often stated in the Veda to be a means to right knowledge of the Self, in such passages as, "The Self should be heard about, pondered over and meditated on continuously (nididhyāsana)."(205) We find a circumstantial description of yoga practice along with thoughts about posture and kindred topics in the Śvetāśvatara Upanishad, in the passage beginning, "Holding chest, neck and head upright, and keeping the body evenly balanced." (206) And there are many incidental references to yoga in the Veda, such as, "They regard that concentration of the organs as yoga" (207) and "(Having acquired) this enlightenment and whole yoga discipline." (208) And in the Yoga system, too, yoga is taken as the means to knowledge of truth, as is shown by the text, "And now yoga, the means to vision of reality." (209) From this one might suppose that because part of the teachings given from the standpoint of the Yoga system in the Smṛti was accepted as authoritative, all of it must be accepted as authoritative, on the analogy of what happens in the case of the Eighth Day Offerings to the Ancestors (aṣṭakā). (210)

It is to combat this (view that the Yoga system agrees entirely with the Veda) that the foregoing refutation of the Sāṃkhya system is formally extended to the Yoga system. For it was earlier seen that although one part of the teachings of the Sāṃkhya system must be accepted as authoritative, another part disagreed with the Veda.

Although there are many passages in the Smṛti giving teaching about the spiritual constitution of man, the author of the Sūtras singles out the Sāṃkhya and Yoga systems for special refutation. The reason is that the Sāṃkhya and Yoga systems are widely believed to be the means to the highest end of life, are accepted by men of culture, and seem to receive the support of the Vedic passage which runs, "Knowing that deity (*viz.* the Absolute), that universal cause which is apprehended through Sāṃkhya and Yoga, he is released from all bonds." (211)

The idea behind the refutation is that one cannot attain the highest end of man either through the knowledge offered by the Sāṃkhya system or through the practical path offered by the Yoga system if these systems are taken independently of the Veda. The Veda denies that there can be any other means to the highest goal in life apart from the knowledge that only the one Self exists, knowledge that can only be derived from the Veda. It says, "Only through knowing Him does one go beyond death. There is no other way to go." (212)

The adherents of the Sāṃkhya and Yoga systems are dualists. They are not possessed of the vision that only the one Self exists. It is true that the passages quoted from the Śvetāśvatara Upanishad attributed such a vision to Sāṃkhya and Yoga when it spoke of "that universal cause which is apprehended through Sāṃkhya and Yoga." But we have to understand that it is only the knowledge and meditation taught in the Veda that is here meant, and that they are referred to by the words "Sāṃkhya" and "Yoga" because the latter are convenient approximate terms.

As for the parts of the Yoga and Sāṃkhya texts which do not conflict with the Veda, we willingly accord them full scope. For instance, Vedic texts like, "This Spirit is untouched by any associations (asaṅga)" (213) show that the Spirit (puruṣa) is pure consciousness. The adherents of the Sāṃkhya system acknowledge this when they say that souls (puruṣa) are qualitiless (nirguṇa). Similarly, the Veda teaches a path of withdrawal from the world, as is evinced by such passages as, "And so the wandering monk, wearing a pale robe, shaven and shorn, accepting no gifts ..." (214) The adherents of the Yoga system follow this when they prescribe wandering forth from home as a monk and kindred forms of discipline.

All the texts of the Smṛti that are based on mere reasoning (215) should be confronted with the same line of argument. If they support true metaphysical knowledge with dialectical argumentation, well and good. But true metaphysical knowledge can only arise from the texts of the Upanishads, as is shown by such Vedic passages as, "One who is not versed in the Vedas cannot understand the Great Principle" (216) and "But I am asking about the Spirit that is proclaimed in the Upanishads." (217)

* * * * *

13. But the rationalists, who abandon the authority which resides in the Vedic texts, obscure the Vedic doctrine by contradictory lines of reasoning, issuing in contradictory conclusions, such as "It is," "It is not," "An agent," "Not an agent" and so forth. All this makes it hard to determine the true meaning of the Veda. But those who place their entire reliance on the Veda, subduing their pride, they obtain quite definite convictions as to the meaning of the Veda in regard to matters like the deities which transcend empirical cognition, just as if they were matters of immediate perception to them. (218)

* * * * *

14. Some (219) maintain that the reasoning of the Vaiśeṣikas and other philosophers of kindred views is enough to show that desire and other such feelings are qualities of the Self. But this is wrong. For such reasoning runs directly counter to such specific Vedic statements as, "(Desires) that dwell in the heart (= intellect)...". (220) All reasoning is

fallacious if it contradicts the Veda. Moreover, the theory stands in contradiction with the self-luminosity of the Self. And as desire and the like are found in dream, (221) when only the subject is present, it follows that the self-luminosity of the latter stands proved and cannot be contradicted. If desires and the like inhered intimately (samavāyin) in the Self (as its qualities), as the Vaiśeṣikas assert, they could not be objects of the Self's vision, any more than the peculiar characteristics of the eye are visible to the eye itself. The fact that that which the Witness apprehends is totally different in nature from the Witness proves that the Witness is self-luminous, (222) and this fact would be contradicted if desire and the other mental feelings were taken as qualities inhering in the Self. And the Vedic teaching as a whole would also be contradicted. If it were assumed that desire and the like occupied a certain corner of the Self, that would undermine the whole Vedic teaching. (223) All this has been explained at length in the Second Book. (224)

All theories about desire and other feelings inhering as qualities in the Self must be carefully refuted if the Vedic teaching that the Self of man is one with the supreme principle underlying all is to be substantiated. The Vaiśeṣikas and Naiyāyikas, with their arbitrary conception about the qualities of the Self, are not in harmony with the doctrines of the Upanishads, and this theory of theirs (about desire inhering in the Self) should not command assent. For it contradicts the Upanishadic doctrine. (225)

TEXTS ON THE VEDA, THE SMṚTI AND REASON: GROUP D

15. We have already (i.e. in the first Adhyāya of the Brahma Sūtras) refuted the objections brought on the authority of the Smṛti (in particular of the Sāṃkhya system) against the doctrine that the Absolute is both the material cause and the

efficient cause of the world. The author of the Sūtras now goes on to refute similar objections on purely rational grounds.

First, however, let us enquire into the question of how objections based on purely rational considerations could have been brought against a matter that has been determined on the authority of revelation. One might suppose, for instance, that revelation was the sole authority as to the nature and existence of the Absolute, just as it is in regard to ritualistic actions bringing merit and prohibited actions bringing demerit, affecting one's experiences in future lives. But this idea, (says our opponent) will not stand examination. It would be true (he thinks) only if the Absolute were a matter completely beyond the reach of all other means of knowledge, and accessible through the revealed texts alone, as is the case with the ritualistic actions bringing merit and the prohibited actions bringing demerit in future lives, where such actions are not yet in being and require to be accomplished in the future. But the Absolute (he says), when known at all, is known as an already existent being. And in the case of already existent beings there is a place for the operation of other means of knowledge besides revelation, as is true, for example, in the case of the perception of earth and the other elements by the senses. And just as, when Vedic texts conflict, one has to be singled out as the main one and the rest to be treated as subordinate to it, so, when revelation and other means of knowledge conflict, the revealed texts may have to be interpreted in accordance with (and as subordinate to) the other means of knowledge. Moreover, reason approximates closely to experience, because it explains what cannot be perceived on the analogy of what can, whereas revelation (from the Mīmāṃsaka standpoint) stands further removed from experience, because it states its teachings on the basis of mere tradition.

Furthermore, (you Advaitins yourselves, he might say, claim that) knowledge of the Absolute is incomplete without experience, and that it is accepted as having immediately perceptible fruit in the form of destruction of nescience, which is the means to liberation (so that, since your ultimate appeal is to experience and not to dogmatic tradition, you cannot avoid our objections raised from the standpoint of reason, which depends on experience and is an extension of it.) And the Veda itself is witness to the fact that rational enquiries have to be brought in even on the topic of the Absolute, as it speaks of "cogitation" (manana) besides hearing in the text, "The Self has to be heard about and cogitated over." (226) Hence the author of the Sūtras proceeds now to take up further objections for consideration, this time objections raised on purely rational grounds. (227)

* * * * *

16. The Āgama Śāstra (the first of the four Books of Gauḍapāda's Kārikās on the Māṇḍūkya Upanishad) affirmed the sole reality of the non-dual principle through an analysis of the syllable OM. The second Book of the Kārikās established the same point, demonstrating rationally the falsity of the distinctions that go to make up the apparent world of outer objects. And then again in the third Book the principle of non-duality was established positively and directly through Vedic quotation, supported by reasoning; and at the end of the Book the final summary declared that this was the highest truth. And because the dualists and Nihilists, the philosophical opponents of this doctrine of non-duality proclaimed by Vedic revelation, contradicted each other mutually, it was hinted that their world-views were influenced by attachment and aversion and other passions, and were hence false. The doctrine of non-duality was eulogized as true because not

based on passions.

In the fourth Book, which is now begun under the title of "The Extinction of the Waving Torch," the mutually contradictory and consequently false character of these doctrines will be exhibited at greater length, and the truth of non-duality will be established by negating them through negative dialectic. (228)

* * * * *

17. You will perhaps object that if a person is confronted by his opponent with a dilemma and cannot defend his doctrine against the defects implicit in either horn of the dilemma, then further discussion is useless. And you will maintain, further, that it follows from this that if either of the horns of the dilemma prove defensible, or if a third view which is free from defect is found, this must represent the right interpretation of the text being discussed, so that in this case likewise discussion is useless.

But to this we cannot agree. For discussion will be needed to settle whether the proposed alternatives are really free from defect or not. It is quite correct to say that if either horn of the dilemma, or a third view, has been *shown* to be free from defect, further discussion is useless. But in the present case this has not been proved, so critical discussion about it is meaningful, as its purpose will be to settle the meaning of the text finally.

Perhaps you admit that discussion is meaningful to settle the meaning of the text, but claim that we Advaitins just go on discussing and never settle anything. Of course, you will say, it is not as if the Veda prevented anyone from settling anything through discussion by a direct prohibition. But the trouble is that there are many conflicting views. Being concerned chiefly with Vedic teaching, you (Advaitins) will adhere to a doctrine of monism. But there are many secular philosophers holding different views involving plurality. And hence you cannot overcome my objection that discussion will be endless and will not attain a settled conclusion.

To this I reply that the fact that you say that I am one person defending monism in opposition to opponents who hold mutually opposed theories involving plurality redounds very much to my advantage. (229) I shall conquer them all. Let us begin the discussion. (230)

* * * * *

18. It is even possible that the Epics and Purāṇas are based on direct perception and other forms of empirical evidence. For there are things that are not perceptible to us which *were* perceptible to our ancestors. In this connection the Smṛti itself tells us that Vyāsa and others enjoyed conversation with the gods and other supernatural beings. And he who was to claim *a priori* that the ancients could no more enjoy conversation with the gods and the like than we can would be doing less than justice to the wonder and variety of the world: he might just as well say that, because there is no emperor now holding sway over the earth, there never was one in the past. (231) And this would make nonsense of the injunction to perform the Rājasūya and other sacrifices that have world-wide dominion as their fruit. Or he might just as well hold that, because the duties of caste and station of life (āśrama) are today in almost total neglect, (232) they must always have been neglected in the past.

And this would make a mockery of the texts that lay them down. So that we ought to conclude that the ancients were indeed able to converse with the gods and other supernatural beings, owing to their superior merit (dharma).

Moreover, the Smṛti presents the further text, "From repetitions of sacred texts and of OM performed continuously and with deep feeling arises vision of one's chosen deity." (233) One cannot deny that practice of yoga leads to supernormal powers — such as that of assuming an exceedingly small form — on the basis of a mere unsupported guess, as it is taught in authoritative works of the Smṛti. And the Veda itself declares that the practice of yoga leads to extraordinary results, as in the text, "When earth, water, fire, wind and ether have been generated in the body in their subtle form through meditation, and when the subtle powers of yoga are already in play, from then on the body of the yogin is afflicted neither by disease, decay or death, forged as it is in the fire of yoga." (234)

Further, we should in no way compare the powers of the seers (ṛṣi) who "saw" the hymns (mantra) and explanatory texts (brāhmaṇa) of the Veda with our own puny powers. From this it follows that what the Epics and Purāṇas say is well grounded. Nor should the general opinion of mankind (which accepts that the ancient ṛṣis had supernormal powers) be dismissed as baseless when there is nothing to disprove it outright. (235)

TEXTS ON THE VEDA, THE SMṚTI AND REASON: GROUP E

19. If, as the Advaita Vedantin says, I am in fact of the opposite nature, why is it that I have the experience "I am associated with desire and am not the ever self-existent one"? We reply that questioning is only possible with regard to the experience "I am associated with desire and action, etc.," not with regard to the experience of being liberated. In experience, whatever matter stands in contradiction with data yielded by certified means of knowledge must be questioned. The

conviction "I am liberated" arises from a different means of knowledge, namely the Vedic text "Thou art the real." (236) It is the feeling of being the sufferer that deserves questioning, for it arises from the mere semblance (ābhāsa) of perception. One must give an answer to the question that has been raised, an answer to which is desired; and the answer is that which was hoped for, namely, "Pain does not exist." For the answer to the question "How can my sufferings be brought to an end once and for all?" is one that itself destroys suffering. On the topic of the nature of the Self, the testimony of the Veda cannot be questioned, because the Veda is itself the authoritative means of knowledge on this subject. Therefore the Vedic text is what causes one to realize that (in its true nature) one's own Self is ever liberated. That text ("Thou art the real") with that meaning should be given as an answer (to the question about pain), as it is not subject to contradiction by anything. (237) No experience of the Self other than this can be substantiated. The Veda itself says, "It is not known by those who say that they know it (as an object)," and "By what could one know Him by whom all this is known?" (238)

* * * * *

20. Hence duties are prescribed for those in the state of nescience only, not for those who have enlightenment. For with the rise of enlightenment, nescience goes to destruction, like darkness before the light of the sun. Before the rise of enlightenment, nescience is accepted as authoritative and assumes the form of distinct factors and fruits of actions, and thus becomes the cause of action. But when it is not accepted as authoritative it cannot be a cause of action. An active human being only carries out a religious duty when he thinks that the Veda is an authority and that it has prescribed such and

such a duty as something that has to be done. He does not do so when he feels, "All this is nescience, like the night." But the knower of the Self, who thinks that all this world of distinctions is only nescience, dark like the night, is only in a position to renounce all duties, not to carry them out. The Lord will point out later, in the passage beginning "Their minds on Him, with Him for their Self," (239) that such people are perfectly established in devotion to metaphysical knowledge.

Nor would it be right to object that no one could devote themselves to the Self in that state either, because there would be no authority for any course of action whatever. For Self-knowledge bears on itself. The Self does not need an authority to prompt it to act on the Self, as it already *is* the Self, and the "authoritativeness" (pramāṇavattva) of an authoritative means of knowledge comes to an end when the Self is known. For once the true nature of the Self is known, the interplay of knowledge and objects can no longer continue. The final means of knowledge (the highest texts of the Veda, which yield knowledge of the Self) brings to an end the notion that the Self is a knower employing means of knowledge. And the final means of knowledge itself ceases to be a means of knowledge the moment it brings that notion to an end, just as the authoritative means of knowledge that prevailed during a dream cease to exist on waking. (240)

* * * * *

21. If the conviction, "I am verily the real, ever liberated" could never arise, then why does the revered Veda declare it, like a compassionate mother?

The function of teachings like "That thou

art," associated with reasoning on their content, is merely to negate the not-self element from this Self, the latter being already existent and evident as "I". The process is like the negation of the idea of a snake falsely imagined in a rope. The fact of the (sole) existence (and reality of the non-dual Self) is knowable (only) because of the reliability of the Veda as a means of knowledge, just as the existence of merit and demerit affecting future lives are knowable only from the same source. (When it is known,) then destruction of evil follows automatically, like the elimination of poison from the body (through meditation on the Gāruḍa mantram). (241)

"I am the real, the Absolute" and "I act" are two contradictory notions witnessed by the Self. Of these two contradictory notions (one will have to be given up, so) it would surely be more reasonable to give up the one springing from ignorance. The notion "I am the real" arises from the Veda, an authoritative source of knowledge. The other notion arises from a mere semblance (ābhāsa) of an authoritative means of knowledge (*viz.* perception). Note, however, that mere appearances, such as perception and the other empirical means of knowledge, are later cancelled, like one's erroneous sense of direction. (242)

Whenever the Veda speaks of the Self as "The agent"or "The experiencer" it does so in order to conform to worldly ideas (and so to be intelligible to human hearers). The notion "I am the real," on the other hand, arises from the Veda alone. The former notion is cancelled by the latter. (243)

Here an opponent intervenes and propounds the following view. (244) No permanent liberation results from the mere statement "Thou art the real." In order to achieve permanent liberation one must therefore practise prolonged meditations combined with reasoning (prasaṃkhyāna). Even the one who comes to understand the meaning of the holy texts does not do so at a single hearing. So, as we have just said, he requires something more. And that "something more" is two-fold (i.e. prolonged meditation and reasoning). Because there is no fruit in the form of direct perception of the non-dual Self from the mere hearing of the text, there must be an injunction (niyoga), as in the case of (obligatory) rituals. Nor is there anything to contradict this (if knowledge *does* arise as a fruit) as long as knowledge remains fitful. (245) Moreover, if no injunctions were binding, and a man could acquire knowledge of the Self while behaving just as he liked, it would follow that the Vedic injunctions for self-control and the like would be useless (which is absurd). Therefore, meditation on and reasoning over the Upanishadic texts are enjoined acts that have to be performed until there is direct experience of the Self. The powerful impressions (saṃskāra) arising from sense-perception certainly contradict the knowledge "I am the real" derived from hearing the text, and then one is attracted toward the realm of the external by psychological defects. A cognition derived from sense-perception and yielding particular and concrete knowledge of its object is certainly liable to obstruct indirect cognitions derived from hearing or inference, since these latter yield but a general knowledge of their objects. (246)

No one (continues the Prasaṃkhyāna Vādin) is found to become free from pain merely through comprehending the meaning of a text. And if someone were found to become free from pain merely through hearing the content of a text, it would be inferred that he has performed meditation on it in past lives. Indeed, if anyone could become free from pain through the mere comprehension of a text, it would follow that there was no Vedic warrant for our traditional Vedic discipline, and that would be unacceptable.

Besides, the Upanishadic statement "Thou are the real" amounts to a statement of the "fruit," so that a means must also be enjoined for the attainment of that fruit. (247) Hence the aspirant should practise repeated meditation and reasoning (prasaṃkhyāna) diligently for the sake of realizing the Self, possessed of inner control (śama), etc., (248) and giving up (self-interested action and) whatever (else) is incompatible either with his discipline or its goal.

But this whole view (rejoins the Advaitin) is misconceived. The secret doctrine of the Upanishads culminates in "Not thus, not thus." Goals which depend on activity are revealed (not primarily in the Upanishads but) in the earlier (249) Vedic texts. But liberation is not such, for it is eternally in being.

Just as a father erroneously superimposes the troubles of his son onto himself, though he is without those troubles, so is the ego-sense erroneously superimposed onto the Self, which is ever devoid of pain. This superimposition, though not a fact, appears to be a fact, and the text "Not thus, not thus" serves to prohibit its practice further. After that, no later injunction to perform acts is explicable on any ground whatever, for all acts involve such a superimposition. (250) In this context, there can be prohibition of superimposition of the Self in the same (loose) sense that there can be superimposition on it. The prohibition is used in the same sort of sense in which extremely ignorant people who superimpose impurities on the pure ether of the sky (i.e. who think of the pure, taintless ether of the sky as a perceptible object subject to contamination by dust-clouds and the like) are advised to abstain from doing so. (251) If the prohibited superimposition had been a reality, liberation would certainly be transient. (252) So this must be a prohibition of something that is not a reality, like the prohibition found against constructing an altar in the sky. (253)

A word or an idea can refer to an object, but not to a non-object. They cannot refer to the Self, since it is their own Self; (254) and neither can the ego-sense reveal the Self, for the same reason. Everything, such as the sense of being an agent and the like, which the ego-sense superimposes on pure Consciousness is denied in the words "Not thus, not thus," together with the ego-sense itself. There then remains awareness, the self-luminous one, the Seer, the actionless innermost reality, the Witness (sākṣin) present within all, the illuminator (cetā), eternal, without empirical qualities, non-dual. (255)

3. THE APPROACH TO THE TEACHER

The modern student who is interested in Advaita Vedanta as a practical spiritual path will want to observe with care the qualifications demanded by its classical exponent of the competent spiritual Teacher. These go beyond the mere business acumen needed to open a modern Āśrama. Already Bhartṛhari had given the warning, "There is little penetration in the wisdom of those who have not studied the Veda and Purāṇas, who have not served the elders, who just give voice to whatever their momentary fancies dictate." (254) Śaṃkara avers that a spiritual Teacher must be ignored completely if he does not belong to a recognized spiritual tradition (sampradāya). (257) The term "sampradāya" was defined by Śaṃkara's Naiyāyika predecessor Uddyotakara, at the end of his gloss on the opening Nyāya Sūtra, as "Acquisition of a science handed down from Teacher to pupils in an unbroken line." (258) The mere possession of a wide familiarity with texts, a capacious memory and a power to recite them does not of itself qualify one to communicate a traditional science. For if one does not understand them by one's own inner light (prajñā) one cannot see to guide one's pupils, being in the position, as one old text puts it, "of a ladle, which does not itself taste the broth."(259) And Sureśvara's commentator, Ānandapūrṇa, claims that enlightenment springs from hearing the holy texts from one who has himself received enlightenment from another. (260)

Thus the celebrated Eckhartian distinction between a "Lesemeister" and a "Lebemeister" was in force. The Teacher from whom one learned the texts by rote was not necessarily the same as the one to whom one repaired, fuel in hand as a token of service, for instruction in the wisdom that confers immortality. The foundations of the great Vedanta tradition were laid not in big cities, but in the huts or forest-hermitages of sages. The sages of the Upanishads might attend at the courts of kings for purposes of teaching or debate, but were not permanently domiciled there. The flavour of the forest-hermitage seems to be preserved in Śaṃkara's commentaries, where there is none of the urban atmosphere that confronts us in some of the literary masterpieces of his time.

Professor Hacker has advanced arguments suggesting that the foundation of Advaita monasteries in the four quarters of India dates from the time of Vidyāraṇya (fourteenth century) rather than that of Śaṃkara. (261) Whatever the truth on this question, Śaṃkara has left a blue-print of how he thought a Teacher should operate. We find it in the prose section of the Upadeśa Sāhasrī, and it certainly suggests a dialogue between the Teacher and an individual pupil or a small class and not a monk pontificating before a large audience. The aim is clearly to make the pupil reflect acutely over the metaphysical implications of his own experience, and not to instil dogma into a passive audience.

The texts that follow illustrate in various ways the attitude that Śaṃkara expected of a pupil.

TEXTS ON THE APPROACH TO THE TEACHER

1. This "means to liberation" is knowledge. The content of the teaching has to be presented again and again until it is firmly entrenched. And the pupil to whom it is taught must be of pure character, of Brahmin caste, and must have approached the Teacher in the traditional way, submitting to enquiries about his caste, rituals, way of life and relatives. He must be one who has grown indifferent to the pursuit of all secular ends and means, who has given up desire for sons, wealth and the attainment of a "world" (262) through ritualistic sacrifices, who has entered the state of houseless mendicancy (paramahaṃsa-pārivrājya), who is possessed of inner and outer control and the other virtues, (263) and who has the general qualities laid down in the authoritative works as required for a pupil.

The Veda, too, says: "Having scrutinized the worlds (that are built up by ritualistic action), a Brahmin should arrive at indifference. For the sake of this knowledge let him go, fuel in hand, to a spiritual Teacher (guru) who is learned in the Vedic texts and established in the Absolute. Such a perfectly enlightened Teacher communicates knowledge of the Absolute in its strict metaphysical form — the knowledge whereby one knows the imperishable Spirit, the real, — but only to one who has approached him in the traditional way, whose mind is tranquil and who has acquired the virtue of inner control (śama)." (264)

The spiritual knowledge that is firmly entrenched leads to the soul's highest welfare and serves to perpetuate the holy tradition.

And the presence of the holy tradition has to be maintained for the welfare of all living beings, as it is like a boat to those who want to cross a river. The Veda itself says: "(Verily, a father may teach this to his eldest son or to a worthy pupil, but to no one else). Even if someone should offer him this earth encompassed by the ocean and filled with treasure (gems and minerals), he should say, 'This, truly, is more than that.'" (265)

Moreover, the teaching cannot be acquired in any other way, but only through a Teacher. This is shown by such Vedic texts as, "One who has a Teacher comes to know," "The knowledge that has been obtained from a Teacher (best helps one to attain one's end)," "The Teacher is the ferry-man, (right knowledge is said here to be the boat)."(266) And there are texts to this effect from the Smṛti, such as, "(Know this: through enquiry and through service, those men of wisdom who have realized the truth) will teach thee wisdom." (267)

The Teacher may notice from certain signs that the pupil has not assimilated the knowledge. The causes of failure to assimilate the knowledge are failure to observe the spiritual law (dharma), carelessness in the course of worldly activities, (268) lack of a firm theoretical grounding at the outset in the distinction between the eternal and the transient, devotion to worldly cares, pride in one's high caste, and other similar evils. The Teacher should eradicate these causes of failure by prescribing antidotes taken from the Veda and the Smṛti, as well as by enforcing general rules of good conduct, such as avoidance of anger and practice of harmlessness, and also by indicating such particular courses of special discipline as are not contradictory to knowledge. (269) He should also give sound instruction in avoidance of pride and in other such means to knowledge mentioned at Bhagavad Gītā XIII.7-11.

What is the nature of the Teacher (ācārya)? He has compassion, sympathy, inner and outer control, power to understand arguments and retain them in his memory, skill in dialectical defence and attack and other such qualities. He is indifferent to enjoyments, whether of this world or of another. He has given up the paraphernalia of ritualistic action. (270) He is without such shortcomings as hypocrisy, pride, deceit, craftiness, trickery, jealousy, untruthfulness, egoism and possessiveness. His only purpose is service of others. His only desire is to promote spiritual wisdom.... (271)

When the pupil has learned the characteristics of the supreme Self, and is eager to escape from the sea of transmigratory experience, the Teacher should ask him, "Who are you, my dear one?"

Suppose the pupil says, "I was the son of a Brahmin from such and such a family, and am an unmarried student of the Vedic texts (brahmacārin)" — or else, if the case be so, "I was a householder, and am now a wandering monk (parivrāṭ) of the Paramahaṃsa order, desirous of escaping from the ocean of transmigratory existence with its great sharks of birth and death."

The Teacher should then reply: "Verily, here (in this world of transmigratory experience), my dear one, when your body dies it will be eaten by crows or will decompose into the earth. How, then, can you hope to escape from the ocean of transmigratory experience? For if you have been reduced to ashes on the bank of a river, you will not afterwards be able to cross over to the other side."

Suppose the pupil then says: "I am other than

the body. The body, it is true, is born, dies and is eaten by crows, decomposes into earth, can be destroyed by weapons and fire and so forth, and is subject to disease and other evils. But I am the one who, from the force of the merit and demerit of my past actions, entered into the body like a bird entering into a nest. And on the death of the present body I again and again proceed to other bodies through the force of merit and demerit, as a bird proceeds to other nests after the first one has been destroyed. Similarly, in this beginningless cycle of transmigration, I acquired and lost many a body through the force of merit and demerit arising from my deeds, appearing and disappearing as god, man and beast, revolving helplessly on the wheel of birth and death like a bucket fixed to a machine at a well. Eventually I arrived at my present body. And having become nauseated by this revolving on the wheel of transmigration, I have come to you, holy Sir, to put the revolutions of this wheel to an end. Therefore I am eternal and verily different from the body. Bodies come and go like clothes."

The Teacher should then reply, "You have said right. You have seen the truth...." (272)

* * * * *

2. This being so, (273) the Spirit as experiencer or individual soul, perched on the same tree of the body as the Spirit, the Witness, in the manner already explained, is weighed down by the grievous burden of nescience and desire and attachment to the fruits of works, and drifts about helpless, like a bottle-gourd floating on the water of the sea. It identifies itself with the body. It wrongly supposes itself to be so and so, the son of such and such, the grandson of so and so, lean, stout, virtuous, without virtue, happy or miserable as the case may be, and

imagines that it has no deeper nature than this. In this condition it suffers repeated birth and death, and is connected with and severed from relatives in different births. It grows miserable and suffers through such feelings as "I am good for nothing, my son has perished, my wife is dead, what is the good of further life?" It is bemused, which means it is worried over troubles of various kinds because of its failure to discriminate (274) its true nature from external factors. In this condition, it hurtles about from birth to birth as animal, man or departed spirit (preta). (275)

Sometimes, after many births, and through the influence of much purity and accumulated merit, it receives instruction in the path of yoga from some compassionate soul. (276) The next stage is to acquire the virtues of non-injury, truth-speaking, continence, renunciation of all benefits and the spiritual equipment of inner and outer control and other qualities, along with concentration of the mind in meditation (samādhi). In this condition he may perceive in meditation that "other" being, differentiated from himself through a different adjunct as explained in the simile of the two birds on a tree, the Lord, whom he has propitiated (as if external to himself) with meditation and ritualistic acts. The Lord is not the transmigrating entity, because He is beyond hunger, thirst, grief, delusion, old age and death. He is the Lord of the world. And the meditator now identifies himself with the Lord and feels, "I am this Self of all that stands unchanged within all creatures. I am not that other illusory self (māyā-ātman), limited by adjuncts arising from nescience." Eventually he sees the entire world-appearance as belonging to himself, the supreme Lord. When this final stage has been reached, he has gone beyond sorrow, he is saved from the ocean of sorrow, he has done all that is needful." (277)

* * * * *

3. Consider the case, my dear one, of how in the world some thief might bandage someone's eyes and take him away from the land of the Gāndhāras (278) and deposit him with his eyes bandaged in some distant spot in the jungle far away from all human life, and how that person, having lost his sense of direction, might yell at the top of his voice straight out in front – or the word might mean "to the east" – and to the rear – or the word might mean "to the west" – and might say, "I am from Gāndhāra: my eyes have been bandaged and I have been left here by a thief." Suppose, then, that some compassionate person freed him from his eye-bandages and said, "Gāndhāra is to the north from here. You must first go to such and such a place." He, being thus freed by the compassionate person from his bandages, would go from village to village, asking the way to the next village each time. For we assume him to be an educated and intelligent man, able to understand the instructions for proceeding to another village. Such a man would eventually reach Gāndhāra, though not a person too foolish to understand the instructions, or a person carried away by his desire to see some other place.

Think, again, of the person described in this example. He is separated from his country, Gāndhāra. His eyes have been bandaged by a thief. He has lost his sense of direction and feels bemused. He is suffering from hunger and thirst. He has been taken into the jungle which is infested with many evils and dangers, such as tigers and robbers. Overcome with misery, he simply stands still, crying out at the top of his voice, longing to be released from his bandages. Somehow or other, by great good fortune, he is released from his bandages by some compassionate person and eventually arrives back at his own country, Gāndhāra, to his immense joy and relief.

Such also is the case of the one who is torn away from his real condition as the Self of the universe by the merit and demerit arising from former deeds, and deposited in the jungle of the human body. The latter is composed of the five elements, and is the abode of wind, bile, phlegm, blood, fat, flesh, bones, marrow, sperm, worms, urine and excrement. Various pairs of opposites assail it, such as heat and cold. Here such a one resides, with his eyes bandaged by the thick cloth of infatuation, and afflicted with thirst for tangible objects such as wife, sons, wealth, cattle, relatives and the like, as well as for the intangible benefits of the future life.

He is entangled in the net of a hundred thousand evils in the form of such thoughts as "I am a man," "This is my son," "These are my relatives," "I am happy," "I am miserable," "I am foolish," "I am wise," "I follow the spiritual law," " I have powerful relatives," "I am born," "I die," "I am old and decrepit," "I am a sinner," "My son has died," "I have lost my wealth," "Woe, alas! I am done for, how can I go on living?" "How can I escape?" "Who will save me?"

Somehow, through very great merit arising from past deeds, while crying out thus, he manages to find refuge in some supremely compassionate person who has direct knowledge of the fact that his own real Self is pure Being or the Absolute, who is established in the Absolute, and who is free from bondage. From this supremely compassionate person of perfect enlightenment he receives instruction in noting the defects attaching to the objects encountered in transmigratory life. Eventually, when he has become indifferent to the objects of the world, he is taught, "Thou art not a denizen of the world, with worldly characteristics such as 'being the son of so-and-so.' Thou art pure Being." In this way he becomes released from his bandages of nescience and delusion and reaches his own true Self, as the inhabitant of Gāndhāra reached Gāndhāra, and becomes happy.

This is what the text means when it says, "One who has a Teacher acquires knowledge." It is of such a person only, who has a Teacher, and whose bandages of nescience have been removed, that it is said, "In his case the delay will only extend until he is released from the body." It means (the delay in) realization of pure Being, one's own true nature. (279)

* * * * *

4. The next verse of the text explains the nature of one qualified for the supreme knowledge, who has become indifferent to all empirical life, consisting in ends and means.

"Having scrutinized the 'worlds' to be attained through ritual ...". That is, there is a certain course of ritual that it is taught in the Ṛg and other Vedas as "lower knowledge," and which has to be performed by the man afflicted with desire and with merit and demerit and other such evils, (280) as a result of natural nescience. Fulfilment of such ritual produces 'worlds' (states of experience), such as those to which one is conducted along the Southern or Northern Paths. (281) And there are other worlds (or states of experience) which arise through neglecting to perform what is prescribed and perpetration of what is forbidden, such as the various hells, or the states in which one becomes an animal or an unshriven ghost (preta). "Scrutinizing" these worlds mean weighing them up in every way through perception, inference, comparison and revelation. (282)

These worlds belong to the domain of empirical experience. Some are unmanifest, others belong to the manifest world, and range from the consciousness of Brahmā to that of stocks and stones. They go on giving rise to one another like seed and sprout. They bristle with a million evils. They are as empty as the spiky seeds of the plantain, comparable to a mirage or to a cloud-city, to a dream or to a bubble or foam. Every moment they collapse at a glance. They are amassed through merit and demerit, arising from acts prompted by desire and other evil states associated with the nescience that one has now put behind one.

The text uses the word "Brahmin" because the Brahmin in the true sense is one who has a special right to knowledge of the Absolute since he has given up all else. Scrutinizing these worlds, he should feel profound indifference towards them, and should reason as follows. In this world there is nothing that is not made (and consequently transient). All the 'worlds' arise through action and are hence of limited duration. There is nothing constant. Action is the instrument for procuring the transitory only. There are only the four (well known) effects of action, and no others, namely, producing, procuring, purifying and altering. (283) But what I desire is something eternal, immortal, beyond danger, firm as a rock, fixed and immovable, and not that which is the reverse of all this. So what is the use of action? It is extremely troublesome to perform, and only brings further evils in its train.

Overcome thus with profound indifference to the world, the Brahmin should approach a spiritual Teacher who has compassion and is equipped with inner and outer control and the rest of the spiritual wealth. The text uses the particle "eva" to emphasize that he *must* approach a Teacher, the rule being that no one should attempt to realize the Absolute independently, even if they were familiar with the requisite texts.

Holding a load of fuel in his hands (as a sign of humility and readiness to serve), he should approach a spiritual Teacher who is both conversant with the meaning of the Vedic texts and also devoted exclusively to the Absolute. This means that, having given up all ritualistic activity, he remains exclusively devoted to the Absolute, in the same sense that one speaks of someone as "exclusively devoted to austerity." No one who is still engaged in action for the sake of individual ends can be called exclusively devoted to the Absolute. For action for the sake of individual ends and knowledge of the Self are contradictory. Brahmins should approach such a spiritual Teacher in the traditional way, and should ask about the Indestructible Principle (akṣara), the Spirit (puruṣa) and the Real (satya).

The text goes on to say that the Teacher who has realized the Absolute should give the right teaching, which means teaching according to the true meaning of the Vedic texts. That is to say, he should give it to the one who approaches him in the proper way, with a calm mind, with pride and other psychological defects rooted out, possessed of inner and outer control, which implies indifference to everything empirical. He should teach him truly that supreme knowledge, that knowledge of the Absolute whereby one comes to know the Indestructible Principle (284) which is also called the Spirit (puruṣa) because it is infinite (pūrṇa) and because it lies in the city of the body (puri śayana). It is the Real (satya) because its nature is such. It is called the Indestructible Principle (akṣara) because it is unalterable (akṣaraṇa), in no way subject to damage (akṣata) and inexhaustible (akṣaya). And there is a law even for the (enlightened) Teacher that he should rescue from the ocean of nescience those good pupils who approach him in the proper way. (285)

* * * * *

5. But how is this special knowledge gained? Listen, says the text, to the way it is gained. First one must betake oneself to a spiritual Teacher (ācārya). Then there must be complete prostration and long-drawn obeisance. There must be questioning all round the subject, such as "How does bondage arise?", "How does liberation arise?", "What is knowledge?",and "What is nescience?". There must also be service of the Teacher. When the Teacher is drawn over by these acts of devotion, he will impart to you this special knowledge. The text specifies Teachers who know the truth by immediate intuition, as some Teachers have this, while others do not. It is the former (only) who will impart effective knowledge to you.

From this more follows, as the next verse shows. When you have assimilated the knowledge that they impart to you, you will never again become victim of delusion (moha), as you are now, O descendant of Pāṇḍu (Arjuna). Through this knowledge you will have direct apprehension of (the true nature of) all beings from the creator-god Brahmā to the meanest clump of grass. You will see them as present in your own inmost Self, and will be aware "They exist in me." Hence you will also be aware that they exist in Me too, Vāsudeva, the supreme Lord, and thus will be aware of that identity of the Knower of the Field (286) with the Lord, which is the ultimate theme of all Upanishadic teaching. (287)

* * * * *

6. He now goes on to explain how knowledge destroys demerit, introducing an example. "Just as a well-lit fire turns its fuel, the wood, into ashes, O Arjuna ...". Here the fire stands for knowledge. And when it is said that it burns up all actions, it means that it deprives them of their seed-bearing character. (288) The fire of knowledge cannot burn up action literally, like a fire burning up its fuel. Hence the meaning is that right knowledge is the cause of all actions losing their seed-bearing character. It is clear that the mass of (previous) action that was responsible for initiating the enlightened man's present birth has already begun to bear fruit and can be exhausted only by being experienced out to the end. (289) But all the acts committed in the present birth before the enlightenment, and all actions performed after enlightenment, and all the actions of the many past births (that were not involved in the initiation of the present birth) are "reduced to ashes" by knowledge of the Self.

Hence, the Lord goes on to affirm, there is no purifier like knowledge. The one who purifies himself and makes himself fit for release through success in the Yoga of Action (karma-yoga) (290) and in the Yoga of Concentration (samādhi-yoga) attains this knowledge after a long time.

Now the Lord goes on to explain the sole means by which one can attain this knowledge. It is the man of faith who attains it. Even when they have faith, some people are still slack, so that the Lord says that only he obtains the knowledge who applies himself whole-heartedly to the means, such as service of the Teacher. Even one who has faith and whole-hearted application may yet fail to control his senses. So the Lord specifies further that the senses must be controlled, which means withdrawn from objects. He who is in this way equipped with faith, and who is whole-hearted in his application, and who has controlled his senses, will certainly attain this knowledge.

The mere external means of obtaining spiritual knowledge, such as prostration, etc., are not infallible, as they may be performed hypocritically. But, when faith and the other characteristics just mentioned are present, hypocrisy and so on are ruled out, and then prostration and the rest become an infallible means. (291)

* * * * *

7. I have taught this science (śāstra) to you (says Kṛṣṇa to Arjuna), for your true benefit, to put an end to your transmigratory life once and for all. This science should never in any circumstances be taught to anyone who has not performed austerity, (292) nor to one who, though he performs austerity, lacks deep devotion to the Teacher and to his chosen deity (deva), nor to one who, though devoted, and a man of austerities, is disobedient. Also unfit to receive this teaching is anyone who thinks that I, Vāsudeva, am but an ordinary man, and accuses Me of self-praise and other defects, and cannot, in his ignorance, accept the fact that I am the Lord of all. This teaching should not be given to him either.

From this we conclude that the one to whom this science is to be taught must be devoted to the Lord (bhagavān), a man of austerity, obedience and subservience. There is another text in which it is said that this science may be taught *either* to an intelligent man *or* to a man of self-discipline, and we must interpret this to mean "either to an intelligent man *or* to a man of self-discipline *who is at the same time obedient.*" The teaching should not be given to anyone who is not obedient or devoted, even if he be a man of self-discipline or intelligent. If a person feels resentment against the Lord, he should not receive the teaching, even if he has all the other virtues under the sun. It should be given only to one who is obedient and devoted to his Teacher. This is the rule for the traditional transmission of this science. (294)

4. THE TEACHER AND THE TEXTS

In this section, the Extract in Group A discusses a question of principle. It is a principle that is of great service to the Advaita Teacher, and which was not always observed by Śaṃkara's Vedantic predecessors or by later Vedānta commentators of other schools. (295) It lays down that there are three main divisions among the Vedic texts, not two. There is the Karma Kāṇḍa, dealing with ritual. And beyond this, the texts which deal with knowledge of the Absolute must themselves be divided into two sections. There are those of the Upāsana Kāṇḍa. Like the ritualistic texts, they give injunctions to act. But the action which they enjoin is not ritual, but meditation on the Absolute in association with this or that finite form, usually relating directly or indirectly to the ritualistic texts. From the purely logical standpoint, therefore, the view of the Absolute they imply conflicts with that given in another group of Upanishadic texts, those of the Jñāna Kāṇḍa, which treat of the Absolute in its true nature, void of all finitude and distinctions. The Absolute, so understood, is beyond the scope of all action, and cannot be the object of a prescribed meditation. Passages in the Upanishads containing mere texts for meditation are often recognizable by the appearance of the particle "iti" at the end of them, the Sanskrit equivalent of our inverted commas.

The texts of the Upāsana Kāṇḍa may be taken as conveying truths when and in so far as they do not contradict the texts teaching non-duality. But they exist for the benefit of a different kind of pupil from the one whose concern is with the highest texts. The meditations of the Upāsana Kāṇḍa are examples of teaching that is in a sense provisional. They may be used to purify the mind and prepare it for the path of knowledge (jñāna). Or they may be taken as ends in themselves, in which case they constitute an "indirect" or "gradual" path to the type of liberation called krama-mukti. (296) But as the Upanishads teach the existence of the Absolute in its pure form, preparation for this latter teaching must be the ultimate purpose of all parts of the Veda, even the ritualistic hymns. So it is wrong to treat any part of the Veda as dogmatically affirming duality in such a way that non-duality would be contradicted.

The Extracts in Group B illustrate directly some of the ways in which the Advaita Teacher arranges and communicates the texts of the Veda to the pupil. The detailed examination of his presentation of the very highest of the texts, "That thou art," will be reserved for Chapter XV in Volume VI. Meanwhile, fourteen, mostly short, Extracts in Group B of the present chapter will show the Teacher active in elevating the pupil to the point where he is ready to embark on the final stage of the discipline.

The Extracts mostly raise theological issues. For example, the first one delimits the sphere of Vedic revelation and sense-perception as separate, and observes that one cannot make assumptions about the Vedic ritual which are themselves intrinsically improbable, and which are not supported by the texts, merely through arguments based on analogy with what sometimes happens in the world. The second Extract shows how the eulogistic passages (artha-vāda) must be accepted as giving true information, except when the information they give conflicts with other certified knowledge. In the latter case, they must be interpreted figuratively. The third Extract establishes that all the characteristics attributed to anything anywhere in the Veda must invariably be attributed to it collectively wherever it is mentioned, unless there is some special reason for not doing so. The fourth Extract establishes the theological point that if a text negates *some* characteristics of the Absolute it is to be taken as implicitly negating *all* characteristics, while if it affirms some characteristics of it, it is to be taken as implicitly affirming *all* the characteristics that are attributed to the Absolute anywhere in the Veda.

The fifth and sixth Extracts explain and illustrate the value of the story-telling method of teaching which often occurs in the Upanishads. It not only makes difficult points easier to understand but impresses moral teaching on the hearer with the help of visual images. The seventh Extract shows how even non-Brahmin Teachers can give spiritual teaching to pupils, though they cannot give them the initiation ceremony for learning the Veda by heart. It adds the point that the Teacher can arouse the understanding of the pupils by asking questions.

The eighth Extract illustrates the value of similes. The ninth illustrates the method of teaching by successive approximations, as the eyes of the bridal couple are directed to the tiny star Arundhatī (Alkorin).(297) Extracts ten to twelve illustrate the method of teaching by false attribution followed by subsequent denial, already met with in the first Volume. (298) The thirteenth Extract explains the treatment of texts found in the Upanishads apparently affirming the creation of a world of plurality. They have to be seen in the wider context of the metaphysical teaching of the Upanishads as a whole. They conform to the metaphysically ignorant standpoint of the hearer, and have to be corrected or seen as figurative in the light of other texts of deeper metaphysical import. The fourteenth and last Extract furnishes an example of determining where a particular topic begins (upakrama) and ends (upasaṃhāra), and how the main topic of a passage gives the guideline for its interpretation.

The section is necessarily scrappy, on account of its subject-matter. It aims to do no more than illustrate the theological activity of the Teacher through examples of interpretative work taken from Śaṃkara's own texts. The Teacher's other, and more vital, role as spiritual director is reserved for Chapter XV in the next Volume. The section also illustrates Śaṃkara's use of some of the traditional exegetical maxims of his day. For a more thorough account, the reader may be recommended to turn to the articles listed in the Bibliography under the names Devasthali and Renou. Here a few observations will be appended which may throw some light on the technicalities to come.

Śaṃkara inherited the scholastic framework of stating a text, raising a doubt, offering a *prima facie* view (pūrva-pakṣa) and eventually arriving at a conclusion (siddhānta), which could be preceded and followed by subordinate doubts and rejoinders, from the grammarian Patañjali, as supplemented by the work of the Pūrva Mīmāṃsā. Renou says that, though the framework was adhered to in almost all philosophical and exegetical writing at that period in India, nowhere is it found adhered to so firmly as in the work of Śabara and Saṃkara. (299)

Within this framework, Śaṃkara leaves the Advaita Ācārya fairly free to exercise his individual powers of insight into the meaning of the texts. In general, it is the exponents of the *prima facie* view in his Brahma Sūtra Commentary who appeal to exegetical and grammatical maxims, while the final view may depend on taking a wider view of the context (prakaraṇa) than they had done, or may take account of an indirect hint (liṅga) in the text they had missed. (300) It is true that Śaṃkara quotes Pūrva Mīmāṃsā Sūtra III.iii.13, a maxim which states that in the interpretation of a text the literal meaning (śruti) takes precedence over all others. But it also makes provision for appeal to an indirect meaning (liṅga), to a special interpretation based on relationship with the preceding sentence (vākya), to the wider context (prakaraṇa), to the order of a series of injunctions elsewhere which may enable one to interpret the present text by analogy (krama or sthāna) and to inference based on the name of a ritual(samākhyā). (301) Appeal may only be made to these different criteria successively, introducing further criteria as each earlier criterion fails to yield a satisfactory meaning. (302) But these criteria were, after all, devised for the interpretation of ritualistic texts, not of texts containing the final metaphysical truth. Śaṃkara remarks that the rules for interpreting ritualistic texts do not always hold in the context of metaphysical instruction. For instance, there can be alternatives (vikalpa) in the former but not in the latter. (303) And Śaṃkara gives the impression of using the different criteria quite freely, without feeling bound to observe the laws of relative priority.

Throughout the first Book of the Brahma Sūtra Commentary, interpretation of the Upanishadic texts proceeds largely through appeal to indirect hints (liṅga) that the dualistic Sāṃkhya opponent has missed, and through refutation of the non-existent "hints" (304) to which he has appealed. An example of a special interpretation based upon appeal to relationship with the previous sentence (vākya) is found at the close of the Commentary to Brahma Sūtra I.i.24. At another place the *prima facie* view is based on an interpretation of the subject-matter as determined at the beginning of a new topic (upakrama). But this view is set aside through appeal to the wider context (vākyānvaya). (305) At the Commentary to Brahma Sūtra I.i.29 appeal is made, based on the Sūtra itself, to the principle of "abundance of connections" (saṃbandha-bhūman). (306) As the term "Cosmic Vital Energy" is connected with the Absolute in innumerable places throughout the Veda, it may (on the ground of "abundance of connections") be taken to be so connected in the present case also, although no explicit mention of the fact is made. However, in many cases the points in the text that mark the beginning and end of a topic are a sufficient criterion in themselves to determine the interpretation of the passage. For example, at Brahma Sūtra I.i.1 Śaṃkara appeals to this criterion alone to show that the texts at the beginning and end of the third chapter of the Kauṣītaki Upanishad enclose a passage that forms a single topic, knowledge of the Self, and that all the intervening material must be interpreted as subordinate to this end, and must not be regarded as initiating new topics.

Another technical term of the Pūrva Mīmāṃsa exegesis that appears in Śaṃkara's theological discussions is that of "vākya-bheda" or "splitting up of the passage." The Pūrva Mīmāṃsa maintained that a long imperative passage, which, from the purely grammatical point of view, could be taken either as one long complicated injunction or as a series of separate ones, *could* be interpreted as constituting a series of separate injunctions, but only if grounds for doing so could be shown. (307) Other things being equal, it is better to take the whole passage as forming a unity (vākya-ekatā). The principle of "splitting up the passage" is a two-edged one, capable of being used either in an approving or a disapproving sense according to whether the splitting is or is not considered justified. Examples can be found in Śaṃkara's texts where he argues for as well as against splitting up a long injunctive text into separate injunctions. For example, at Brahma Sūtra III.iii.58 he argues that the Upanishadic injunctions to meditate and to know should not all be treated as subdivisions of one all-comprehending injunction to meditate on the Absolute, but that it is more justifiable to regard each injunction as separate, since their subject-matter is different, and the different words they use for meditation or knowledge imply different degrees and kinds of knowledge. On the other hand, at Brahma Sūtra II.ii.14 he argues that verses I.iii.10-17 of the Kaṭha Upanishad constitute different aspects of one meditation on the Self, and should not be broken down by "splitting up the passage" and made to refer to separate meditations, each bearing on one separate member of a series of different cosmological principles.

The Advaita Teacher appeals to the maxims of the Grammarians and Logicians as well as to those of the exegetes of the Pūrva Mīmāṃsā school. Śaṃkara appeals also to illustrative stories, like that of "the tenth man," (308) which must have been current amongst earlier Vedanta teachers, as they are referred to without explanation, as if they would be already familiar to the student.

Śaṃkara makes great use of the Law of Contradiction in refuting Bhartṛprapañca, and also in refuting the Jainas. The fact that he was able (309) to refer the doctrine back to the Brahma Sūtras themselves (Sūtra II.ii.33) is interesting, and puts a question mark over the common belief that the later Bhedābheda Commentators represent the true view of the Sūtras, while Śaṃkara does not. For the whole world-view of the Bhedābheda Vādins rests on the denial of the validity of the Law of Contradiction.

Throughout his refutation of opponent's views, Śaṃkara repeatedly appeals to the Law of the Excluded Middle. For example, if the Sāṃkhyas posit the existence of the three "constituents" (guṇa) in a state of equilibrium before the manifestation of the universe, then the constituents must either pass or not pass into a state of imparity, any third possibility being excluded. (310) Thus Śaṃkara appeals to the Law of Contradiction and to the Law of the Excluded Middle. And (at least in sketching an alternative view) he appeals to the Law of Identity in the words "For whatever object is critically determined to have a given characteristic as an essential property retains that characteristic through all changes of time and place. If it could lose it, all critical knowledge would be at an end." (311)

The Veda exists to throw light on how men can attain their ends. They can secure favourable material conditions in the after-life through the performance of ritual. They can enter into association with the divine forces presiding over the ritual through the performance of prescribed meditations on the symbolic significance of certain elements in the ritual. And they can throw off ignorance and realize their true nature as the immortal, infinite Self through adherence to the discipline of hearing, cogitating over and continuously meditating on the supreme texts of the Upanishads. As exegete, the Advaita Teacher has to pick his way amongst the texts, assigning to each its due place and weight, using the traditional maxims that are available, some coming from the Grammarians, some from the

Logicians, some from the professional exegetes of the ritualistic portion of the Veda, the Pūrva Mīmāṃsakas. Without denuding the ritualistic texts or the texts concerned with prescribed meditations on symbolic themes of their true meaning, he must nevertheless show that the great mass of the texts of the Upanishads are concerned, directly or indirectly, with teaching the true nature of the Self. And the essence of the method, as we have so often seen, is to take the affirmative texts, where they ascribe any finite features to the Absolute, as preparatory to the negative ones. Even the supreme text "That thou art," as we shall see, (312) is in practical effect a negation, although it is an affirmation in its grammatical form.

But beyond his exegetical function, the Teacher also has the role of spiritual educator. He is not only concerned with arranging texts, but also with training the mind of the pupil first to understand them and then to become 'no-mind' through intuitive apprehension of their metaphysical content. In this role, he casts aside the paraphernalia of traditional maxims and awakens the *reason* of the pupil directly, with a view to developing that power of discrimination (viveka) without which final enlightenment from the supreme texts cannot come. We have already had a glimpse of the Teacher in this role.(313) In the sixth and final volume to come, after an intervening chapter on the indirect path to liberation, we shall rejoin the Teacher in Chapter XV as he strives once more to awaken the pupil to a direct intuition of reality through preparing his mind for the understanding of the highest texts by forcing him to reflect upon the implications of his ordinary experience.

TEXTS ON THE TEACHER AND THE TEXTS: GROUP A

1. The Absolute must be known as being without finite attributes such as colour, etc., not as

having them. Why? "Because," as the author of the Sūtras puts it, "that (is how it is described in the texts) primarily (concerned with expounding its nature)." Thus we have: "Not gross, not subtle, not short, not long," "Void of sound, tangibility or colour, it is undecaying, not subject to diminution," "The ether (i.e. the Self) is what brings out name and form: that in which these two stand is the Absolute," "The Divine Spirit is immortal, it includes all that is within and all that is without, unborn," "This Absolute has nothing before it, nothing after it, nothing within it, nothing outside it. This Self is the Absolute (brahman), which experiences everything from within." (314) In these and other such (negative) texts, the main purpose is to expound the metaphysical principle of the Self, the undifferentiated Absolute, and not any other principle. And this was established earlier in the Sūtras, "But that (i.e. the Absolute) (is the ultimate purport of the Upanishadic texts), because of the harmony of the texts (when conceived as all directly or indirectly communicating the Absolute". (315)

Thus, in this class of texts, the Absolute must be known as verily formless, just as the texts teach. In the other class of texts, which deal with the Absolute as associated with finite forms, the Veda is not concerned with expounding the Absolute in its true nature. Such texts are concerned with prescribing subjects for meditation (upāsana-vidhi). They may be accepted as true where they do not contradict the texts expounding the Absolute in its true nature. But where there is a contradiction, the latter must be taken to prevail. This is the ground for the definite conclusion, "Though there are both texts attributing form to the Absolute and also texts denying form, the Absolute must be known as, verily, without form, and not the reverse." (316)

(XIII.4) THE VEDA AND THE TEACHER (TEXTS)

TEXTS ON THE TEACHER AND THE TEXTS: GROUP B

1. You spoke earlier of ritualistic action being able to produce different results from usual when associated with meditation, just as poison and curds produce different results from usual when associated with spells and sugar respectively. (317) We do not contest the assertions about the behaviour of poison and curds, and this matter is to be settled by perception and inference. But in regard to a matter that can only be settled by Vedic revelation (such as the question of whether or not liberation is attainable through ritual supported by meditation), one cannot, without the support of any relevant Vedic text, just lightly assume that the usual results of anything (318) can be modified in special circumstances, (319) in the way that the usual results of poison or curds are modified in certain circumstances. Nor should the Veda be regarded as authoritative (in its literal meaning) if it were to contradict truths already ascertained by other means of knowledge, for example, it it were to say, "Fire is cool and dampens what it burns." (320) But where the revealed text is dealing with its own peculiar province (of revealing truths not accessible to other means of knowledge), then, if the other means of knowledge are applied in this context, they are not genuine means of knowledge, but mere appearances of such. (321) We can illustrate how means of knowledge can be mere appearances of such from ordinary life. Some simple souls perceive fireflies as flashes of fire, and the sky as literally having the form of a dome and the pure ether in it of being subject to contamination (by dust and murky clouds). These are perceptions, and even determinate perceptions. But when the truth about them has been ascertained by another means of knowledge (*viz.* inference), these determinate perceptions of such simple souls turn out to have been mere appearances of perception. Hence, since every text in the Veda is authoritative in some way or other,

those texts in which it deals with its own peculiar province must be left as they stand, and not interpreted according to human ingenuity. No amount of human ingenuity will prevent the sun from illuminating colour. And, in the same way, no amount of human ingenuity can alter the content of what the Veda actually says. (322)

* * * * *

2. Here a further objection might be raised against the possibility of the gods and other supernatural beings being eligible for the holy knowledge. (323) Āditya and other names suggesting a luminous deity, such an objector might claim, in fact refer only to the mere physical disc of light which changes position continually, day and night. For this is what is generally agreed in the world, and is what the sequel to the Vedic passage previously quoted shows. (324) It cannot be supposed that a disc of light has a heart, or consciousness, or that it is capable of hearing supplication, as it is taken to be non-conscious, just like clay and other material substances. And similar remarks apply in the case of fire (agni) and other deified natural forces....

The Epics and Purāṇas, too, being of human authorship, (325) require the support of some authority before they can be accepted as evidence. The eulogistic passages of the Veda are syntactically connected with the injunctions, and cannot be accepted as proof that the gods and other supernatural beings have bodies, because their purpose is quite different from true statement of fact, being merely to eulogize the ritual. The Vedic hymns (mantra), too, which are shown by the recognized tests to have their proper place in the ritual, and which only have the function of (empty) assertion and reminding, (326) are said to have no authoritative power to communicate information. From all this it follows that the doctrine that the gods and other supernatural beings are eligible for the holy knowledge is wrong (since they do not exist).

The author of the Sūtras indicates that he rejects the view with the word "but"....

It was further maintained that the hymns and eulogistic passages had no power to instruct us about the bodily forms assumed by the gods, because their purpose was something different. (327) To this our reply is that it is the presence or absence of an idea in our minds that causes belief in the existence or non-existence of an object, and the question of purpose does not come into it. One who goes on a journey for some other purpose may very well notice the presence of grass and leaves on the road as he goes.

You might object against this that the case was not parallel. In the case of the grass and leaves, you might say, perception was in play, and their existence was known through this. In the case under discussion, on the contrary, we have only an eulogistic passage syntactically connected with the expression of an injunction, and one cannot establish that any other means of knowledge is in play that has a different purpose and is concerned with the establishing of fact. For where a longer grammatical unit conveys one idea, it is not in the power of a subordinate phrase included within it to convey a different one. In a text like "Do not drink alcohol!", which contains the word 'not', one takes all the words together and arrives at one meaning only, a prohibition against drinking alcohol. One cannot *also* single out two words only and arrive at the meaning "Drink alcohol!".

To this we reply that the case *you* cite is not parallel either. It is correct to say that in the text prohibiting the drinking of alcohol one must not pay attention to the meaning that some small group of words within it would have if taken in isolation, as here the words (of the prohibition) form a single grammatical unit. But it is otherwise in the case of an injunction and an accompanying eulogistic passage. Here the words in the eulogistic passage form a separate grammatical unit from those in the injunction, and acquaint one (not with anything one has to do but) with facts. It is only when they have already performed this function, and one goes on to enquire into their purpose, that they are found to act as an eulogy of the injunction. For example, in the case of the injunction, "Desirous of welfare, one should offer up a white goat consecrated to Vāyu," (328) all the words are grammatically connected with the injunction. But this is not true of the words of the eulogistic passage which comes next, "Vāyu is the swiftest deity. The sacrificer runs to Vāyu with appropriate gifts and Vāyu grants him welfare." It is not that Vāyu has to offer anything up, or that "the swiftest deity" has to offer anything up. On the contrary, the words form a special subordinate phrase of their own, designed to explain the nature of Vāyu: and thus they act as an eulogy of the injunction, conveying the idea, "This sacrifice is offered to a splendid deity."

Where the matter stated in a subordinate phrase of this kind is accessible to any other means of knowledge we have an eulogistic passage (artha-vāda) based on restatement of what is already known (anuvāda). When it stands in contradiction with other means of knowledge, we have an eulogistic passage based on a figure of speech (guṇa-vāda). But what about the (most numerous) cases where the matter stated in an eulogistic passage is neither corroborated by, nor in contradiction with, other means of knowledge? Should we say that we have figurative speech because of the absence of any corroborating means of knowledge? Or should we say we have direct revelation about something which actually exists because there is no evidence contradicting it? Those who take refuge in faith (329) must surely accept that these passages constitute direct revelation about something which actually exists, and are not to be dismissed as mere figures of speech. Similar reasoning should be applied to the hymns.

And one can go further. The very injunctions themselves, in so far as they enjoin the offering of oblations to Indra and other deities, imply that Indra and the other deities each have their own distinct form. For, if they did not, they could not be represented in the mind, and, if the deities did not have separate representations in the mind, one could not offer oblations specifically to this or that deity. And there is the text, "One should meditate on the deity to whom one is offering the oblation, saying 'vaṣaṭ'." (330) Nor can the mere name do duty for the object, as the name and the object are different. No one, therefore, who accepts the validity of the Vedas as a means of knowledge is in a position to deny that the forms of Indra and the other gods are exactly what they are known to be from the hymns and eulogistic passages. Even the Epics and Purāṇas are able to establish in the same sort of way how the gods have bodies, as the passages in which they treat of these subjects are based on the hymns and eulogistic passages of the Veda. (331)

* * * * *

3. In the passages in the Bṛhadāraṇyaka and Chāndogya Upanishads (332) mentioning the Quarrel

between the Senses, it is laid down that the Vital Energy (prāṇa) has to be meditated on because it has superior qualities. Speech and the other organs, too, are credited with excellence and other qualities, but these qualities are then attributed in greater measure to the Vital Energy, in such words as, "You are even more excellent in respect of that in which I am excellent." On the other hand, there are other passages in the traditions of other Vedic schools, such as the Kauṣītakas, dealing with the Quarrel of the Senses, in which the Vital Energy is said to be superior, but in which no "excellence" or other quality is admitted in respect of the other senses. One might instance such passages as, "And now follows the section on the attainment of supremacy. These deities (the senses) quarrelled about who was superior." (333) And here the doubt might arise whether or not the "excellence" and other virtues which are mentioned at one place should be understood at other places, where they are not mentioned, as well.

And one might initially suppose that they should not be understood. This is on account of the presence of the words "thus" in the phrase, "And so he who knows thus, knowing that superiority lies in the Vital Energy."(334) For the word "thus" refers to what has been said recently, and cannot be made to refer to groups of qualities that are only mentioned by other schools in different places of the Veda. Hence one should not seek to draw in from elsewhere other qualities beyond those explicitly mentioned in the text.

Against this view, the author of the Sūtras teaches that the qualities of excellence, etc., spoken of at one place in this context (of the Quarrel of the Senses) should be understood as being taught at other places where the Quarrel of the Senses is being mentioned too. (335) For one can recognize that it is the same one Vital Energy that is being taught throughout, and the conversation between the senses, and all other circumstances, are similar. And if the meditation is the same, how could these qualities fail to be understood on all other occasions, if they are mentioned on one occasion? True, the word "thus" occurring in the Kauṣītaki Upanishad cannot refer to the group of qualities mentioned in the Bṛhadāraṇyaka Upanishad, because they are not mentioned in close enough proximity. Nevertheless, they are included by the force of the word "thus" (evam) when it occurs in the (second) Bṛhadāraṇyaka passage (336) in the course of expounding the same meditation. And the groups of qualities which are included in an identical meditation when it is mentioned in the texts of another school cannot be excluded from the meditation as taught in one's own school. Nor does this result in the fault of suppressing what does occur in the Veda and vainly introducing what does not. For qualities taught in one Vedic school are to be understood as being taught everywhere else where teaching in the same context occurs, as that which has the qualities (as object of meditation) is a constant factor. When Devadatta, who is famous for qualities of courage and the like in his own land, journeys to another land where his qualities are not noticed, it does not follow that he loses these qualities. And just as with more familiar acquaintance the qualities of Devadatta come to be recognized even in the foreign land, so, with a special effort, the qualities that are meditated on in one school have to be meditated on by members of other schools as well. Hence it follows that the qualities that belong to an object of meditation have to be understood everywhere the meditation is dealt with, even if they are only mentioned in one of the various places where the meditation is taught.

(XIII.4) THE VEDA AND THE TEACHER (TEXTS)

In some places of the Veda, and in particular Vedic schools, we find texts concerned (not with meditation but) with a statement of the metaphysical nature of the Absolute, and which speak of the latter as being of the nature of bliss, as being a mass of pure Consciousness, as being omnipresent and as being the Self of all. And here the doubt might arise whether bliss and the rest were qualities attributed to the Absolute only in the places where they were specifically mentioned, or whether they had to be understood as all present in the Absolute throughout. And one might initially suppose that the qualities of the Absolute had to be accepted only when and where they were specifically mentioned.

Against this the author of the Sūtras affirms that bliss and other qualities of the Absolute (337) have to be understood as all present wherever the Absolute is taught. For in each case it is the same identical Absolute. Hence the example of the ferocity of Devadatta mentioned in the previous topic (of meditation on the Absolute applies here also and shows) that all the qualities of the Absolute that are mentioned anywhere have to be included in one's conception of the Absolute everywhere.

Does this mean that qualities like "Having joy for its head" have to be understood in every case of meditating on the Absolute? For the Taittirīya Upanishad, in the section following on that on the "Self as Bliss," says: "Joy is its head. Delight is its right wing. Divine power (brahman) is its tail and support." (338)

To this the following Sūtra makes reply. "Having joy for its head" and the other qualities mentioned at that point in the Taittirīya Upanishad are not to be understood as included in the Absolute wherever it is presented as an object of meditation. For joy, delight, extreme delight and bliss represent different grades of joy both in themselves and in relation to other experiencers. Where there are different grades there can be differences. But the Absolute is free from all internal distinction, as we know from such texts as "One only, without a second." (339) Furthermore, these qualities of "having joy for its head" and the like belong not to the Absolute but to the bliss sheath, (340) as we have already explained at Brahma Sūtra I.1.12. (341) And they are only imagined at all by way of a device to help introduce the mind to the Absolute in its highest form. It is not at all the case that they are taught as actually existing in the Absolute. All the less, therefore, can such qualities be supposed to be implied whenever the Absolute is mentioned. In speaking of them as qualities of the Absolute, the Teacher (i.e. the author of the Sūtras) was (not asserting the presence of these qualities in the Absolute but) only drawing attention to a general rule. This rule also applies in the case of other well-authenticated qualities attributed to the Absolute for purposes of meditation, such as "being the centre of all that is delightful" and being "one whose desires come true." (342)

In these cases, the object of the meditation, the Absolute, is admittedly one, but the meditations are different, as they have different starting-points, and hence the qualities mentioned as present at one place are not to be assumed as present in the others also. Two wives may offer service to one and the same king, one by holding the parasol and the other by wielding the fly-whisk. Here the object of the devotion is one and the same, but the manner of the devotion in the two cases is different, and each activity has its own peculiar nature. And the same can hold good in the case of different meditations performed on the same one Absolute. Different grades of a given quality are possible in the case of the Absolute as associated with qualities, as here we are in the realm of experience of distinctions, but not in the case of the Absolute in its highest form, void of all qualities. Hence "having true desires" and other such qualities that are occasionally ascribed to the Absolute are not to be assumed as taught for *all* meditations on the Absolute.

But the other qualities such as bliss, etc., (343) are mentioned for the sake of conveying the true essence and nature of the Absolute (and not to supply themes for meditation). They are all mentioned for the same purpose, and the substance in which they are said to inhere is one and the same, the Absolute, namely, whose true nature is being proclaimed. Hence they are all to be understood, everywhere, every time that any one of them is mentioned. For they are mentioned only to expound the nature of the Absolute. (344)

* * * * *

4. The Bṛhadāraṇyaka Upanishad says: "This, O Gārgī, is what the Brahmins call the Imperishable Principle, not gross, not fine, not short, not long, not red (like fire), not clinging (like water)." (345) And the Atharva Veda says: "But the higher knowledge (parā vidyā) is that whereby the Imperishable Principle is known, the Principle which is invisible, inapprehensible, without a source, indescribable." (346) And the Imperishable Principle, which is the Absolute in its highest form, is conveyed in other places too, by the negation of particular characteristics. Now, one might wonder whether all notions of particular characteristics were to be regarded as negated in all passages, or only those that were mentioned specifically at a given place. And one might initially suppose that only those

mentioned at a given place were to be regarded as negated, because the Veda mentions them at a separate place.

The present Sūtra opposes this idea and says that *all* notions of particular characteristics are to be understood as negated in all the passages, because, as he puts it, "The passages have the same purpose, and the subject-matter is the same." In each case, they are communicating knowledge of the Absolute by the negation of particulars, and we recognize that in each case the subject-matter is the same identical Absolute. In such circumstances, the ideas that hold good at one text certainly hold good at the others too.

And the principle enunciated here also holds good for the Sūtra, "Bliss and other qualities pertaining to the Supreme." (347) The only difference is that there it was texts affirming qualities positively of the Absolute, whereas here it is texts negating qualities of the Absolute that are under consideration. They are considered separately only according to requirements of exposition.

The author then refers to rules surrounding the Upasad ceremonies by way of example. (348) He refers to the fact that in the Upasad ceremonies, in the complete (four-day) form of the sacrifice originated by Jāmadagni, the formulae such as "O Agni, accept the offering, accept the sacrifice," which are used in offering the cakes, come from the Veda of the Udgātṛ priests (i.e. the singers of the Sāma Veda) and yet are used by the Adhvaryu priests (specialists in the low-voiced prayers of the Yajur Veda). This is because the Adhvaryu priests perform the actual offering of the cakes, and because the texts enjoining subordinate elements of the ritual have to be interpreted so as to harmonize with the ritual as a whole. The same principle operates here too. Whatever is said about the Imperishable Principle at one place applies in all other places as well. And in this connection it has been said in the ritualistic section, "Where the principal and subordinate instructions conflict, the Veda sides with the principal instructions, as the subordinate instructions are only for their sake." (349)

* * * * *

5. The figure of the Brahmin Gārgya, who identifies himself with this standpoint, (350) is set up as its imaginary spokesman. The opposite standpoint, that of the one who has an intuitive vision of the Self, is represented by Ajātaśatru, the (imaginary) listener to the discourse. For it is when some doctrine is presented in the form of an imaginary dialogue embodying various *prima facie* views and a considered conclusion that the audience is able to master it. Otherwise, if it is just presented through a plain connected argument, as in the purely logical treatises, it can become hard to understand if the point at issue is a very subtle one. It is in this spirit that texts like the Kaṭha Upanishad, in such a passage as "Many do not even give it their hearing and attention," (351) indicate in some detail how the Absolute can only be understood by a highly purified and spiritual intellect, and is quite incomprehensible to a mere average intellect. Morever, there are such reminders as the "A man who has a Teacher comes to know" and "Knowledge comes only from a Teacher" of the Chāndogya Upanishad, (352) as well as the text of the Bhagavad-Gītā, "Those men of enlightenment who know the metaphysical truth will teach thee." (353) Later in the work at present under comment, too, (354) there is going to be a most lively presentation of the Absolute in all its abstruseness and profundity

through the medium of an imaginary conversation between Śākalya and Yājñavalkaya. Hence, (since the topic is abstruse), there is every reason for devising an imaginary dialogue as a means to present *prima facie* views and settled conclusion.

The passage has the further object of teaching spiritual conduct. It is when the participants in the imaginary dialogue are shown conducting themselves in the proper way that the doctrine expressed in the dialogue will be understood in its full bearing. And the story is also intended to discourage the belief that the truth can be known through resort to mere logic. "This insight is not to be gained through dry logic," (355) says the Veda: "This should not be given to a hard-bitten logician," says the Smṛti. (356) The inner implication of the present story is that faith is the supreme means to knowledge of the Absolute, as both Gārgya and Ajāśatru are presented as men of extreme faith. And we have the text from the Smṛti, "He who has faith wins knowledge." (357)

* * * * *

6. And the conversation of speech and the other faculties amongst themselves is just a piece of imagination given to help the student become convinced of the superiority of the Vital Energy, by supplying examples on the basis of agreement and difference (anvaya and vyatireka). (358) It is conceived on the analogy of human beings who meet in the world amongst themselves to argue over who is the best, and finally appeal to some acknowledged expert. The expert then tells them to attempt some task one by one, and says that whichever of them can succeed will be the best; and each one then tests himself to see whether he or another is the best, by attempting this task. This is how the Vedic text here imagines this conversation between speech and the other

faculties. The idea is that when the student sees that life still remains even after speech and the rest of the faculties have departed one after the other, but that it does not remain after the Vital Energy has departed, he will be bound to see that the Vital Energy is the best. And there is a text to the same effect in the Kauṣītaki Upanishad. (359) "One can live when the power of speech has gone, as witness the dumb. One can live when the sense of sight has gone, as witness the blind. One can live without hearing, as witness the deaf. One can live without mind, as witness infants. Even those who have lost their arms or the whole of their legs continue to live," and so forth. (360)

* * * * *

7. He said, "I will give you the answer tomorrow, in the morning." And, understanding the king's intention, they came before the king the next day at the earliest hour, with fuel in their hands. (361) Thus, great learned Brahmins as they were, they laid aside their pride and approached the king humbly as pupils, even though he was below them in caste. And the text hints thus that others who desire knowledge should behave in the same way. And he (the king) gave them knowledge, without initiating them as pupils in the regular manner. The idea behind giving the story is that others, too, should give knowledge to pupils in this way. (362)

How did he speak to him? He (the king Aśvapati Kaikeya) asked, "O Aupamanyava, who is that Vaiśvānara Self you meditate on?" But is it not wrong that he, being the Teacher, should ask his pupil a question? No, there is nothing wrong. For we find the text, "Come to me with (tell me) what you know, and I will tell you what is beyond that." (363) And in another place we find the Teacher Ajātaśatru addressing a question to a pupil, who did not understand a certain matter, to arouse his understanding, in the words, "(When this being was asleep) where was it? And whence did it return?" (364)

* * * * *

8. By analogy with the creative cosmic powers (adhidaivata), the Absolute is declared, by way of a simile, to have the quality of speedy illumination, like a flash of lightning or a wink of the eye. (365) By analogy with the individual soul (adhyātma), it is said to have the quality of manifesting itself simultaneously with the cognitions of the mind. That is the teaching through similes. The Absolute is taught through similes because, when so taught, it is more easily grasped by dull minds. The Absolute cannot be understood by dull minds in its true form, shorn of all external adjuncts. (366)

* * * * *

9. But the claim made earlier that the bliss-self (ānanda-maya-ātman) could not be the true Self, as it was a member of a series of false selves, was wrong, because the bliss-self is the inmost principle existing within all. (367) The sole purpose of the Vedic text in the whole passage is to affirm and expound the true Self, approaching the matter from the standpoint of the ordinary worldly understanding. It begins by provisionally accepting the view of very stupid people that their true "self" is nothing but the physical body made of food. It then goes on to speak of a whole series of further "selves," each lying within the last like a cast within a mould. And this can most

reasonably be explained as an attempt to teach as simply as possible the existence of the true Self as the last one inside all the others. In pointing out the (minute) star Arundhatī (to the bridal couple at a wedding ceremony), a lot of larger stars other than Arundhatī (Alkorin) are pointed out first (as approximating to Arundhatī),and then the real Arundhatī is pointed out last in the series. And in the same way here, the bliss-self is the real Self, as it is the inmost "self" (and therefore the last of the series). (368)

* * * * *

10. (The Absolute is that which ultimately has to be known.) So, in order to show that it exists, it is first spoken of in its false form set up by adjuncts, and fancifully referred to as if it had knowable qualities in the words "with hands and feet everywhere." For there is the saying of those who know the tradition (sampradāya-vid) "That which cannot be expressed (in its true form directly) is expressed (indirectly) through false attribution and subsequent denial."(369)

* * * * *

11. Whoso knows the Self, thus described, as the fearless Absolute (brahman), becomes the Absolute, beyond fear. This is a brief statement of the meaning of the entire Upanishad. And in order to convey the meaning rightly, the fanciful alternatives of production, maintenance and withdrawal, and the false notions of action, its factors and results, have been falsely attributed to the Self. And then the final metaphysical truth has been inculcated by negating these characteristics through a comprehensive denial of all particular superimpositions on the Absolute, expressed in the phrase "Not this, not this."(370)

Just as a man wishing to explain numbers from one to a hundred thousand billion says, "This line is 1, this line is 10, this line is 100, this line is 1,000," and all the time his only purpose is to explain numbers, and not to affirm that numbers are lines; or just as one wishing to explain the sounds of speech as represented by the written letters of the alphabet resorts to indirect means (upāya) in the form of a palm-leaf on which he makes incisions, which he later fills with ink to form letters, (371) and all the while, (even though he point to a letter and say "This is the sound so-and-so" his only purpose is to explain the nature of the sounds referred to by each letter, and not to affirm that the leaf, incisions and ink are sounds, even in just the same way, the one real metaphysical principle, the Absolute, is taught by resort to many indirect means (upāya), such as attributing to it production (of the world) and other powers. And then afterwards the nature of the Absolute is restated through the concluding formula "Not thus, not thus," so as to purify it of all particular notions accruing to it from the fanciful means used to explain its nature in the first place. (372)

* * * * *

12. The Upanishad first denies all particulars of the Self in the text "And so there is the teaching, 'Not thus, not thus.'" (373) Then, perceiving that if the Self is taught thus (merely in negations) it is scarcely intelligible, the text proceeds to a series of other positive explanations, resorting to various indirect means. And then, once more, it denies everything said (positively) about the Absolute in the course of the explanations. It negates everything that is knowable, everything that has an origin, everything that

is the object of a mental cognition.

In other words, in its successive reiterations of the phrase "Not thus, not thus" the Upanishad shows that the Self is not a perceptible object. It openly declares that the Self is unknowable, lest the one who did not realize that the various symbols were only introduced as a means (upāya) to convey the symbolized (and were not anything real in themselves) should think that the Absolute was knowable in the same way as the symbol was (i.e. as an object). This is the meaning of Gauḍapāda's verse.

And then, (after the negation has been completed), for the one who realizes that the symbol was used merely to convey the meaning to be symbolized, and that the nature of the symbolized was in no way affected by the use of the symbol, the unborn Self shines forth of its own accord, as the metaphysical reality, present within and without. (374)

* * * * *

13. True, there are distinctions in the portion of the Veda dealing with ritual (karma-kāṇḍa) that imply distinctions among objects. They come before the Upanishadic texts on creation, like "From which these beings come forth," etc., (375) and are not to be regarded as proclaiming the final truth. They are figures of speech like the figurative reference to a (purely fanciful) distinction between "the great ether" and "the ether in the pot," (376) or like the statement, "He's cooking a dish of cooked-rice," when there will be no cooked-rice until *after* the grains have been cooked. For the texts that ostensibly imply distinctions can never be shown to have the final purport of teaching the

existence of distinctions. They are doing no more than conform to the natural tendency to see distinctions, a tendency found in all living beings who are afflicted with nescience.

What then is the case with the texts found (not in the ritualistic portion of the Veda but) here in the Upanishads which speak of the rise and dissolution of the world? Their purpose is to help teach the identity of the individual soul with the supreme Self, just like such other texts as, "That thou art" and "He does not know who thinks 'He is one and I another.'" (377) The purpose of the Upanishads being to teach the unity of all, mention of plurality here also is figurative, and is made in conformity with the natural tendency to see distinctions found amongst the beings of the world. But it is preparing the way for the notion of unity.

Or else the verse may be explained otherwise as follows. The doctrine of the unity of all is voiced in the words, "One only without a second" (378) before the texts proclaiming creation, namely, "He took thought" and "Then he projected fire." (379) Afterwards again will come the text, "That is the real that is the Self, that thou art" (380) proclaiming unity, and any statements coming in between and ostensibly involving a distinction between the individual soul and the supreme Self will have to be taken as figurative statements concerning something that will only emerge later, as in the sentence "He's cooking a dish of cooked-rice." (381)

* * * * *

14. Perhaps it will be said that, since the example of sparks issuing from fire appears in the Upanishads themselves, this is enough to show that the supreme Self *must* undergo some form of

real modification to produce the individual souls. But this is not so. For the function of the Veda is only to inform. It does not in any way alter the constitution of objects. It simply gives correct information about what exists but could not otherwise be known. (382)

You ask what follows from this? Listen and hear what follows. There are certain concrete and abstract entities in the world which have well-known characteristics and properties. What the Vedic teaching does is to take these well-known entities as examples and use them to convey information about other unknown things that have analogous properties. It does not take worldly examples to illustrate matters that are not analogous to what is found in the world. If it did this, the example would be useless, as it would not agree with what it was supposed to exemplify. You cannot teach that fire is cold, or that the sun does not scorch, by even a hundred examples (of cold or non-scorching substances), as it would be clear from other means of knowledge (perception, etc.,) that what was being taught was not in fact true. Therefore no one following the well-known rules of logic can claim that the supreme Self has parts and can be exhibited as a whole with parts.

You may ask, then, for the meaning of such phrases in the Veda and Smṛti as "minute sparks" and "a ray (part) of Me." (383) But there is no difficulty here, as the passages in question are only concerned with conveying the essential identity of the individual soul with the supreme Self. A spark of fire is seen in the world to be nothing other than fire, and hence can be conceived as identical with fire. (384) Similarly, the part may be conceived as identical with the whole on the same basis. This being so, the words of the Upanishad which speak of the individual soul (vijñāna ātman) as a modification and a part of the supreme Self are really meant to convey the identity of the individual soul with the supreme Self.

This is also shown by the criteria of the beginning (upakrama) and conclusion (upasaṃhāra) of a topic. In all the Upanishadic passages in question, we find that there was first a declaration of the topic as the identity of the individual soul with the supreme Self. This was followed by worldly examples and reasoning based on them, in which the supreme Self figures as that which underwent modification to assume the form of the world, or was the whole of which the world was a part. Finally, there was a concluding retrospective passage summing up the topic as the identity of all with the supreme Self. As, for example, a passage to follow in the present Upanishad, where the topic opens with a statement of the identity of all with the supreme Self in the words, "All this is the Self." (385) This is followed by argumentation in favour of the identity of all this world with the supreme Self on the basis of its being a "modification" (vikāra) of it or a "part" of it, and so forth, arguments and examples (386) being introduced in connection with the creation maintenance and withdrawal of the world. And finally there follows a retrospective summary determining the topic in the words, "Without an inside or an outside" and "This Self is the Absolute." (387)

Hence it can be determined from the opening declaration and final summary of the topic that the texts proclaiming the creation, maintenance and withdrawal of the universe are inserted (not to teach creation, etc., as a fact, or to implicate the Self in modification, etc., but) only to support the notion of the identity of all with the supreme Self. Any other interpretation would involve the fault of (unjustified) "splitting up the sentence." (388) Indeed, there is universal agreement amongst all followers of the Upanishads that the Upanishadic teaching as a whole contains an injunction to think of the individual soul as identical with the supreme Self. (389) No proof can be adduced to show that the texts mentioning creation, etc., belong to any other topic, as they can all be construed in relation to this injunction. (390) Even if one could produce proof that the creation texts were subordinate to some injunctions other than the one to "see" the Self, one would be faced with the difficulty of deciding what fruit they were concerned with producing. (391) Hence we should conclude that the texts mentioning the creation, maintenance and withdrawal of the world are really concerned only with expounding the identity of all with the Absolute. (392)

NOTES TO CHAPTER XIII

(1) Cp. B.S.Bh.II.i.6, Gambhīrānanda p.314 (2) U.S. (verse) XVII.61 (3) Kumārila, Ś.V. Nirālambana Vāda verses 157 ff. (4) B. Sid. p.13 f. (5) To be more exact, Bhartṛmitra's objection was: "If the Self is known through means other than verbal authority, verbal authority is superfluous; and if it is not known through means other than verbal authority, words cannot communicate it, as words depend on extra-verbal cognition for a knowledge of their meaning." Cp. S.L. Pandey, p. 234 f. Śaṃkara bypasses this objection by saying that the ultimate function of the Veda is to negate. (6) Taken to be the founder of the Sāṃkhya system. (7) The founder of the Vaiśeṣika system. (8) Scholars have wondered whether Śaṃkara knew the verse of Bhartṛhari, Vākya Padīya I.34. "A point which has been explained with great trouble and by skilful logicians in one way will invariably be shown by others more skilful to have another explanation." Cp. Staal p.32, who gives a more detailed account of the evidence in P.E.W., 1960, pp. 53-57. (9) Manu Smṛti XII. 105-6 (10) The Indian conception of inference is inductive. It depends on the perception of signs known from previous experience to be invariably connected with the thing to be inferred. For example, "This hill has smoke, therefore it has fire." As the Absolute has no empirically knowable characteristics, it cannot be known through experience to be invariably connected with any perceptible signs, and hence it cannot be the object of an inference. (11) B.S.Bh. II.i.11 (12) Kaṭha I.ii.9 (13) R.V. X.129.6 and 7 (from the Creation Hymn) (14) That is, R.V. X.129.6 and 7. (15) Bh.G. II.25 (16) The word "maharṣi" is bandied about rather freely as a kind of courtesy title for a number of revered sages today, but in classical India it was reserved for the

great Seers like Bhṛgu to whom the hymns of the Veda were believed to have been revealed. (17) Bh.G. X.2 (18) B.S. II.i.11, part of Śaṃkara's commentary to which has just appeared in the previous Extract. The present Extract is from B.S.Bh. II.i.6 (19) Cp. above, Vol. IV Chapter XI. (20) Keith (Mīmāṃsā p.29) formulates the doctrine of inference succinctly: "Something is perceived, and recognized as invariably connected with something else...". Inference differs from mere presumption (arthāpatti), which consists in the formation of hypotheses to harmonize apparently contradictory data. (21) Bṛhad. Bh. I.i.1 (intro.) (22) The crime of murdering a Brahmin, the peculiarly heinous nature of which can only be known from the Veda, can only be performed by one afflicted with nescience. This is generally admitted. Similarly, the obligatory rituals, known only from the Veda, can also only be performed by those afflicted with nescience (for all action presupposes nescience). (23) Unless the Self is perceived as distinct from the body, says the P.M. opponent, no one will see the point of obeying the Vedic injunctions, which concern the after-life. (24) The P.M., who does not subscribe to the Advaita view that we are ignorant of the Self, maintains that we have direct apprehension of it, through the ego-sense, as different from the body. When we say, "I am tired," he believes, we are quite conscious that it is only the body that is tired, but we refer tiredness to the soul deliberately, either for emphasis or else through custom and convenience. Advaita denies that anyone but the enlightened person knows his true Self as separate from the body. In natural unregenerate human experience they are always confused and intermixed. (25) Kauṣītaki II.11 (26) Devadatta is a fierce warrior, "the little fellow" is a bright-faced Brahmin boy-student of the Veda. (27) In other words, the premises of the P.M. lead, not to his own doctrine which takes the Self as a separate agent using the body as its instrument, but rather to the doctrine of Advaita and of some passages in the Bh.G., according to which the Self is actionless. (28) But this is what we do with the body and its organs, which shows that this latter identification must be based on nescience. (29) Quoted by the opponent above. (30) Bh. G. Bh.XVIII.67 (intro.)

(31) For the context, see B.S.Bh. I.i.4, trans. Gambhīrānanda p.41. (32) B.S.Bh. I.i.4 (33) Īśvara Kṛṣṇa 62, Vācaspati's Comm. (34) Bh.G.Bh. XVIII.67 (introduction) (35) It is of interest to note the contrast between Śaṃkara and his contemporary Maṇḍana Miśra in their handling of this topic. Śaṃkara accords each means of knowledge validity in its own sphere. Maṇḍana does the same (B.Sid. p.17). But, unlike Śaṃkara, he does not claim that it is possible to rise beyond the empirical means of knowledge while yet in the body. Consequently he makes provision for the possibility that the impressions of sense-perception may efface the spiritual knowledge even of the enlightened man (B. Sid. p.35). And he feels bound to *defend* the teachings of the Upanishads against the suggestions of perception, etc. (B. Sid.p.40 ff.) This leads him to display his dialectical powers in areas where Śaṃkara did not venture, such as the *a priori* refutation of the possibility of the perception of difference. The dialectical work of Vimuktātman, Ānandabodha, Śrī Harṣa, Citsukha and Madhusūdana on this topic rests largely on foundations laid by Maṇḍana. Śāṃkara does not broach the topic at all. He simply argues that, because the Absolute is inaccessible to perception or inference, it is not subject to refutation asserted on the basis of them. (36) The Logicians of Śaṃkara's day relied on the Vaiśeṣikas for their physics. The Vaiśeṣikas of that time emphasized the unity and homogeneous character of the ether. Because it was too subtle to be perceived by the senses perception revealed no evidence of distinctions in it, while inference showed it was homogeneous and partless as the universal vehicle of sound. Śabda-liṅgāviśeṣād ekatvam siddham, Praśastapāda, p.58 — trans. Jha p.129. Cp. Frauwallner, G.I.P. Vol. II pp.205 ff. (37) Chānd VIII.xiv.1 and VI.iii.2 (38) Bṛhad. Bh.II.i.20 (39) Śaṃkara lists perception, inference, revelation, presumption and comparison, Bṛhad. Bh.III.iii.1, intro., trans. Mādhavānanda p.449. He omits non-perception (anupalabdhi). (40) Ātmasvarūpa attributes these verses to a certain Sundara Pāṇḍya (on whom cp. above, Vol.I p.33 f.) in his comm. to P.P. (Madras ed., p.373). The verses are valuable evidence that others besides Gauḍapāda had interpreted the Upanishads on strict Advaita lines

before Śaṃkara's day. See Kuppaswami Śāstrin in J.O.R.M. I p.5 ff. (41) B.S.Bh. I.i.4 *ad fin* (42) Chānd. VI.i.4 (43) Bṛhad. III.ix.28, Taitt. II.1 (44) G.K.Bh. III.32-33 (45) Śvet. III.8, Chānd. III.xiv.2, Bṛhad. IV.iii.9 (46) The principle behind this interpretation has been explained above, Vol. I. pp.137-140, (47) Kaṭha I.iii.15 (48) Śvet. IV.20 and Kaṭha I.iii.15 (49) For the terms "intellect" and "lower mind" in this connection, cp. above Vol. III p.29. For the doctrine that we identify ourselves with intellect, lower mind, senses and body through a series of reflections, see above Vol. III p.54. (50) Bh.G.Bh. XVIII.50. The argument continues with the passage given above, Vol.I p.117 (Extract 1). (51) The P.M.(52) Birth, existence, growth, development, decay, destruction. (53) Bh.G.Bh. II.20. It would be a mockery of this text if liberation were declared impossible. (54) I.e. the P.M. (55) Bṛhad. IV.iv.19 (56) Bh.G.Bh. II.21 (57) Muṇḍ. III.ii.9 (58) On the villager, cp. above, Vol.I p.160. (59) Taitt. Bh.II.1. Part of the passage has already appeared above, Vol. I p.160 (Extract 4). (60) See Chānd. III.xii.7-9 (61) The Absolute can never be an *object* of perception: yet the mind can be aware of the presence of the Self within as inner Witness, cp. Sureśvara, T.B.V. II.111-113. (62) Taitt. Bh. II.1 (63) Sureśvara interprets this to mean that, when the inmost Self is known, objects no longer have to be known, as their outer form is now known not to exist, and their inner reality is the inmost Self, which is now known, B.B.V. I.iv.969-979. (64) When we know a universal, we know the particulars comprehended within it even though we may not be acquainted with them individually, for they are nothing other than (nothing over and above) the universal. And the universals themselves are nothing over and above massed Consciousness. Cp. above, Vol.I. p.188 f. (65) Bṛhad. Bh. I.iv.7 (66) For the two "visions" here referred to, cp. above Vol.I p.217. (67) Bṛhad. III.iv.2 (68) The Self, the knower, cannot know itself, or it would make itself into an object and so no longer capable of being at the same time the knowing subject. (69) Bṛhad. Bh. I.iv.10 (70) See Kena I.2 and 5. (71) Cp. U.S. (verse) XVI.13 (72) Bṛhad. III.viii.11 (73) Chānd. VIII.vii.4

(74) Kaṭha I.iii.15 (75) Bṛhad. III.ix. 28.7, II.iv.12, Taitt. II.1, Ait. III.i.3. The word "vijñāna" comes in the first two texts, though the English translation has to be different in different contexts. (76) For Śaṃkara's conception of the Unmanifest Principle, see above, Vol. II p.138 ff. (77) Bṛhad. III.iv.2 (78) Sac sees here a reference to the doctrines of Bhartṛprapañca, and refers to Bṛhad. Bh. III.iv.2. (79) Bṛhad. III.ii.28, Ait. III.i.3 (80) For one thing, there is no particular place where a memory could inhere. Cp. above, Vol. IV p.234 (81) Bṛhad. III.ix.26, Bh.G. XIII.14 (82) Bṛhad. IV.iv.23, Bh.G. X.15 (83) Bṛhad. IV.iii.30, Muṇḍ. I.i.6, Bṛhad. IV.iv.25. The Extract is from Kena Bh. II.1-4 (84) Reading karaṇa, according to an alternative reading of R.T's Comm. supplied by D.V. Gokhale. (85) "Nothing beyond it" — R.T. affirms that the meaning is that there can be no second Witness of the Witness whereby it could affirm "I am that (other) Witness." For this would lead to infinite regress, as there would have to be another Witness to witness the second one and so on to infinity. (86) The body, etc., are but accidental and adventitious characteristics (upādhi) of the Self, not essential characteristics (viśeṣana). Where there is insight into the essential nature of the Self, therefore, the sense of identification with accidental characteristics is cancelled. The process is analogous to the cancellation of the notion "I am the one with the ear-rings" when that accidental characteristic is removed. (87) Although from the purely logical point of view they are just a pair of contradictory notions, and the acceptance of either would cancel the other. (88) U.S. (verse) XVIII. 158-162 (89) As often, in this context, the term asatya connotes both the unreal and the untrue, the deceptive. (90) A rope mistaken for a snake. The objector claims the occurrences in the realm of illusion have no practical effects, so that the Vedic discipline will not have the practical effect of producing liberation. (91) The dream-objects and the dream-cognitions as such are contradicted and cancelled. But the presence of "knowledge" or "consciousness" in dream is not contradicted or cancelled in waking. So the illusory Vedic texts can awaken one to the real Self as Consciousness. (92) The cognitions of dream (the dream-houses, etc.,) are of course contradicted and cancelled by waking experience.

But the presence of pure knowledge as such is not contradicted, and is felt to be continuous with the presence of pure knowledge in the waking body. Thus pure knowledge is constant, and therefore separate from the body of the waking state and the various bodies of dream states. The latter are not constant from the standpoint of the one who identifies himself with them, as even the body of the waking state disappears in dream and dreamless sleep. (93) Chānd. V.ii.8 (94) Aitareya Āraṇyaka III.ii.iv.17 (95) The symbol is efficacious only if it is taken *as* the symbolized: yet if it is taken as the symbolized it is illusory in the sense that it is, in truth, not the symbolized but only the symbol. On the eternality of the syllables, cp. the P.M. theory mentioned above, Vol.IV Chapter X Note 293. (96) Chānd. VI.viii.7, Bṛhad. I.iv.10 (97) Chānd. VI.xvi.3 (98) B.S.Bh. II.i.14 (99) Bṛhad. II.iii.6, Kena I.4, Taitt. II.iv.1 (100) The text in question is lost, and there are variant readings of the proper names in the different editions of Śaṃkara's text. (101) Bh.G. XIII.12 (102) M.Bh. XII.339.45, G.P. Ed. Vol. III p.705 (103) B.S.Bh. III.ii.17 (104) B.S.Bh. I.iii.29 (105) Cp. von Glasenapp, Einführung p.362 (106) See Extract 4 below. (107) E.g. Śabara Bhāṣya I.iii.30, quoted Biardeau, Connaissance p.80 f. (108) B.S.Bh. IV.i.3, Gambhīrānanda p.821 (109) Bṛhad. IV.iii.22 (110) Below, p.247, cp. Devasthali, Śaṃkara's Indebtedness, p.23 (111) sāvakāśa-niravakāśayor niravakāśam balīyaḥ (112) Devasthali, *loc. cit.* p.23 f. (113) Chānd. Bh. VIII.v.4, prāk sad-ātmapratibodhāt svaviṣaye 'pi sarvaṃ satyam eva. Cp. U.S. (verse) XI.5 (114) Śabara at P.M. Bhāṣya IX.i.9 says that the deities invoked in the sacrifices have no bodies, have no possessions and cannot give anyone anything. A text like "O Indra, I take hold of your right hand" must not be taken literally, as Indra does not have a right hand. Cp. Jha, pp.335-7 and 361 (115) p.258 below (116) *Ibid.* (117) Below, p.224 (118) Bhāṣya on P.M. Sūtra I.i.5, introduction, quoted by Biardeau, Connaissance p.83. (119) Cp. above, Vol.III p.27 (120) rūpādy abhāvāt, B.S.Bh. II.i.6, Gambhīrānanda p.314. (121) *Ibid.* (122) Below p.254 (123) B.S.Bh. IV.iv.8, Gambhīrānanda p.902 (124) Cp. B.Sid. p.79, quoted M.V. p.276 (125) Cp. above, Vol.IV p.148 ff.

(126) Sac, Salient Features p.22 (127) B.S.Bh. I.i.2, Gambhīrānanda p.16 (128) Bṛhad. Bh I.v.3 (129) The Prātiśākhyas are ancient treatises on pronunciation of the Veda in different schools. Four such treatises survive. (130) The Seer of the opening hymn of the Ṛg Veda. (131) Ārṣeya Brāhmaṇa, ed.Burnell p.3. Ānandagiri says it means "Will either sink to the level of stocks and stones or fall into hell." The Extract is from B.S.Bh. I.iii.30 (132) Chānd. I.i.1 (133) Chānd. Bh. VIII.xv.1 (134) R.V. X. 71.3. On ākṛti, and for the whole of the present Extract, cp. above, Vol. II pp.171 ff., to which the present passage is a sequel. (135) M.Bh. XII.210.19, G.P. Ed. p.548. The Extract is from B.S. Bh.I.iii.29. (136) An allegorical representation of R.V. IX.62.1, see B.S. Bh. I.iii.28, trans. Gambhīrānanda p.210, footnote. (137) Bṛhad. I.ii.4. Śaṃkara comments: "Having desired thus, he brought about the union of Speech, or the Vedas, with the mind that had already appeared. In other words, he reflected on the Vedas, that is, the order of creation enjoined in them, with his mind." (Mādhavānanda) (138) M.Bh. XII.232.24 (G.P. ed. p.578) (139) The words of the Veda are not invented anew at the beginning of each world-period, but merely re-manifested. In themselves, they are eternal. (140) M.Bh. XII.232.25 ((141) Manu Smṛti I.21 (142) Taittirīya Brāhmaṇa II.ii.4.2 (143) B.S.Bh. I.iii.28 (144) Chānd. VI.ii.1. (145) The Mīmāṃsaka view. (146) T.S. I.v.i.1. See Note 54 to Chapter X (147) Īśa 7 (148) Chānd. VII.i.3 (149) These latter are the texts which the Mīmāṃsaka regards as authoritative *par excellence* because they enjoin action. But their results cannot be verified in the present life. Judged by the test of producing indubitable and beneficial knowledge, they fall well behind the texts producing knowledge of the true nature of the Self, which take the qualified hearer beyond grief here *in this very world*. (150) Bṛhad. Bh. I.iv.7 (151) Cp. above p. 182 (152) Inference is authoritative insofar as it reveals what cannot be known through perception. The Veda is authoritative insofar as it reveals what cannot be known through any empirical means of knowledge whatever. (153) Cp. above p. 181 f. (154) The Mīmāṃsaka, whose doctrines are at present under fire, admits that the eulogistic passages at the end of the injunctions are not true in

themselves, but that they are significant and beneficial because they promote a desire in the sacrificer to carry out the ritual. The Advaitin can also appeal to this principle to safeguard the authority of the texts dealing with the ritual, even though he dismisses them as belonging to the sphere of nescience. (155) Bh.G.Bh. XVIII.67 (introduction) (156) The older Upanishads contain injunctions to meditate on the symbolic significance of certain factors in the ritual. The authority of all this is undermined, says the objector, in the light of the metaphysical texts denying duality altogether, if the latter are accepted at their face value. (157) Because their ultimate function is to negate the illusory world. Cp. above, Vol.I p.30 f. All the difficulties raised fall away if it is seen that the function of the Upanishads is not to convey knowledge of some transcendent Self up in the clouds but simply to negate false superimpositions on the Self that is immediately evident. (158) Above, p.222 (159) P.M. Sūtra II.i.46, cp. Jha. Pūrva Mīmāṃsā in its Sources, pp.189 ff. (160) The statement "Fire is hot and cold" may be erroneous but is not self-contradictory. This is because the proposition "Fire is hot" is not a statement in the strict sense of a proposition conveying information new to the hearer, but is a mere reminder of what he knows already. So we do not have two mutually contradictory statements, but merely a reminder that fire is hot plus an (admittedly erroneous) statement that "Fire is cold." Similarly, the metaphysical statements of the Upanishads cannot contradict the validity of the ritualistic section of the Veda, because they have a different sphere. Their function is to teach that all is the one Self from the standpoint of the highest truth, not to negate the validity of the ritualistic section of the Veda from the standpoint of the world of nescience. See B.B.V.S. II.i.180, Vol.II p.1312. (161) The "others" are mainly the New and Full Moon Sacrifices. These "obligatory" rituals form a different class from the "optional" rituals which are deliberately and explicitly formed for the sake of gaining a specific end. (162) For instance, no one will perform ritual who does not know that the soul is eternal and can reap the fruits of it in heaven, or who does not know what ritualistic acts have to be performed in what way for what particular ends. But *this* kind of knowledge is of course for Śaṃkara not contradictory to nescience. (163) The answer to the objection is that the point that the objector makes will only be true when there is knowledge of the Absolute, and then it is irrelevant. (164) Bṛhad. Bh. II.i.20 (165) Kauṣītaki III.8 or 9 (166) Ait.III.i.3 (167) Ait. Bh. I.i.1 (introduction) (168) U.S. (prose), section 42 (169) The theme of meditation on the Cosmic Vital Energy as purity. (170) Any view adopted by a Vedic commentator that can be shown to imply that the Veda is useless or harmful can be ruled out *a priori* as an absurdity. (171) Ānandagiri here quotes Chānd. VII.i.5, "He who meditates on Name as the Absolute...". The "etc." includes Strength, Food, Water, Heat etc. which are subjects prescribed for meditation on as the Absolute in the course of Chānd.VII. (172) The idea of the Mīmāṃsaka is that no Vedic injunction to worship or meditate on anything *as* another thing is to be taken as literally true. The injunction is simply to meditate on or worship the thing, and the part about meditating on it *as* something glorious is only added to encourage one to obey the injunction. The examples the Mīmāṃsaka chooses support his position if considered from his own standpoint, as he maintains that no human being can have any conception of a deva or ancestor (pitṛ) or of the Absolute (the existence of which he denies), so that there is no question of meditating on anything "as" them. Against this view, Śaṃkara quotes a text enjoining meditation on something as "the earth", a thing well-known to all. This undermines the argument used by the Mīmāṃsaka to support his position, as it shows that it is not based on a universal rule. (173) Chānd. I.vi.1 (174) Because in both cases there is an implicit injunction to meditate on A as B. (175) A figurative meaning of a word is an alteration of its usual meaning based on generally accepted convention. The altered meaning could never become generally intelligible without general knowledge of and agreement about the "primary" or usual meaning, which in turn implies that what the word designates in its primary sense really exists. (176) As at Chānd. V.x.1-10 (177) This example is chosen with the Mīmāṃsaka in mind: he is especially concerned with the large-scale sacrifices and with the Veda as authority for our knowledge of their results. (178) The Veda is an unchallengeable authority in matters transcending other means of knowledge. In matters that are in principle open to natural means of knowledge it is not regarded as a special authority. (179) Sureśvara argues here that an idea must have an object and that that object must be real unless it can be shown to be erroneous. B.B.V. I.iii.68. (180) For example, for the sake of heaven you must sacrifice with the Prayāja and other rites. Āpadeva, Ed. Abhyaṅkara Śāstrin, Editor's Comm. p.10. (181) In the case of anything which transcends the natural means of knowledge, such as the future results of rituals, the only authoritative means of knowledge is a Vedic text. The Vedic text is authoritative precisely because it is the only possible authority. (182) The argument of the Mīmāṃsaka is the extremely pragmatic one that sentences are intelligible only as forms of urging. Sentences in the Veda having the form of statements of fact must be construed as auxiliaries to some injunction if they are to be intelligible. As such, they lose all independent authority as sources of information. They may well be mere eulogistic passages designed to facilitate or encourage obedience to the injunctions to which they are subordinate. (183) B.B.V. I.iii.82 (184) Taitt. II.i.1 and Muṇḍ. II.ii.9 (185) The phrase "nescience and other evils" refers in Śaṃkara's writings to the "passions" (kleśa) mentioned at Yoga Sūtra II.3, namely nescience, egoism, attachment, aversion and headstrong clinging to life. (186) The passage "He whose ladle is made of Palāśa wood never hears an evil verse" (T.S. III.v.vii.2) is an eulogy, because it is a statement subsidiary to an enjoined rite. (Mādhavānanda) (187) And, as will be explained below, p.264, the metaphysical statements of the Veda are themselves prohibitions "prohibiting" erroneous knowledge, and therefore, by implication, prohibiting all action, since action flows from erroneous knowledge. (188) Ānandagiri quotes Bh.G. VI.3, "For the one who has climbed the heights of yoga, cessation of action is said to be the means." (189) These restrictions applying to monks are laid down in the appropriate sections of the Law Books. (190) Bṛhad. Bh. I.iii.1 (191) The term "Tantra" here refers to the Shāstras of the Sāṃkhyas. There may be a specific reference to the Śaṣṭi Tantra of Vṛṣagaṇa, cp. above, Vol.IV p.175 f. (192) Ait. I.1, etc.

NOTES TO CHAPTER XIII

Such texts exclude the dualistic Sāṃkhya view that non-conscious Nature is the cause of the world. (193) Śvet. V.2 (194) Bh.G. VII.6 (195) P.M. Sūtra I.iii.3. Cp. Keith, Mīmāṃsā p.82 f. (196) Vālmīki Rāmāyaṇa I.xl. f., trans. H.P. Shastri, Vol.I, p.84 ff. (197) The passage from Śvet V.2, quoted by the opponent in favour of the omniscience of Kapila, is primarily concerned with knowledge of the Lord. The name of Kapila is only brought in to help specify the Lord, and the passage cannot be quoted as containing true information about Kapila if it is not confirmed from other sources. (196) T.S. II.ii.10.2 (199) Manu Smṛti XII.91 (200) This view probably first occurred in the Sāṃkhya with the Śaṣṭi Tantra of Vṛṣagaṇa. Cp. above, Vol. IV p.176. (201) M.Bh. XII.350.1-3, G.P. Ed. Vol.III p.729. From the standpoint of modern philology, this text could have been composed well after the time of Vṛṣagaṇa. The pluralistic Sāṃkhya probably took shape as a *philosophical* doctrine a little before the Christian Era, (cp. above, Vol.IV p.176). But it no doubt flourished side by side with the perpetuation of older, monistic *religious* forms of the doctrine (cp. above, Vol.IV p.173), and we know that parts of M.Bh. XII were composed far later than the beginning of the Christian Era. They may therefore contain texts in which the later pluralistic philosophical form of the Sāṃkhya is criticized from the standpoint of the older monistic religious form of the Sāṃkhya. (202) M.Bh. XII.351.4-5, G.P. Ed. p.730 (203) Īśa 7 (204) B.S.I.iv.1 (205) Bṛhad. II.iv.5. For Śaṃkara, "yoga" was basically "adhyātma-yoga", and he practically equates this term with dhyāna-yoga and mano-nigraha and uses them to mean nididhyāsana. See M.V. pp.147 ff. Some relevant Extracts are quoted at Chapter XV section 1 below. (206) Śvet. II.8 (207) Kaṭha II.iii.11 (208) Kaṭha II.iii.18 (209) An untraced text. (210) On the eighth day after the full moon, especially in the two winter months, "aṣṭakā" offerings were made to the ancestors. The offerings are prescribed in the Gṛhya Sūtras only, and are not mentioned in the Veda. They became the stock case cited to illustrate the principle, already mentioned, that where there was no overriding reason to the contrary, it should be assumed that passages in the derivative literature for which there was no support in the extant Vedic texts were based on Vedic texts now lost. Here they are cited by an opponent to show that even apart from those parts of the teachings of the Yoga System which have already been shown to be supported by the Veda, the rest of the system, too, must be assumed to be based on lost Vedic texts. (211) Śvet. VI.13 (212) Śvet. III.8 (213) Bṛhad. IV.iii.16 (214) Jābāla Up.5 (215) Such as the Vaiśeṣika system of Kaṇāda and the Nyāya system of Gautama. (216) Taittirīya Brāhmaṇa III.xii.9.7. (217) Bṛhad. III.ix.26. The present Extract is from B.S.Bh. II.i.1-3. (218) Bṛhad. Bh. I.iv.6 (219) Bhartṛprapañca is meant, cp. above, Vol.IV p.89. (220) Bṛhad. IV.iv.7 (221) Dream-experience proves the self-luminosity of the Self because there can be bright daylight in the dream when there is the darkness of night round the body in which the dreamer is dreaming, so that the light in dreams cannot proceed from any external luminary. Cp. above, Vol.III p.105."Desire and the like" refers to mental experiences witnessed by the Self as objects in dream. (222) Cp. U.S. (verse) XV.20, "The knower must be different from the objects and instruments of his knowledge, such as (a non-sentient object like) a pot." Cp. above, Vol.III p.50. (223) By attributing parts to the Self, the fault of Bhartṛprapañca's doctrine. (224) Cp. above, Vol.IV p.87 f. (225) Bṛhad. Bh. IV.iii.22 (226) Bṛhad. II.iv.5 (227) B.S.Bh. II.i.4 (228) G.K.Bh. IV.1 (introduction) (229) First of all it shows the need for a discussion. And secondly it shows that the dualists will never arrive at a settled conclusion of their own wherewith to refute the position of the monist. (230) Taitt. Bh. II.viii.5 (231) Little can be squeezed out of this reference for Śaṃkara's chronology, see Kunjunni Raja, The Date of Śaṃkarācārya, p.127. Harṣa's empire covered a large part of India, and he died in 647 A.D. The Gupta Empire flourished a few centuries earlier. But it has been thought likely that Śaṃkara was thinking of the Maurya Empire if not of more distant legendary kings. (232) We have already seen another example of the severe judgement of the religious negligence of his contemporaries — cp. the present volume, above, p.11 f. (233) Y.S. II.44 (234) Śvet.II.12 (235) B.S. Bh. I.iii.32 and 33 (236) Chānd. VI, in which the text "That thou art" occurs, begins with and consists of a discussion of the nature of the real (sat). Though the words "Thou art the real" do not occur as a connected phrase in the Upanishad text, they stand for the "That thou art" of Chānd. VI.viii.7. (237) From the standpoint of the highest truth, perception, etc., are mere appearances, cp. above, Vol.I p.109. (238) Kena II.3 and Bṛhad. II.iv.14. The Extract comprises U.S. (verse) XVIII.215-221 (239) Bh.G. V.17 (240) Bh.G.Bh. II.69 (241) The Commentator Rāma Tīrtha sees a reference to Tāntrika magical practices here. But the Commentators Ānandajñāna and Bodhanidhi refer to meditation on the Gāyatrī, as Mayeda has shown in the Notes here to his translation of the U.S. (242) Perception and all other empirical means of knowledge presuppose a knower who uses them,and this presupposes a superimposition of (in the form of an identification with) a conscious principle onto a non-conscious body and its organs. Hence all the empirical means of knowledge, beginning with perception, the most important and that on which the others depend, are based on illusion and are semblances of means of knowledge. Cp. above, Vol.I p.96. Losing one's sense of direction was apparently a standard case of error for the theories of the time. We find it in Maṇḍana's B. Sid. p.35. (243) An authoritative means of knowledge (pramāṇa) is such only in relation to matters not already known from some other source. You cannot draw a genuine inference of the presence of an elephant from its footprint if you have already perceived it. (B.Sid. p.30). Hence the Veda is not an authoritative means of knowledge when it speaks of an agent and experiencer, as these are already established by interior perception. So one cannot quote such texts as proof that an agent and enjoyer really exists. On the other hand the Veda *is* an authoritative means of knowledge when it teaches "I am the Absolute," because this knowledge can be had from no other source. Perception being but a semblance of a means of cognition, its notion "I am the agent and enjoyer" is cancelled by the notion "I am the Absolute" arising from the Veda, which, on this particular point, is an authority properly so-called. (244) The opponent propounds "Prasaṃkhyāna Vāda" throughout, for which see above, Vol. IV p.51, with the references there given. (245) From the opponent's standpoint, a mere statement of fact occurring in the Veda is not authoritative, as the authority of the Veda derives, according to him, from its commands. The Prasaṃkhyāna Vādins were more conservative than Śaṃkara in that they still thought it possible to adhere to the positions laid down by the Mīmāṃsakas about the authority of the Veda depending on command. Merely hearing a metaphysical statement, they thought, does not bring liberation. The latter will not come unless there is action in obedience to a Vedic injunction which promises liberation as the fruit of performance of the action enjoined. The Upanishads contain injunctions to meditate, such as "One should meditate, verily, on the Self which is dear." The notion of action continuing after the conviction "I am the Absolute" has arisen is not absurd for the Prasaṃkhyāna Vādin, as it is for Śaṃkara, because the Prasaṃkhyāna Vādin regards this knowledge as inevitably fitful before the death of the body. He therefore contends that it is necessary to continue with meditation and reasoning and the performance of caste duties even on the part of those who have acquired the conviction "I am the Absolute," in order to avoid the demerit of neglecting duties and to guard against relapse. It is noteworthy that Maṇḍana and Vācaspati, the chief later champions of a form of the Prasaṃkhyāna view amongst the Advaitins, were both householders. (246) Knowledge derived from hearing or inference is abstract, it is mere knowledge by description, not knowledge by acquaintance, to use Bertrand Russell's terms. A mere abstract idea is always subject to effacement through the perception of a concrete contradictory particular. One's abstract knowledge that honey is sweet is liable to be effaced by one's concrete sensations if one eats it with a disordered liver. Thus meditation and reasoning are required to strengthen the abstract idea received from revelation that one is the Absolute. Otherwise it will be overpowered by the sensations derived from sense-experience. Similar remarks apply to knowledge derived from inference, which is also abstract. In inferring the presence of fire from the presence of smoke, we apprehend that fire in general is present, but do not have concrete knowledge of a particular fire. So argued the Prasaṃkhyāna Vādin. (247) Śaṃkara himself maintained that the Upanishadic texts were authoritative only if they yielded some fruit of benefit to man. And in the case of the metaphysical texts that were apparently mere statements of fact he specified the fruit as the removal of ignorance and fear etc. Cp. above p.222. This is to make the metaphysical statements an exceptional case. Normally, the fruits promised in the Veda pertain to the distant future and depend on ritual activity for their coming into being, which will only occur after the ritual has been performed. Here the Prasaṃkhyāna Vādin is made to bring the fruit of "Self-realization" under the general rule of being dependent on resort to some active means (sādhana). But because the universal Self is an already existent entity, it does not require to be produced by action. Only a new *awareness* requires to be produced, and this by mental rather than by physical activity, *viz.* by meditation. So the Prasaṃkhyāna Vāda argument runs. Against this view, Śaṃkara later maintains that awareness of the Self no more requires to be produced by activity than the Self itself does, and that it would be transient if it did. All that is required is destruction of the obstacles preventing its manifestation. (248) Śaṃkara also recommended inner and outer control (śama and dama) and pursuit of other spiritual qualities. For him they were *prerequisites* for enquiry into the Absolute, but after realization of the Absolute they no longer had to be practised deliberately, but were the very nature of enlightened man. Cp. G.K. Bh. IV.86, as shown below, Vol.VI p.289 f. Śaṃkara here puts them into the mouth of the Prasaṃkhyāna Vādin on a different basis, that he would not himself accept. The Prasaṃkhyāna Vādin regards them as enjoined practices which have to be carried out deliberately until the death of the body as an act of obedience to a rule. (249) Not "earlier" in the modern philologist's sense of being composed earlier (for Śaṃkara the Vedic texts were all beginningless and were repeatedly breathed out anew at the beginning of each world-period) but "earlier" in the sense of coming earlier in the traditional order of being learned. Every Brahmin was supposed to learn the whole or part of the mantras of the Veda by heart in order to perform his daily ritual: but only some went on later to learn the texts of the Āraṇyakas and Upanishads. (250) On superimposition, cp. above, Vol.I p.96. (251) Nothing is really done by the one who falls into illusion and thinks the ether of the sky is dark, say, because the clouds are dark. The colourless ether itself remains unaffected. Even so, it makes sense to tell someone to stop such an action. So with superimposition onto the Self, which the Veda prohibits when saying "Not thus, not thus." All commands, deeds, prohibitions, and abstentions fall within the realm of illusion (avidyā-viṣaya). Cp. above, Vol.I,p.96. (252) Because it would be a real change of state brought about by a real act. Whatever has a beginning in time has an end also. (253) Śaṃkara here shows that the Upanishads are not ultimately concerned with injunction (vidhi), as the Prasaṃkhyāna theorists hold, but with prohibition (pratiṣedha). A prohibition, however, bears normally on a real act. In the previous verse, therefore, Śaṃkara gave an example from worldly experience of an act that was no act in that it had absolutely no effect on the external world. In the present verse he points to a Vedic example of a prohibition of an act that is not an act. The strange prohibition occurs at T.S. V.ii.7. (254) Nothing can act on its own Self. (255) There are reminiscences of Śvet.VI.11 here. Leading on from the previous verse, the present one speaks of the Self. It is that which cannot be negated and does not require to be taught positively because it is self-luminous and affirms its own existence. But it cannot be known without the authoritative teaching of the Veda, as its true nature is concealed by nescience. Cp. U.S. (verse) XVIII.134 ff. The present Extract comprises U.S. (verse) XVIII.3-26. (256) Bhartṛhari, V.P.II.487 (257) Bh.G. Bh. XIII.1, trans. A Mahādeva Śāstrin p.330 (258) Quoted by Lakṣmīpuram Śrīnivāsācāra, Darśanodaya, p.7 (259) *Ibid.*, p.2 (260) Cp. Ānandapūrṇa on Sureśvara's Sambandha Vārtika 254, ed. and trans. Mahadevan p.120, bodhita-vākya-ja-bodha. (261) Hacker, Kleine Schriften p.479 (262) Cp. above, p.37 (263) Cp. above, p.102, 105 (264) Muṇḍ. I.ii.12 and 13 (265) Chānd.III.xi.5-6 (266) Chānd.VI.xiv.2, U.S.3 (267) Bh. G. IV.34 (268) R.T. says "loose practice in speech and eating." (269) R.T. specifies the qualities to be cultivated as "Inner and outer cleanliness, contentment, austerities, Vedic recitations and the practice of offering all to God," a list taken from Y.S. II.32. The Vivaraṇa attributed to Śaṃkara on Vyāsa's Yoga Sūtra Commentary at this point mentions: washing of the body, eating pure food such as clarified butter and other milk products, care not to hear impure talk or to see impure sights, meditating on the opposites of lust and anger and other vices, contentment with what comes to hand even when inadequate to the body's needs, putting up with excessive heat and cold and deliberately eating and drinking little, disciplines such as refraining from speech or from using the hands, study of the Upanishads, repetition of OM. (270) Notably the sacred thread, cp. U.S. (prose) 30 (271) The text then quotes a long list of passages from the Veda and the derivative literature stating the true nature of the Self. These the Teacher must present to the pupil. (272) Here, however, the teaching of the pupil has only just begun. In the sequel it is shown that he must come to understand exactly *how* he is different from the body. It is not enough if he just jumps to the conclusion that he must be. The Extract is from U.S. (prose) sections 2-13 (selected). (273) That is, once it has been admitted, according to the explanations of the previous verse, that the individual soul as experiencer and the Lord as Witness are comparable to two birds perched on the same tree (the body), one eating the berries and the other not. (274) Reading with Sac "vivekitayā" for "vivekatayā". (275) A being which has not received the prescribed obsequies at death and which consequently haunts the earth like our "unshriven" ghost. (276) The only motive of the true Teacher of Advaita is compassion. (277) Muṇḍ. Bh. III.i.2 (278) Near the modern Kandahar, considered in Upanishadic times as typical of somewhere distant. (279) Chānd. Bh. VI.xiv.1-2. (280) Merit is an evil in the sense that it implies further worldly experience which debars one from realizing one's own true nature, even though that experience may be, from the worldly standpoint, of a relatively desirable kind. (281) For the Southern Path, cp. above, p.19 ff. For the Northern Path, see below, Vol.VI Chapter XIV section 2. (282) One of the few places where Śaṃkara makes a list of pramāṇas or means of knowledge. Cp. above, Vol.IV Chapter X Note 156. (283) Cp. U.S. (verse) XVII.50, and Sureśvara's N. Sid. I.53. (284) See Muṇḍ. I.i.6. (285) Muṇḍ. Bh. I.ii.12-13 (286) Kṣetrajña — the witnessing Consciousness present in the human personality. (287) Bh.G.Bh. IV.34 (288) Every act performed egoistically leaves a seed of future worldly experience in the soul. The doctrine is that spiritual knowledge has the power to efface or at least burn these seeds so that they do not fructify and the enlightened man faces no more involuntary births in the world. A parched seed does not fructify. (289) An affirmation of the doctrine of "prārabdha karma". (290) Conceived by Śaṃkara essentially as the performance of all action in a spirit of duty and as an offering to the Lord.

NOTES TO CHAPTER XIII

(291) Bh.G.Bh. IV.37- 39 (292) On austerity or discipline, cp. above, pp.133 ff. (293) Untraced (294) Bh.G.Bh. XVIII.67 (295) Cp. Sac, Misconceptions p.93 (296) For which see below, Vol.VI Chapter XIV. (297) Cp. Sac, Misconceptions p.33 (298) Above, Vol.I p.147 f. (299) Renou, Grammaire et Védanta, p.132 (300) Renou, p.125 (301) B.S.Bh. III.iii.25, Gambhīrānanda p.689 (302) Cp. Keith, Mīmāṃsā p.89 (303) Cp. M.V. p.133 (304) Lit. "apparent hints" (liṅgābhāsa), B.S.Bh. I.iv.28 (305) B.S.Bh. I.iv.19, Gambhīrānanda p.282 f., cp. Renou, p.126 (306) Renou *ibid.* (307) Keith, Mīmāṃsā, p.82 (308) Cp. above, p.194 f. (309) Above, Book IV Chapter XI Note 378 (310) Above, Vol.IV. p.188 (311) Bṛhad. Bh. II.i.20 . Cp. Mādhavānanda Svāmin's trans. p.294. (312) Below, Vol.VI Chapter XV (313) Vol.I p.199 f. (314) Bṛhad. III.viii.8, Kaṭha III.15, Chānd. VIII.xiv.1, Muṇḍ. II.i.2, Bṛhad. II.v.19 (315) B.S. I.i.4 (316) B.S. Bh. III.ii.14. Cp. Sac, Misconceptions p.92 (317) Cp. above, Vol.IV p.56 (318) In this case, the ritual. (319) In this case, association with meditation. (320) The Veda is always authoritative in the sense of conveying information useful to man: but where the surface meaning of a sentence in the Veda contradicts truths already known from another source, the sentence has to be interpreted figuratively. (321) Cp. above, p.261 and Note 242 (322) Bṛhad. Bh. III.iii.1 (323) The objector is the P.M., for whom rituals and their results were the essential teaching of the Veda, and who rejected the mythological element as fiction. (324) The reference is to Chānd. III.vi.4, "Āditya rises in the east and sets in the west...". (325) They are Smṛti, which can only be accepted where it does not contradict the Veda. Cp. above, p.246 f. (326) Narrowly concentrated on the ritual and its results, the P.M. denies any serious function to the verses or hymns accompanying the ritual. He will not admit that they are intended either to please or invoke the gods, as for him results flow not from the gods but from the ritual. He reduces the hymns to mere assertion (not necessarily true) and reminding of what has been asserted. Keith, Mīmāṃsā p.81; Jha, Pūrva Mīmāṃsā pp. 179 ff. (327) According to the rules of Vedic exegesis, if the purpose of a text was "eulogy" (the recommendation, direct or indirect, of a course of

action) it could not also be the communication of information. (328) T.S. II.i.1.1 (329) The right course, according to Śaṃkara. (330) Aitareya Brāhmaṇa III.viii.1 (331) B.S.Bh. I.iii.33 (332) Bṛhad. I.iii. ff. and Chānd. V.i.1 ff. (333) Kauṣītaki II.14 (334) *Ibid.* (335) E.g Chānd. V.i.1 as well as Bṛhad. I.iii.1 ff. (336) Bṛhad. VI.i.14, following on Bṛhad. I.iii.1 (337) Bliss is treated as a quality of the Absolute in the Sūtra at present under comment. For Śaṃkara, and also for the main Teachers of his school, the Absolute *was* bliss and did not *possess* bliss as a quality. Cp. Prakāśātman, Vivaraṇa (Madras Ed.) p.675, "The Absolute is bliss which is itself of the nature of Consciousness." (Vijñāna-svabhāva ānando brahmeti). In the present passage, however, Śaṃkara is following earlier tradition about qualities that have to be attributed to the Absolute in meditation. (338) Taitt. II.5 (339) Chānd. VI.ii.1 (340) On the bliss sheath of the Self, cp. above. Vol.III pp.38 ff. (341) Deussen remarks that this agrees with B.S.Bh. I.i.12 but not with the reconsidered view inserted at the end of B.S.Bh. I.i.19. Here, as in certain cases elsewhere, Śaṃkara first gives the traditional interpretation of the B.S.Bh. and then quietly follows it with a correction embodying a deeper philosophical view. Cp. above, Vol.I p.22 f. (342) Chānd. IV.xv.2, VIII.i.5 (343) When Reality, Knowledge, Infinity, Bliss or Selfhood are attributed to the Absolute, the idea is not to endow it with a variety of different qualities for purposes of meditation, but to help proclaim its true nature by excluding false ideas. Cp. above, Vol.I Chapter IV section 1. (344) B.S.Bh. III.iii.10-13 (345) Bṛhad. III.viii.8 (346) Muṇḍ. I.i.5-6 (347) Cp. the immediately preceding Extract. (348) The Upasads were ceremonies forming part of the Jyotiṣṭoma sacrifice. They lasted several days and preceded the pressing of the soma. (349) P.M. Sūtra III.iii.9. The present Extract is from B.S.Bh. III.iii.33 (350) The standpoint of self-identification with body and organs. (351) Kaṭha I.ii.7 (352) Chānd. VI.xiv.2, IV.ix.3 (353) Bh.G. IV.34 (354) Bṛhad. III.ix.1 ff. (355) Kaṭha I.ii.9 (356) M.Bh. XII.246.18, G.P.Ed. Vol.III p.590 (357) Bh.G. IV.39. The Extract is from Bṛhad. Bh. II.i.1 (358) The present Extract is inserted to illustrate how the Veda teaches through stories which required interpretation through reason. (359) Kauṣītaki

III.3, cp. *ibid.* II.14 (360) Chānd. Bh. V.i.15 (361) Every Brahmin boy was expected to learn at least one Veda by heart, so that he could perform his own household sacrifices and so that human memory of the Vedic texts, preserved entirely by oral tradition, should be kept in being. The Veda had to be learned by rote from a Brahmin Teacher who already knew it, a lengthy day-to-day task lasting many years. The Brahmin Teacher of the Veda was thus typically a householder, and the typical service of the pupil was to tend his sacrificial fires in the sacred precincts of his house. A vestigial memory of the old Aryan practice of maintaining a sacred fire in one's house survives in the modern English expression "hearth and home". Thus, coming before a Teacher "with fuel in the hand" came to be regarded as the correct formal way of approaching a Teacher for any kind of spiritual Teaching. (362) That is, non-Brahmins who have direct knowledge of the spiritual truth should teach it to worthy pupils, but without the upanayana ceremony, which only a Brahmin can administer. (363) Chānd. VII.i.1 (Sanatkumāra speaking to Nārada) (364) We today would think it obvious that a Teacher can ask a pupil a question as part of the process of evoking receptive attitudes in him. But the Extract throws light on the degree of reverence accorded to the Teacher in Śaṃkara's tradition. It is from Chānd. Bh. V.xi.7 and V.xii.1 (selected) (365) This refers to the immediately preceding teaching at Kena IV.4 (366) Kena Bh. IV.5 (367) Normally Śaṃkara differentiates the "bliss-self" (ānandamaya-ātman or ānandamaya-kośa) from the true Self with some emphasis, cp. above, Vol.III p.38 ff. His procedure in the B.S.Bh. is to accept the identification of the bliss self with the true till I.i.19, at the end of his commentary on which he shifts his ground and argues for his own view as a preferable alternative. Cp. above, p.298 and Note 341. (368) B.S. Bh. I.i.12. There is a parallel passage regarding indication of the new moon at Chānd. Bh. VIII.xii.1, trans. Gambhīrānanda p.650 f. (369) The principle behind this short Extract has been explained above, Vol.I p.24, and the Extract itself has occurred there, p.147f. It is from Bh. G. Bh. XIII.12. (370) Occurring at Bṛhad. II.iii.6, III.ix.26 and IV.iv.22. (371) This confirms other evidence that Śaṃkara was born in the south. Cp. above, Vol.I p.44 and Note 113. (372) Bṛhad. Bh. IV.iv.25 (373) Cp. the references at Note 370 above. (374) G.K. Bh. III.26, which has also appeared above, Vol.I p.144 f. (375) Taitt. III.1 (376) Cp. above, Vol.III p.20 f. (377) Bṛhad. I.iv.10 (378) Chānd. VI.ii.2 (379) Chānd. VI.ii.3 (380) Chānd. VI.viii.7 (381) G.K.Bh. III.14 (382) Cp. Sureśvara N. Sid. I. 30 (prose introduction) and III.93 (prose introduction) (383) Bṛhad. II.i.20 and Bh.G. XV.7 (384) A sort of "non-reciprocal" identity. The spark is identical with the fire in the sense of being nothing other than the fire. But it cannot be said that the fire is nothing other than the spark. (385) Bṛhad. II.iv.6 (386) For instance, the example of the drum at Bṛhad. II.iv.7. (387) Bṛhad. II.v.19 (388) Vākya-bheda. Cp. above, p.285 f. Śaṃkara held, as he explains at B.S. Bh. I.i.4 (Gambhīrānanda p.37, "Puruṣa is the primary object to be revealed by the Upanishads"), that the texts of the Jñāna Kāṇḍa of the Upanishads constituted one connected topic, namely a statement of the true nature of the Self. All digressions should be interpreted as subordinate to this end and not as conveying independent information in their own right. (389)"The Self is to be seen, heard, reflected on, meditated on," Bṛhad. II.iv.5 (390) In the Extracts already given, Śaṃkara has mentioned that there could be no injunction to know the Self, cp. above, Chap.X section 2. But here he is meeting the P.M. on the latter's own ground. He is accepting for argument's sake the latter's rule that statements in the Veda have to be construed as subordinate to some command, and showing that, on that basis, the creation-texts in the Veda cannot be regarded as statements of fact but only as "eulogistic" passages (artha-vāda) designed to encourage or otherwise aid the student to carry out the injunctions to meditate on the Self. (391) No text in the Veda can be supposed useless to man. But what solid good could a knowledge of the mode of creation yield to man? If texts on this topic are taken as subordinate to the injunction to "see" the Self, this difficulty disappears, as the texts are then seen as ways of bringing home to the mind the identity of all with the Absolute. Even if they are taken as subordinate to some other injunction, it is in any case "fruitless" to take them as literally true. (392) Bṛhad. Bh. II.i.20

LIST OF GENERAL ABBREVIATIONS

In principle, works are referred to under their author's names throughout the Notes, and the abbreviations occasionally used to distinguish between an author's different works should not cause any difficulty. Except for the two entries R.T. and Sac, the following list comprises those abbreviations that are used independently of any author's name. The list excludes the names of Upanishads on which Śaṃkara wrote commentaries, which are listed under his name in the Bibliography of Vol.I and readily identifiable there.

A.B.O.R.I. .	Annals of the Bhandarkar Oriental Research Institute, Poona
Ā.D.S. . . .	Āpastamba Dharma Sūtra
Ā.S.S. . . .	Ānanda Āśrama Sanskrit Series, Poona
Ā.Ś.S. . . .	Āpastambīyam Śrauta Sūtram, Mysore University
A.V. . . .	Atharva Veda
B.B.V. . . .	See Sureśvara in Bibliography to Vol.I
B.B.V.S. . .	See Vidyāraṇya in Bibliography to Vol.I
Bh. . . .	Bhāṣya (i.e. Commentary)
Bh.G. . . .	Bhagavad Gītā, q.v. under Texts of Śaṃkara in Bibliography to Vol.I
B.S. . . .	Brahma Sūtras, see under Śaṃkara in Bibliography to Vol.I
B.S.Bh. . . .	See Śaṃkara in Bibliography to Vol.I

LIST OF GENERAL ABBREVIATIONS

B.V.S.	i.e. B.B.V.S., see Vidyāraṇya in Bibliography to Vol.I
G.K. . . .	Gauḍapāda's Kārikās on Māṇḍūkya Upanishad. See under Śaṃkara in Bibliography to Vol.I
G.O.S. . . .	Gaekwad's Oriental Series, Baroda
G.P. . . .	Gītā Press, Gorakhpur
I.H.Q. . . .	Indian Historical Quarterly
I.I.J. . . .	Indo-Iranian Journal
J.A. . . .	Journal Asiatique
J.A.O.S. . .	Journal of the American Oriental Society
J.B.B.R.A.S. .	Alternative form of J.R.A.S.B.B., q.v.
J.B.O.R.S. .	Journal of the Bihar and Orissa Oriental Society
J.O.I.B. . .	Journal of the Oriental Institute, Baroda
J.O.R.M. . .	Journal of Oriental Research, Madras University
J.R.A.S.B.B. .	Journal of the Royal Asiatic Society of Great Britain and Ireland, Bombay Branch
J.U.B. . .	Jaiminīya Upanishad Brāhmaṇa
M.Bh. . . .	Mahābhārata. G.P. Mūla-mātra Ed., 4 Vols.
M.V. . . .	Method of the Vedanta, see Saccidānandendra in Bibliography

LIST OF GENERAL ABBREVIATIONS

N.S. . . . Nirṇaya Sāgara Press

N.Sū. . . . Nyāya Sūtras. See Vātsyāyana in Bibliography to Vol.I

P.E.W. . . . Philosophy East and West, Honolulu

P.M. . . . Pūrva Mīmāṃsā

P.P. . . . Pañcapādikā, q.v. in Bibliography to Vol.I

R.T. . . . Rāma Tīrtha (seventeenth century commentator)

R.V. . . . Ṛg Veda

Sac. . . . Saccidānandendra Svāmin, modern author, (d.1975) q.v. in Bibliography to Vol.I

Ś.B. . . . Śatapatha Brāhmaṇa

S.B.E. . . . Sacred Books of the East Series, Oxford, recently re-issued Delhi

T.B.V. . . . See under Sureśvara

T.S. . . . Taittirīya Saṃhitā (Black Yajur Veda)

U.S. . . . Upadeśa Sāhasrī. See under Texts of Śaṃkara in Bibliography to Vol.I

V.P. . . . Viṣṇu Purāṇa, q.v. in Bibiliography to Vol.I

W.Z.K.O. . . See W.Z.K.S.O.

W.Z.K.S.O. . Wiener Zeitschrift für die Kunde Süd- und Ostasiens

LIST OF GENERAL ABBREVIATIONS

Y.D. . . . Yukti Dīpikā, q.v. in Bigliography to Vol.I

Y.S. . . . Yoga Sūtras. See Patañjali in Bibliography to Vol.I

Z.D.M.G. . . Zeitschrift der Deutschen Morganländischen Gesellschaft

Z.I.I. . . Zeitschrift für Indologie und Iranistik

Z.M.R. . . Zeitschrift für Missionswissenschaft Münster/Westfalen

B I B L I O G R A P H Y

The texts of Śaṃkara here used are those listed in Vol.I of the Śaṃkara Source-Book, Śaṃkara on the Absolute, p.241 f. In regard to the secondary literature, only those works are listed below which did not appear in the Bibliography of Vol.I.

Aitareya Āraṇyaka: Ed. and trans. Keith, Oxford, 1909

Aitareya Brāhmaṇa: Ed. Aufrecht, Bonn, 1879

Ānandapūrṇa, *Nyāya Kalpa Latikā*, ṭīkā on B.B.V., Tirupati, Vols. I and II, 1975

Āpastamba Dharma Sūtra: For text, see Vol.I Bibliog. under Cinnaswāmī Śāstrī. Eng. trans. G. Bühler, S.B.E. 2 (1879, reprinted recently, Delhi)

Chāndogya Upanishad: Ed. and trans. with Comm. of Śaṅkarācārya by Swāmī Gambhīrānanda, Calcutta, 1983

Deussen, P., *Erinnerungen an Indien*, Kiel and Leipzig, 1904

Devasthali, G., *Śaṃkara's Indebtedness to Mīmāṃsā*, J.O.I.B., 1951-2, pp. 23-30

Eckhart, Meister, *Sermons and Treatises*, Ed. and trans. M. O'C. Walshe, London (Watkins), Vol.II, 1981

Gambhīrānanda: See above, *Chāndogya Upanishad*, and also Vol.I Bibliog.

Gautama Dharma Sūtras: Eng. trans. G. Bühler, S.B.E. 2 (1879, reprinted recently, Delhi)

Gokhale, D.V.: See Vol.I Bibliog. under *Bhagavad Gītā Bhāṣya* (p.237)

Hacker, P.: *"Texte" = Untersuchungen über Texte des frühen Advaita Vāda*, Wiesbaden, 1951

BIBLIOGRAPHY

Jaimini, *Śābara Bhāṣya* (on P.M, Sūtras), trans. Ganganath Jha, G.O.S., 3 Vols., 1933, reprinted 1973-4

Kullūka: See Vol.I Bibliog. under Manu Smṛti

Mahānārāyaṇa Upanishad: See Vol.I Bibliog. under Rāghorām

Pūrva Mīmāṃsā Sūtra: See under Jaimini

Rāhula: See Vol.I Bibliog. under Sāṃkṛtyāyana

Renou, L.: *Grammaire et Védanta*, J.A., 1957, pp.121-32

Ṛgveda-Saṃhitā with Comm. of Sāyana: Vedic Research Institute, Poona, 5 Vols. 1933-51

Śatapatha Brāhmaṇa: Trans. Julius Eggeling, S.B.E., Oxford, 5 Parts, 1882-1900, recently reprinted Delhi

Śabara: See under Jaimini

Saccidānandendra, *Intuition of Reality*, Holenarsipur, 1973

— *The Method of the Vedanta* (abbreviated M.V.), Eng. trans. of *Vedanta Prakriyā Pratyabhijñā*, K.P.I., London, 1989

Sūra Dāsa, *Sūra Sāgara*, ed. Vājapeyī, Vārāṇasī, 2 Vols., 1953 and 1956

Sureśvara, *Sambandha Vārtika*, ed. and trans. T.M.P. Mahadevan, Madras, 1958

Taittirīya Brāhmaṇa: Ed. Rājendralāl Mitra, Calcutta, 1870

Taittirīya Saṃhitā: Trans. Keith, Harvard Oriental Series, 2 Vols., 1914

Vāsishtha Dharma Sūtra: Trans. G. Bühler, S.B.E. 2 (1879, reprinted recently, Delhi)

CONSPECTUS OF CONTENTS OF THE SIX VOLUMES OF THE ŚAṂKARA SOURCE-BOOK

VOLUME I

ŚAṂKARA ON THE ABSOLUTE

CONTENTS OF THE ŚAṂKARA SOURCE-BOOK

CONTENTS OF THE ŚAṂKARA SOURCE-BOOK

CONTENTS OF THE ŚAṂKARA SOURCE-BOOK

VOLUME VI

ŚAṂKARA ON THE PATH TO ENLIGHTENMENT

ERRATA VOL.IV

At Chapter XI Note 99, read II.ii.1-10; at Note 234, read II.iii.7; at Note 257 read deśānānugata and kālānugata; at Note 334 insert "the" to read "to know the cognition...". The following entries should be added to the Bibiliography: Jaya Deva, *Gītagovinda Kāvyam*, ed. Nārāyaṇa Rāma Ācārya, Bombay, 9th ed. 1949; P.N. Srinivasachari, *The Philosophy of Bhedābheda*, Madras, 1934.